Further praise for *Strong Passions*

"*Strong Passions* is that rare delight—a fascinating, beautifully written story grounded in research rigorous enough to satisfy the most exacting historian. Barbara Weisberg's book is more than a riveting legal drama about gender and power in old New York; it is also a thoughtful commentary on the anxieties created by the shifting boundary between private behaviors and public selves that beset Americans today."

—Joan Shelley Rubin, author of *The Making of Middlebrow Culture*

"The story of *Strong v. Strong* is a fascinating, disturbing, and page-turning dip into a divorce of the messiest sort. Barbara Weisberg marshals her facts and exposes nineteenth-century New York divorce laws and the suffering of women who experienced them firsthand."

—Deirdre Sinnott, author of *The Third Mrs. Galway*

STRONG
PASSIONS

ALSO BY BARBARA WEISBERG

*Talking to the Dead: Kate and Maggie Fox
and the Rise of Spiritualism*

Waverly: Oil painting of the Strong family homestead in Newtown, Queens, 1852, by Jasper Francis Cropsey. *Image courtesy of Freeman's*

For Katie —
Wonderful to meet you
at this beautiful club,
and I'm so happy
you enjoyed my
book!

With warm
regards,
Barbara

STRONG
PASSIONS

A Scandalous Divorce
in Old New York

Barbara Weisberg

Barbara Weisberg
Acorn Club
4/30/24

W. W. NORTON & COMPANY
Independent Publishers Since 1923

For information about permission to reproduce selections from this book,
write to Permissions, W. W. Norton & Company, Inc.,
500 Fifth Avenue, New York, NY 10110

For information about special discounts for bulk purchases, please contact
W. W. Norton Special Sales at specialsales@wwnorton.com or 800-233-4830

Manufacturing by Lake Book Manufacturing
Book design by Buckley Design
Production manager: Lauren Abbate

ISBN 978-0-393-53152-7

W. W. Norton & Company, Inc., 500 Fifth Avenue, New York, N.Y. 10110
www.wwnorton.com

W. W. Norton & Company Ltd., 15 Carlisle Street, London W1D 3BS

1 2 3 4 5 6 7 8 9 0

FOR DAVID

Contents

Contents

Introduction

> Was not all morality based on a convention? What was the staunchest
> code of ethics but a trunk with a series of false bottoms? Now and then
> one had the illusion of getting down to absolute right or wrong, but it
> was only a false bottom—a removable hypothesis—
> with another false bottom underneath.
>
> —*Edith Wharton*, "A Cup of Cold Water"

MARY EMELINE STEVENS STRONG abducted her younger
daughter, four-year-old Allie, in the second week of June 1864.
They had been living at the Manhattan townhouse of Mary's parents when they suddenly vanished. There's no record of how they
managed their flight—whether they slipped away to Long Island
by night in a private carriage, took a train up the coast to Boston,
or boarded a steamer on the Hudson River for Albany. Mary's
hitherto strict and law-abiding mother and father were her cocon-
spirators. They never let on where she went and, if they had any
evidence, destroyed it. Indeed, they may not always have known
her various destinations throughout the years. Her safe havens
changed the longer she was hunted.

Mary ran a day after the delivery of a writ of habeas corpus,
issued at her husband's request, demanding that she produce Allie

in court. Peter Remsen Strong had sued his wife for divorce, an action he had previously tried to avoid. *Strong v. Strong* came to trial in November 1865, more than a year after Mary and Allie disappeared, and the nation from Boston to San Francisco was riveted by the headlines. Seven months after Abraham Lincoln's assassination, the case provided a war-torn country with a shocking distraction and an unusual glimpse into the private world of New York's powerful and privileged elite. Not only was divorce virtually nonexistent among the upper echelons of mid-nineteenth-century American society, but women such as the accomplished, well-bred, and beautiful Mary Emeline Stevens Strong were also presumed to never violate the sacred marital bond—or, at least, never allow their transgressions to become public.

I was researching another project when I first encountered *Strong v. Strong* in the diary of George Templeton Strong, who was Peter's cousin and a prominent lawyer. His nineteenth-century journal presents an extraordinary window on New York life. I found myself as fascinated by the trial's twists and turns as readers were at the time. I immersed myself in the pages of *The New York Times*, *The New York Herald*, and other newspapers of the day to learn more. The plot of the Strongs' family story—for a family saga it is—seemed to me as if it should have been recounted in a nineteenth-century novel rather than bluntly reported on the front pages of newspapers.

Told in bits and pieces of trial testimony, the story unfolded as a set of overlapping narratives by the witnesses—the same story told from disparate points of view—with different events emphasized and analyzed, chronology altered, character traits and motivations debated. Witnesses were summoned from all walks of life, an assortment that included, among others, a governess, a detective, a judge's daughter, an undertaker, an abortionist's spouse, a laundress, and Teddy Roosevelt's uncle. The series of dramatic incidents that precipitated the divorce suit were clouded by a divergence in bitterly contested versions of what occurred. Did Mary seduce Peter's brother into an affair? Or did he—a pillar of the community—rape her? Was Mary forced by Peter to undergo an abortion, or did she suffer a miscarriage? Did the abortionist who took care of New York's high society have an affair with Peter? Or was she bribed to say so by Mary's lawyers, who threatened to have her arrested for murdering a client? As I searched for the answers, it seemed to me that I was struggling with the very essence or nature of a trial: that indeed every trial might be viewed as a single story fractured into a prismatic one. A jury and judge consider the versions, examine various scenes and episodes, weigh supporting evidence, and most often reach a conclusion.

In that spirit, I began to think about key witnesses' testimony as a set of discrete narratives, each a piece or version of what happened. In the account that follows, quoted testimony is primarily drawn from the trial's extensive press coverage and, in a few instances, from the small number of surviving court documents, primarily depositions, in New York City's archives. If lawyers' objections and questions substantially enhanced or contradicted a witness's testimony, I note and analyze those shifts.

The trial itself, however—a matter of weeks—is only part of the larger, decades-long story of the Strongs. This narrative begins years before the trial starts and ends well after its conclusion, when little Allie is a grown woman. It involves two powerful New York families intertwined through marriage, the conflict between Peter and Mary echoing across three generations, with parents, siblings, and children swept up in the drama, as were the couple's servants and friends.

Through its coverage of the suit, the press imparted a frank portrait of life within the Strongs' unhappy household before and during the Civil War, accounts that rocked genteel society with a mounting succession of scandalous revelations. The publicity around *Strong v. Strong* also helped focus attention on issues, attitudes, and laws related to marital roles, abortion, divorce, and child custody that continue to resonate as they remain in contention today. The Strongs' divorce demonstrated to a society at war with itself that the "perfect union" was as much a fiction in marriage as it had proved to be for the nation, an analogy that did not escape Americans at the time. From the earliest days of the Civil War, the sectional crisis was compared, as one journalist wrote, to "a divorce for incompatibility." Mary Boykin Chesnut, the wife of a Confederate general, saw familial and national conflict through an even darker lens. "We are divorced, North from South," she wrote in her diary, "because we have hated each other so. If only we could separate politely, and not have a horrid fight for divorce."

To frame the Strongs' divorce suit in context, I have drawn on many different sources, including—in addition to court documents and newspaper articles—genealogies, letters, diaries, New York histories, legal treatises, and nineteenth-century novels. Like a juror, I have done my best to weigh all the evidence in an effort to make reasoned assumptions wherever the truth is deeply disputed. I hope that you, after reading about this trial and its aftermath, will reach your own conclusions about the Strongs' troubled marriage, assess it in relation to their times, and consider which spouse—if either—inspires your empathy across more than 150 years.

PART 1

A Perfect Union

CHAPTER 1

A Marriageable Girl

THE TOUCH OF A MAN'S HAND transformed the life of Mary Emeline Stevens Strong not once but twice. The first time, in a passing gesture, she touched the hand of her brother-in-law—a moment that ignited a fiery and forbidden passion between them. The second time, her husband gently took her hand in his after one of their daughters died—a rare show of tenderness that unleashed his wife's distraught confession of adultery.

Mary Stevens was nineteen years old when she met her husband, Peter Remsen Strong, in 1852. A graceful girl, 5'3" with silky brown hair and gray eyes, she was said by her affectionate Aunt Em to be "sweet as a rose." Peter was ten years older and five inches taller, with brown hair and gray eyes—his coloring almost a mirror of hers. A handsome, worldly, and personable bachelor, he had fallen, according to friends and family, desperately in love with Mary.

Ideally matched, a storybook couple, Mary and Peter came from the privileged world of New York City's social elite, a thriving class of well-to-do merchants, lawyers, bankers, and doctors. These prosperous citizens of mid-nineteenth-century New

York, whose forebears had built the city into the nation's commercial capital, were an insular group whose members grew up with, worked with, entertained, and often married one another. Their wealth generally went back at least a generation if not two, although no one discussed such matters or flouted good fortune in an extravagant or crass manner—as did certain more opportunistic businessmen like the Vanderbilts, whose riches were greater yet newer. Instead, families such as the Stevenses and Strongs constituted a proud, self-contained, and dignified lot, governed by an unwritten code of proper private and public behavior. Good manners and good breeding mattered. So, too, did Protestant affiliation—Dutch Reformed or Episcopalian preferred. Affluence was assumed, not displayed. These families represented what the writer Edith Wharton later called the world of "old New York." America's grand chronicler of nineteenth-century marital discord and social foibles, Wharton named as an example of "old New York" some of her own relatives, commenting in her memoir *A Backward Glance*: "The Schermerhorns, Joneses, Pendletons, on my father's side, the Stevenses, Ledyards, Rhinelanders on my mother's, the Gallatins on both, seem all to have belonged to the same prosperous class of merchants, bankers and lawyers."

Mary and Wharton were cousins, the two women born a generation apart—Mary in 1833 and Wharton in 1862. Both were descendants of Ebenezer Stevens, a Revolutionary War hero turned merchant who was Mary's grandfather and Wharton's great-grandfather. Although Wharton never knew Ebenezer, she saw his portrait in the rotunda of the Capitol in Washington, D.C., as a child and later wrote that she developed a certain "secret partiality" for him. She admired his "stern high-nosed good looks, his gallantry in war, his love of luxury, his tireless commercial activities."

Ebenezer founded a successful mercantile firm specializing in overseas trade, importing French wines and other luxury items for notable clients such as Thomas Jefferson. He made a fortune and built a mansion in the then rural environs of Queens County, New York. He called his estate The Mount, a name Wharton gave decades later to her own home in Lenox, Massachusetts. Characterized by his joie de vivre, Wharton wrote, Ebenezer married twice and fathered fourteen children. His second wife, Lucretia, gave birth to Mary's father, John Austin Stevens, and six other children. John's sister—whose married name was Mary Stevens Rhinelander—was Wharton's grandmother.

John Austin Stevens inherited his father's visage and propensity for mercantile success. He graduated from Yale in 1813 and rose to prominence as a partner in Ebenezer's firm. Then, in 1824, he married twenty-five-year-old Abby Perkins Weld, whose notable New England family approved the match. John subsequently became a banker, joining in 1838 with other New York businessmen to found the Bank of Commerce.

John's family expanded as his career flourished. By the mid-1840s, Abby had given birth to twelve children, not all of whom lived beyond a few years. Two of Mary's brothers died before she was born; when Mary was eight, her beloved two-year-old brother, Sam, died. In the nineteenth century, before the advent of modern medicine, it's estimated that twenty percent of children died before age five, often from a contagious disease such as cholera, whooping cough, scarlet fever, or diphtheria. That reality did not make loss any easier to bear. Mary and her siblings mourned Sam grievously in the sentimental language of the day. Sam was "too perfect to live," wrote Lucretia, Mary's eleven-year-old sister. "He belonged not to this world of sorrow."

Of the nine surviving Stevens children, Mary was a middle child; she had one older brother, three older sisters, and four younger ones. Mary's oldest sibling, John Austin Stevens, Jr.—

called Austin—was born in 1827; Julia, the youngest, in 1843, a year before Austin started college at Harvard. Mary's best friend was Lucretia, who was almost three years older than Mary and in many respects her opposite. Huge-hearted and extroverted, Lucretia was said to "have so much spirit" that "she kept everyone wide awake." Equally charming but quieter and more serious, Mary was the family's "dear little scholar."

Home was a stately red brick townhouse at 63 Bleecker Street in an area of Manhattan commonly known then and now as Greenwich Village. In the late 1830s and '40s it was the city's most fashionable neighborhood, the street lined with townhouses in late Federal style, many with a multistep front stoop and an imposing doorway flanked by white Greek Revival pillars. Most of the Bleecker Street townhouses stood as straight and upright as their owners, with only a single narrow staircase winding from cellar to attic where family, servants, and guests passed one another as they came and went.

So similar were the homes of the upper middle class that one journalist wrote, "The proprietor of almost any house in New York might wake up in thousands of other houses and not recognize for a half hour that he was not at home." The Stevens house is now gone but, like others in the neighborhood then, probably had a kitchen and family room in the basement, with a few steps leading up to a back garden; a front and rear parlor on the main floor, divided by sliding pocket doors; master's and mistress's separate bedrooms on a second floor; children's shared bedrooms on a third floor; and servants' cramped quarters beneath dormer windows in the attic. A privy would have been located at the back of the garden, set as far as possible from the house. Bedroom chamber pots generally were used for urination only, emptied several times daily by one of the servants.

The Stevens household in 1850 had five servants: four women

and one man. The size of the staff was not unusual, given the Stevenses' social status, and probably included a cook, a laundress, two housemaids, and a waiter who served the family's meals and performed other tasks. With sixteen people—family and servants, children and adults—waking, dressing, working, playing, eating, and sleeping at 63 Bleecker, Mary enjoyed little privacy. On the other hand, privacy was not yet a priority of the nineteenth-century family.

The Stevenses' neighbors included James Roosevelt, great-grandfather of Franklin Delano Roosevelt. Other distinguished families whose names are now familiar resided nearby—among them the Astors, the Delanos, and the Joneses, Edith Wharton's relatives, by some accounts memorialized in the phrase "keeping up with the Joneses."

Mary and her sisters attended Madame Canda's school, a private girls' academy, where they studied history, English, French, geography, and music, among other subjects. They could easily walk the few blocks to it on nearby Lafayette Place, an elegant two-block plaza between Broadway and the Bowery, two thoroughfares packed at all hours with New York's fast-paced crowds. Both streets already evidenced early signs of sedate *old* New York's demise and the birth of a tumultuous *new* New York unique in its diversity of cultures, racial and ethnic kaleidoscope of faces, babel of languages, extremes of wealth and poverty, its cheek-by-jowl juxtaposition within a few square miles of rich and poor, middle and working class, immigrant and native born.

Exploding in area and population, New York was a city on the move, with changes visible even in the neighborhood between Mary's home and school. Taverns, butcher shops, secondhand furniture stalls, and boarding houses lined the Bowery, pushing the city northward. Hotels, music halls, public gardens, and specialty shops selling ribbons, gloves, and sweets proliferated along

Broadway. In 1847, the magnificent Astor Opera House was built on Astor Place, scarcely a block from Madame Canda's academy. Two years later, a riot erupted when rowdy New Yorkers objected to a famous English actor, William Macready, playing the part of Macbeth at the Opera House when his long-time rival, the beloved American actor Edwin Forrest, was appearing nearby in the same play at a different theater. More than a feud between two thespians, the rivalry seemed to symbolize England versus America, the aristocracy versus the working man. The riot began with audience members disrupting Macready's performance by throwing eggs and lemons, escalated when a crowd outside the Opera House started hurling rocks and stones, and ended with gunfire. An estimated twenty-two people died, and more than one hundred were wounded. From the living-room window, young Mary might have seen the rioters and police racing by her house.

Within a year of the riot, Edwin Forrest sued his English wife, Catherine, for divorce. She thought the anger and stress the riot had caused him contributed to his decision. The divorce suit, with its furious charges and countercharges of adultery, made front-page headlines . . . at least at first. The couple's various appeals dragged on for eighteen years.

The Forrest headlines offered a glimpse of misconduct, but illicit sexuality stared New Yorkers in the face daily. Prostitutes, some in tawdry or tattered clothes, others bedecked in opulent gowns, frequented the theaters and, just like society's genteel matrons, paraded along Broadway every afternoon. A commentator for the *Herald* noted that a "strange and disreputable anomaly of theaters, churches and houses of ill-fame" could be found "all huddled together in one block" in neighborhoods throughout the city. A great many men of all classes, regardless of birth or wealth, visited brothels. If elite New York's innocent young maidens and proper wives noticed anything unseemly, such topics remained unmentionable.

Jammed with private carriages, carts laden with goods and produce, and horse-drawn omnibuses, the streets echoed with the noise of hoofs clattering on cobblestones; the calls of vendors hawking their wares; the shouts of schoolboys chasing one another, and the barking of stray dogs chasing the boys. Avenues as well as alleys were foul-smelling from horse manure and littered with garbage. Still, even well-to-do young ladies such as Mary and Lucretia enjoyed strolling to school, shops, and friends' homes, hiking their skirts and stepping carefully to avoid the filth and mud, taking in the dazzling panorama, sometimes savoring an ice cream bought along the way. Unlike some of his wealthier and less frugal colleagues, the girls' father never considered owning a carriage. He could hire one as needed.

For leisure activities after school, young girls like the Stevens sisters practiced piano, played card games, and read novels—always carefully monitored for virtuous content. *Godey's Lady's Book*, the most popular woman's magazine of the day, warned that a passion for reading needed to "remain a healthful appetite for mental food rather than a morbid craving for mental stimulation." Choices had to nurture young minds "which must have food; so we have the Bible for bread, school books for meat . . . and then we have Goldsmith, Addison, Shakspeare [*sic*], Plutarch. . . ."

Too much "mental stimulation" was something of a euphemism. "Lascivious thoughts and imaginations will excite and stimulate the genital organs," advised Sylvester Graham, a noted mid-century voice among a spate of books and pamphlets on the related topics of diet, health, and sexuality by philosophers, phrenologists, freethinkers, physicians, and Christian evangelists. They debated whether enjoyment, temperance, or abstinence was the best approach to sex.

Godey's Lady's Book counseled that fiction, filled with tales of lustful lovers and fallen women, especially threatened to excite the passions and undermine morality, yet the magazine allowed that not all novels were pernicious. Those of Walter Scott and Washington Irving were permitted, the first for his noble heart and sense of honor, the second for his pure mind.

Surprisingly, the magazine recommended that a girl might also want to read her father's newspaper, apparently overlooking the countless articles on violent crime, notices of scandalous court trials, and advertisements for abortions and brothels. Rather than clashing, the genteel and the salacious seemed oddly to coexist in the newspapers, life, and streets of Victorian-era New York. Nevertheless, worried Frederick Hollick, a physician and lecturer, "the sexual feeling is now developed too early. . . . A child cannot walk out, but his eyes and ears are assailed with sights and sounds all bearing on this topic."

In the evening, Mary and her sisters sometimes went to concerts, both the Philharmonic and more intimate chamber music presented at friends' homes. They also joined in gatherings where guests assembled around the piano to sing sentimental parlor songs about love and loss. They sometimes attended lavish parties, too, a socially sanctioned way for the marriageable girls and eligible bachelors of old New York to be introduced and chaperoned by their elders. Gilt-framed mirrors were polished to reflect the warm gleam of candelabras; pocket doors between front and rear parlors were opened; and furniture was pushed aside for dancing. Women showed off the latest fashions, courting couples whispered in corners, and children peeped in from halls and stairways. In the back parlor, men typically crowded around a dining table laden with chickens, turkeys, oysters, sweets, punch, whiskey, and wine. In the front parlor, dancers glided gracefully in the intricately patterned steps of the quadrille, considered more appropriate than vulgar waltzes in which couples held one another too closely and whirled too wildly. Fifty to one hundred guests might attend, coming and going in carriages until two or three in the morning. Although the rooms were spacious, "yet the crowd is so uncomfortably great that the dancers have scarcely room to make a small circle in the middle of the dense mass; while those who do not dance must be content to remain wedged into one compact and solid phalanx," complained James Silk Buckingham, a British visitor apparently accustomed to better-choreographed balls in grander homes.

The Christmas and New Year holidays were especially festive in New York. Indeed, New Yorkers felt they had a proprietary hold on the season. After all, it was a New Yorker—the author Washington Irving—who brought forgotten Christmas traditions to life in his stories, and another New Yorker—Clement Moore—who created the image of St. Nick as we know him today. In the poem now called "Twas the Night Before Christmas," Moore cast him as a jolly elf who travels across the sky in a sleigh drawn by reindeer, leaving presents for all the world's children. Along with lavish parties to celebrate the season, a special tradition marked New Year's Day, when married men and bachelors alike went from house to house, paying their respects to the ladies, who welcomed them with tables groaning with food.

Mary's mother, Abby Stevens, was famed in New York society for her splendid annual holiday gala. Long before Mary met Peter, his cousin George Templeton Strong met his future wife at Abby's 1847 holiday party. Writing in his diary many years after the event, he fondly recalled the festive, hectic atmosphere, and the few moments that, for him, stood out in memory from all the rest. "I was in Mrs. John A. Stevens' house in Bleecker Street, at a big party," he wrote, "in the crowded supper-room, where poor Johnny Parish had lodged himself in a very strong position at the supper table. . . . And I was thinking about the young lady in blue silk (or blue something) I'd been talking with so pleasantly and sympathetically before supper. . . . I remember just where she stood, at the end of a dance." It had taken all his "sheepish courage," he said, to speak with her.

Not everyone approved of glamorous parties. Catherine Beecher, Harriet Beecher Stowe's sister and the author of well-regarded books on women's education, believed that such events distracted young girls from learning what they most needed to know: how to excel in their life's work—she termed it their "profession"—as a wife and mother. She worried that "young girls, especially in the more wealthy classes *are not trained for their profession.* . . . Thus they enter on their most arduous and sacred duties so inexperienced and uninformed . . . that probably there is *not one chance in ten*, that young women of the present day, will pass through the first years of married life without such prostration of health and spirits as makes life a burden to themselves."

Beecher's fretful criticism did not hold true of Mary and her sisters, however, for they were well trained for their future roles: the older girls took care of the younger children, readying themselves for motherhood, and all the children did routine household chores such as mending. Mary in particular excelled as a seamstress. She sewed handkerchiefs, collars, and occasionally even her sisters' dresses from the yards of fabric needed to make the full, bell-shaped petticoats and skirts of the day. While there were festivities and laughter in the Stevens home, they coexisted with discipline and high expectations. Lucretia later remembered her childhood home as having a "high toned puritanical atmosphere . . . many pleasures and some anxieties."

Small family gatherings regularly took place at relatives' homes. Mary sometimes visited her uncle Byam Stevens and his sister, her widowed aunt Mary Stevens Rhinelander (Edith

Wharton's grandmother) at The Mount, the eighteenth-century mansion Ebenezer Stevens built for his family on Long Island. Emeline Weld—the children's Aunt Em, their mother's unmarried sister—also frequently visited The Mount from her home in Brunswick, Maine. Aunt Em routinely played chess while in New York with Albert Gallatin, former Secretary of the Treasury and a Stevens relative by marriage. Just as routinely, Aunt Em won.

Summertime, Mary and her siblings visited Aunt Em and her sister, Aunt Caroline, at their Brunswick home. This tradition gave the children's mother, Abby, some respite because she was pregnant again or simply worn out with caring for her brood. Brunswick was a shipbuilding town, known for its gracious homes, cool summer breezes, and Bowdoin College, which had graduated such distinguished alumni as the writers Henry Wadsworth Longfellow and Nathaniel Hawthorne, the ambitious politician Franklin Pierce, and the physician Luther Bell, a founder of psychiatry in the United States. Bell became known for his diatribes against masturbation—an unhealthy habit, he believed, excessively indulged in by "the pale student of the school, the college, or the theological seminary."

The president of Bowdoin College, Leonard Woods, boarded with Em and Caroline, and some of his students who lived nearby—boys on the cusp of manhood—visited frequently, making dinner the scene of lively conversations. Boasts of triumph in games such as rope pulls mingled with discussions of academic subjects and occasional spirited arguments over serious national issues such as the abolition of slavery. Released from school routines and parental expectations, the girls had more freedom than at home. Aunt Caroline once told the girls' brother, Austin, that "they have run wild the last three months."

For several summers, while John worked in New York, Abby and the children spent time at Newport, Rhode Island, still a modest seaside community of wooden homes, boarding houses, and a few comfortable hotels near the healthful air of ocean and beach. Writing to her father in 1847 about a Newport children's fair, Lucretia admiringly confided that thirteen-year-old Mary was in charge of selling the most popular items—ice cream and lemonade—with "a very businesslike air," only to be teased by a group of mischievous boys "playing their jokes at her table," and complaining "her prices were too extravagant . . . but Miss Mary replied," wrote Lucretia, "'they need not purchase them,' and asserted her price more distinctly than ever." Mary knew how to stand her ground, veering however slightly from the nineteenth-century ideal of the passive, perfectly genteel young lady. The American girl, according to the observant British traveler James Silk Buckingham, was especially noted for her "domestic fidelity, social cheerfulness, unostentatious hospitality, and moral and religious benevolence."

A few years later, in 1850, Mary decided to continue her studies beyond the customary age of sixteen for a girl. Among other subjects, she may have wished to perfect her French, perhaps dreaming of future travel. Lucretia had thought the extra activity was a good idea. "Mary is . . . so strong in habit . . . as we think she may tire of remaining home all winter . . . [school] will seem as an amusement."

As an elderly woman thinking back on her sister, Lucretia commented that Mary had a "will few could withstand." But in 1850, only the slightest hint of that fierce determination shone through Mary's genteel demeanor. There was, after all, so little need to show it.

CHAPTER 2

A Good, Honest, Warm-Hearted Fellow

ON A SWELTERING MONDAY AFTERNOON in July 1838, a rider lost control of his horse, which was galloping headlong down Broadway through Manhattan's business district, the horseman clinging to the reins. As the horse raced forward, a well-dressed businessman stepped from an omnibus and began to cross the street. Careering by him, the horse knocked him to the ground and kicked him with a back hoof, shattering his skull. Horrified onlookers gathered around the victim, who looked at them briefly before his eyes closed. Good Samaritans lifted him and carried him into a nearby shop where a doctor attempted to revive him, but he never regained consciousness. In the confusion that followed the incident, horse and horseman disappeared. The victim, fifty-five-year-old James Strong, died a few hours later, leaving behind his wife, Aletta, and six children between the ages of nine and eighteen. His son Peter was fifteen at the time.

James had been an established member of old New York's powerful merchant elite. As a young man he had joined the mercantile firm founded by his father, the Revolutionary War patriot Selah Strong. Soon afterward, James married Aletta Remsen, a descendant of wealthy merchants and property owners with land and roots in Queens. Aletta brought to her marriage a family homestead of two hundred acres in Newtown, Queens, and James joined the mercantile firm established by Aletta's brother.

Although Queens was accessible by ferry, James and Aletta chose instead to live on Cortlandt Street in lower Manhattan, close to his business and other affluent urban dwellers. Of their six children, Peter—like his future bride, Mary—was a middle child, with two older sisters, one older brother, and two younger ones. Julia, Peter's oldest sibling, was born in 1820, Benjamin, the youngest, in 1829.

By the 1830s, fashionable city dwellers had largely abandoned lower Manhattan's business district and moved further north. Recognizing the wisdom of real estate investments in the burgeoning city, James Strong purchased three townhouses in Greenwich Village on Waverly Place, named in honor of Sir Walter Scott's popular Waverley novels, although—perhaps by mistake—spelled differently. James leased two of the properties—104 and 124 Waverly Place, located near Sixth Avenue—to tenants. The family occupied the third house, 1 Waverly Place, located on the more stylish end of Waverly near Broadway.

After James's death, shock and grief radically transformed the family's life. Aletta retreated to her Queens homestead, now also named Waverly. Much of the time, Peter and his siblings lived there as well, at first because they were young and recovering from the horror of their father's death; later, because they were attached to the property not only by bonds of affection but also by provisions of their father's will. James named Aletta as his heir, with the stipulation that, if she so wished, the children were to receive an annual allowance on coming of age, but only so long as they remained in close proximity to her during her lifetime. They would also receive an inheritance after her death. The will was interpreted rather literally by family members: the Strong children, along with their spouses and, later, their offspring spent an inordinate amount of time living at or visiting Waverly.

Despite the real or imagined constraints of his father's will, Peter soon managed to assert his independence, becoming a young man about town, commuting by coach and ferry to Manhattan, balancing his days between city and country. He enrolled at Columbia College, then located in lower Manhattan, and studied law among other subjects. At his commencement in 1840, he read a poem titled "Freedom," perhaps his own composition, to the assembled audience. On graduation, since neither law schools nor bar associations existed in New York at the time, he was able without further formal training to call himself a lawyer, a well-respected profession among members of his social class. However, he never actually practiced law. Instead, he lived on the annual allowance of $4,000 he had inherited from his father, a substantial amount worth an estimated $130,000 today; helped his mother, Aletta, manage the affairs of Waverly; and oversaw other investments, such as the rental and management of the Waverly Place townhouses in Manhattan.

Otherwise, in the 1840s, Peter enjoyed the life of leisure of a well-to-do gentleman, the occupation of choice for many young men of his class. While the generations of his grandfather, Selah, and father, James, worked diligently to build their fortunes, Peter and many of his peers—the second and third generations—were content to live on inheritances. Peter read Romantic poets—Keats and Shelley were his favorites; he boated, hunted, and socialized with friends. He relished cigars, evenings of masculine conversation, and flirting with pretty girls. One of his friends later caricatured him in a book as a character named *Don Pedro*, implying a taste for pleasures and indulgences more typical of a European bon vivant than of a presumably practical and hardworking American.

Peter also joined several of the gentlemen's clubs forming in the city. He spent especially long hours at the Century Association, a club established to accommodate "Artists, Literary Men, Scientists, Physicians, Officers of the Army and Navy, members of the Bench and Bar, Engineers, Clergymen, Representatives of the Press, Merchants and men of leisure."

Peter's affectionate cousin and good friend, George Templeton Strong, wrote about him in the diary he kept faithfully for forty years. A few years older than Peter, George also graduated from Columbia College, and went on to become a lawyer—but in George's case, an active and successful one. In 1848 George married the young woman he had met the previous year at Abby Stevens's annual Christmas party and considered himself a mature family man. While he also belonged to the Century Association, he belittled Peter's ardent devotion to clubs, calling them "mere Institutions for the Doing of Nothing . . . where a parcel of boys have [sic] larger facilities than elsewhere for lounging and loafing." Equally ironic about Peter's skills as a hunter, George commented after one misadventure, "Pete was indefatigable—rampaged around the Oyster Pond like a kind of Dismal Wild Huntsman in a dirty shooting jacket." Peter also, George confided to his diary, babbled too much about "High Art & Tone." George nevertheless maintained that Peter was a "good, honest, warm-hearted fellow" with many congenial friends.

Like other young bachelors of his social rank, Peter indulged his hunger for "High Art" by setting off on a European Grand Tour, embarking on his adventure in 1848, a year that turned out to be one of momentous events both at home and abroad. A two-year war with Mexico ended in a treaty that awarded the victorious United States more than a half-million square miles of land, including California. The discovery of gold there the same year set off the California Gold Rush, luring thousands of hopeful prospectors west across the continent.

Along with the acquisition of territories and gold, essential issues of rights and freedoms also preoccupied Americans. Territorial expansion heightened the nation's already impassioned debate over slavery. While the South sought to protect its "peculiar institution," abolitionists wanted to eradicate slavery immediately, and others hoped for compromise. The conflict assumed fresh urgency with the question: should these newly acquired territories be admitted to the union as slave states or free?

Less noticed, a small convention in the upstate New York village of Seneca Falls addressed the "social, civil and religious condition and rights of Woman." The convention issued the "Declaration of Sentiments and Resolutions," a document modeled on the Declaration of Independence. Written to outline the ways that men controlled and constrained women's lives, it proclaimed that the "history of mankind is a history of repeated injuries and usurpations on the part of man toward woman, having in direct object the establishment of an absolute tyranny over her. . . ."

He has never permitted her to exercise her inalienable right to the elective franchise.

He has compelled her to submit to laws, in the formation of which she had no voice. . . .

He has made her, if married, in the eye of the law, civilly dead. . . .

He has so framed the laws of divorce . . . as to be wholly regardless of the happiness of women—the law, in all cases, going upon a false supposition of the supremacy of man, and giving all power into his hands. . . .

He has denied her the facilities for obtaining a thorough education—all colleges being closed against her.

He has endeavored, in every way that he could to destroy her confidence in her own powers, to lessen her self-respect, and to make her willing to lead a dependent and abject life.

The convention received relatively little contemporary press. Still, women's rights and anti-slavery advocates such as Lucretia Mott and Elizabeth Cady Stanton had attended, as well as formerly enslaved abolitionist leader Frederick Douglass, and its controversial concerns were beginning to permeate American culture. Tyranny, whether of whites over Blacks or men over women, was coming under attack.

In Europe as well, the call for radical change focused largely on tyranny—the tyrannical rule of despots over their subjects and one country over another. Liberal and democratic revolutions swept the continent. Kings were deposed in Denmark and France; in Germany and Italy, movements against Austrian domination and for national unification and independence gained power. Although most of these revolutions ultimately failed, turmoil and upheaval throughout Europe surely made travel more uncertain and dangerous but might also, to a young man like Peter Strong, have proved exciting.

At the time Peter went to Europe, the transition from an unpredictable voyage by sail to a faster passage by steamship had encouraged a new breed of globe-trotting American tourists. If they left from New York, youthful adventurers usually disembarked at Le Havre, France, after a sea journey of two to three weeks and about 3,500 nautical miles; from there, the itineraries and time spent on the Grand Tour varied but generally included close-by Paris, then cities such as Rome, Heidelberg, Vienna, Amsterdam, and London, as well as Switzerland's scenic Alps, and sometimes even Egypt and other parts of the Mideast. Travelers sought out cities famed for their history, art, monuments, and music; picturesque towns and villages; and sites of sublime beauty. Not all pursuits were staid, for Europe's allure included the chance for men to spend long evenings in gambling houses, cafés, and bordellos. The relatively few women who traveled in the 1840s often went to Paris where they purchased fabulous wardrobes, while men returned with art collections of Old Masters, some real, others forged.

When twenty-eight-year-old Peter returned from his three-year Grand Tour in 1851, he boasted of hunting crocodiles on the Nile and jackals in the desert. Among the treasures he allegedly brought home were a Turkish rug, a dagger, and a mummified human foot.

That year, Peter's twenty-four-year-old brother Edward married. Although Aletta's two daughters, Julia and Elizabeth Jane, had married before Peter went abroad, Edward was the first of Aletta's four sons to do so. The charms of Edward's seventeen-year-old bride, Susan Warren—unusually young but much praised for her elegance and beauty—may have prompted Peter to reconsider his own bachelorhood, or perhaps he simply found the right girl to marry. Whatever the reasons, when he met Mary Emeline Stevens in 1852, he fell in love.

Given their common background, it's surprising they hadn't met earlier. The attraction between them, however, went beyond genealogy and social connections. Good-looking Peter and lovely Mary were both outgoing and appealing, and she was known to be a delightful conversationalist. Curious about the world beyond New York, Mary doubtless was eager to hear about Peter's adventures, listening with flattering attention to his ideas and opinions. She also was a girl comfortable in boys' company because of her brother and his friends and used to their mischief, a girl who was lively and fun-loving. Some men might have preferred a more retiring, passive girl, but Peter was genial, too, and enjoyed his amusements.

Moreover, while both Peter and Mary had led privileged lives, they were not untouched by sorrow. Peter had lost his father under tragic circumstances, and Mary experienced the death of her little brother when she was only eight. Both understood that life had its shadows, a shared sensibility and sympathetic bond.

Lucretia called Peter a devoted beau, but her parents thought nineteen-year-old Mary too young to marry. A banker committed to his work, John Austin Stevens had concerns about Peter's lack of an earned income and well-defined livelihood. Still, it was understood that Peter's family had means, and that, belonging to the world of old New York, he was one of the Stevenses' own kind.

Although not the eldest, Mary was the first of the eight Stevens sisters to marry. A smart and spirited American girl, she was restive with the familiar routines of life on Bleecker Street. Now wooed by her eligible suitor, like other girls of her age, class, and era, she would have imagined herself in the roles of wife and mother, as the mistress of her own household. According to women's magazines such as *Godey's Lady's Book*, "Home is the empire, the throne of woman," as the writer J. N. Danforth proclaimed in an essay. "Here she reigns in the legitimate power of all her united charms." Not everyone agreed. The activist and orator Ernestine Rose argued that marriage degraded women. The moment a woman married, said Rose, she ceased "legally to exist" and became "a purely submissive being." Although lampooned in cartoons, the women's rights movement was beginning to be covered seriously by sympathetic editors such as Horace Greeley of the *New-York Tribune*.

Peter waited a year before asking for Mary's hand in marriage. He did so at the impressive office of her father, by then president of New York's Bank of Commerce. Peter cornered John during the business day and, instead of asking for Mary's hand, announced that she had agreed to be his wife, and that he had $4,000 a year on which to support her. Despite Peter's blithe violation of protocol, John agreed to the match. Peter left in the belief that his future father-in-law had promised the young couple a yearly $10,000 allowance, a sum that many of Manhattan's well-to-do considered just adequate for maintaining a respectable lifestyle with a nicely furnished home and several servants. Later, however, John would recall no such promise.

Mary and Peter's wedding took place at the Stevenses' house on an unseasonably warm Wednesday afternoon in mid-May 1853. Even Peter's ever-acerbic cousin George seemed pleased to attend and celebrate the marriage. Lucretia was a bridesmaid, and the house overflowed with relatives and friends. The ceremony was performed by the Reverend Gregory Thurston Bedell, husband of Peter's oldest sister, Julia, and an Episcopal cleric, rector of the fashionable Church of the Ascension on Fifth Avenue.

Abashed to admit superstition, even to his diary, George confessed relief at the absence of rain or clouds. Sunshine, he thought, was an auspicious sign. He harbored doubts about the compatibility of Peter's in-laws to be, describing the Stevenses in his diary as "lively & cordial," but "always in a state of effort . . . to maintain or establish the exalted social and intellectual position of the family and all its members." Of Mary, however, George wholeheartedly approved. The bride, he wrote, was self-possessed and beautiful, dressed splendidly in lace and pearls.

Peter, on the other hand, was clearly nervous. He missed a step and slipped down the stairs, then dropped the wedding band at the crucial moment.

After the ceremony, Mary moved through the crowd with ease and grace, shaking hands with each of her guests. Touched by the day's events, George mulled over the possibility of a bright future for the bride and groom, writing that night in his diary, "God prosper this to them both. Each has elements of good quite different from the other's, according to my reading of their respective natures; and it may be a most happy union." While recognizing the newlyweds' differences in temperament and personality, he hoped that these would only serve to enhance their lives. "Of course, I know P. far better than I know his wife," he wrote, "but I think I understand both. His kindness & gentleness & generous impulses I'm sure of. She has, I think, the <u>deeper</u> character, but in both are such diverse charms . . . traits of truth and of promise, that one cannot but hope the very best from this."

He concluded with a private and sincere benediction—"So may it be"—that was uncharacteristically lacking in irony. He would remember this wedding day, and mourn its outcome, a dozen years later.

CHAPTER 3

Initiations

FOLLOWING THEIR WEDDING, Mary and Peter took a brief honeymoon in Philadelphia, a popular tourist destination about five hours by train from New York and touted by guidebooks for its fine hotels, historic interest, museums, and libraries. The newlyweds, however, had far more important preoccupations than sightseeing. Especially at a time when only the most transgressive couples lived together before marriage, when parents monitored courtship, and when brides were expected to be chaste, the first weeks of marriage initiated a radical transformation in a man and woman. The groom unveiled the secrets of sexual intimacy for his bride, and bride and groom alike donned their wholly new identities as husband and wife.

In the nineteenth century, a chasm separated male and female marital roles, beginning with differences in sexual knowledge and self-image. A man was presumed sexually experienced on his wedding night, having had at least a sexual escapade or two in his youth. In the United States, the popular image of the "sporting man"—who enjoyed "manly" pursuits such as horse racing, gambling, and boxing, who frequented brothels, and who experienced bodily passions that demanded satisfaction—exerted an influence on men of all classes, even those respectable members of old New York society who discreetly abjured the sporting man's lifestyle. Viewed as lustful beings, men were supposed to need and crave frequent sex. However, sex presented a conundrum, for surrendering too often to desire was considered dangerous, a potentially debilitating waste of male energy and bodily fluids. Thus, men of the reputable sort attempted to moderate their unruly appetites.

No such conflict about sexual desire was thought to burden womankind. Society unapologetically expected a well-bred girl—by implication at the time, a white girl from a family of at least moderate means—to be a virgin at marriage and, ideally, a naïve one at that. Mary, who came from a family with a constantly pregnant mother, most likely understood something of sex and the intimacies of the bedroom. Nevertheless, her wedding night surely was revelatory.

Not that explicit sexual information was unavailable. A host of mid-nineteenth-century publications explained how to fulfill the roles of husband and wife. Along with marriage manuals that focused primly on manners and customs, a few brave treatises described the workings of the human body. Frederick Hollick's 1845 opus *The Origin of Life*, while read more widely by men than women, was detailed and specific, particularly in its appreciation of female anatomy and acknowledgment that sexual activity didn't exclusively mean intercourse.

"The sexual feeling," Hollick wrote, "like every other physical sensation, results from a specific excitement of the nerves in certain parts of the body. In the male this part is chiefly the glans, on the end of the penis. In females, it is either the external lips, the interior of the vagina, or . . . most usually the clitoris." Sexual excitement and pleasure, he explained, resided not only in consummation but in "mechanical irritation, by copulation or otherwise."

Proper wives were expected to *feel* delicate aversion to sex but to *demonstrate* ladylike enthusiasm. The latter was in part for her own protection. In *Love and Parentage*, written in 1851 in the polite language of marriage manuals meant for both sexes, the author Orson Fowler explained the reasons for dissembling. "First, to the reluctant wife!" he counseled. "For you to yield, is to conquer. By showing a desire to do all you can to oblige a beseeching husband, you throw yourself on his generosity, and thereby quell that desire which coldness or refusal would only aggravate." Sympathetic to a woman's plight, Fowler assured "the reluctant wife" that her husband would be sympathetic, also. "Your cheerful submission to what he knows to be disagreeable at once excites his pity and gratitude, and thus awakens his higher faculties in your behalf."

In reality, of course, sexual relations depended on the couple. Sex could be bland or brutal, but it could also be satisfying, for the notion of considerate and mutually pleasurable sex was acceptable. However, a husband's civility and a wife's pregnancy were the only actual restraints on a man's potentially unbridled passion. Sensitive husbands customarily refrained from making sexual demands in the late stages of a wife's pregnancy, and, in an era before effective contraception, pregnancies were frequent. Withdrawal, condoms, sponges, and douches were available but unreliable methods, and society frowned on their use. The concept of marital rape did not exist, and wives were obligated to satisfy their husbands, as William Andrus Alcott, the author of a well-received marriage manual from 1837, made clear. "Nothing, perhaps," he wrote, "will more severely test your forbearance than [the] assumption, on the part of your husband, that might gives right. But what will you do? Will you resent it . . . or will you bear and forbear?"

Submission in sex mirrored a woman's overall role in marriage. American matrimonial law, while different from state to state, basically derived from English matrimonial law, which was rooted in the concept of *coverture*—that is, a married woman's identity was *covered* or subsumed by her husband's. Legally, she had no existence separate from his. Any wages a married woman earned belonged to her husband, and she was neither permitted to sign a contract in her own name nor, in most cases, to sue in a court of law. For the women of New York State, the revolutionary Married Women's Property Act of 1848 corrected some injustices, but a woman's social, legal, and civil statuses remained inferior to those of a man, as she was considered inferior to him in intellect and abilities. She was not admitted to most institutions of higher learning, not allowed to work in most jobs or professions, and not accorded many of a citizen's rights, including the right to vote or sit on a jury. Moreover, from her wedding night on, partly as a matter of law, and partly social custom, she was stripped of whatever autonomy she might have possessed as a single woman. In exchange for her husband's support and protection, a wife was expected to devote herself to his wants and needs. It was considered a wife's duty to obey her husband, submit to his wishes, run his household, maintain harmony, avoid controversy, provide comfort, offer companionship, fulfill her sexual obligations, and, if possible, bear and raise children. These often-challenging expectations held true not only for affluent women with servants and spare time but also for wives who worked long hours, whether at home managing multiple children or at a factory.

Considered in conventional thinking to be superior to a man only in what was deemed to be her naturally virtuous character—although, of course, she could prove weak and corruptible, like

Eve—a woman exercised limited power at home in her role as wife and mother. The domestic realm, whatever its reality, was idealized as gentle and genteel and defined as a "separate sphere" from the heady public, political, and economic sphere of a man. But domestic power, too, a wife held at her husband's indulgence. In 1854, a select committee of the New York State legislature, empowered to make recommendations on the topic of equality in marriage, made its unanimous opinion clear: "Every well-regulated home and household in the land affords an example illustrative of what is woman's proper sphere, and what is man's . . . the husband is the head—the representative of the family."

Whatever the future seemed to promise them, Mary and Peter had married at a time of significant confusion and transition in the relationship between men and women. While the lifestyle of the "sporting man" made the reality of male and female sexuality highly visible, the perception of "separate spheres" glorified the world of polite domesticity and female purity. The situation of working-class and impoverished women of course could turn the notion of separate spheres into an illusion. Moreover, enslaved women and men were denied all legal rights, including the right to marry and have custody of their children. Nevertheless, all women, privileged and otherwise, were subject to one extreme or another to the limitations, deprivations, and demands men imposed on them. While not all women objected to their subordinate and vulnerable status, some women's rights advocates went so far as to compare, with fierce hyperbole, the role of a wife to the much harsher existence of prostitutes or slaves—abused, passive, and deprived of effective agency.

Without agency, that is, except in one significant way. Over the course of the previous century, the yearning for romantic love had become an important element in marriage, previously a rather practical arrangement designed to unite families of similar social class, forge economic ties, and produce children. Ironically, the responsibility for keeping romance alive in a marriage was thought to rest not on the iron strength of a man's devotion but on a woman's frail shoulders and her talent for subtle manipulation. "It is to a thousand little delicacies of conduct that [a woman] must trust to keep alive passion, and to protect herself from that dangerous familiarity . . . incident to matrimony," the popular author Washington Irving wrote in his episodic novel *Bracebridge Hall.* "By these means, though she has surrendered her person, [she] may continue the romance of love even beyond the honey-moon."

ON THEIR RETURN FROM PHILADELPHIA, Peter took his bride home to Waverly, his mother's two-hundred-acre estate in rural Queens. Mary now lived a significant distance from her parents, sisters, and friends, as well as from the familiar urban pleasures of Manhattan. Moreover, she once again found herself living amid a throng of family—only this time, a family of near strangers, her in-laws.

Mary's mother-in-law, Aletta Strong—frail, genial, almost blind—had been a widow for fifteen years. The benignly autocratic head of Waverly, Aletta was a Remsen on her father's side, descended from a family of Dutch and German stock, and a Rapelje on her mother's, descended from French Huguenots. This mingling of bloodlines, according to one nineteenth-century historian of Queens County, allowed family members to combine what he considered characteristic French traits such as gaiety, grace, and intelligence with a Dutch legacy of common sense, frugality, and neatness.

Of Peter's five siblings, four still lived at Waverly. Twenty-nine-year-old Elizabeth Jane, married nine years, resided there with her husband, Edward Livingston Lynch, and their eight-year-old daughter, named Aletta for her grandmother. The son and grandson of distinguished judges, Edward Lynch, like his brother-in-law Peter, was a lawyer who chose not to practice.

Twenty-six-year-old Edward Strong and his wife, the former Susan Warren, had been married only a year. Edward was much admired for his good looks, thoughtful demeanor, and religious interests. Susan, now eighteen, comely and demure, was the closest family member in age to Mary, potentially either a rival for family favor or a friend.

James, the oldest of Aletta's sons, and Benjamin, the youngest, were bachelors. Both would remain at Waverly, along with their spouses, even after their marriages a few years in the future. Thirty-two-year-old James was known to be fun-loving, outgoing, and sociable. Twenty-four-year-old Benjamin, sensible and reliable, would be remembered in years to come as the last Strong to inhabit the family homestead. Like Peter, his three brothers abstained from paid work, preferring to live at Waverly and identify themselves simply as "gentlemen."

Only thirty-three-year-old Julia, oldest of the Strong siblings, a mother hen to them, lived in Manhattan. She and her husband, Gregory Thurston Bedell, an ambitious cleric, resided at the parish house of the Church of the Ascension on Fifth Avenue, where he served as rector. Julia suffered from a painful ailment that made walking difficult, most likely rheumatism, and her first child had died in infancy a few years earlier. Nevertheless, Julia bore her troubles with stoic good cheer and was an ideal minister's wife—capable, religious, affectionate, and devoted to her family. Although the trip to Waverly was tedious, about an hour and a half by ferry and coach, Julia visited her mother and siblings in Queens so often that she might have lived there.

In the early 1850s, Queens was a vastly different world from the urban and commercial behemoth of Manhattan. Not yet consolidated into New York City, Queens County remained mostly idyllic countryside: windy bluffs overlooking clear blue bays, green-gold salt meadows, lush farmlands. On the county's north coast, a high, rocky ridge formed scenic coves. Inland, meandering creeks, forests, and rolling hills forged natural boundaries between various townships. Many of the county's inhabitants made their living in agriculture, fishing, and oyster harvesting, supplying fruits, vegetables, and seafood to satisfy Manhattan's huge hunger. Others in small businesses, such as blacksmiths, grocers, carpenters, harness makers, and wheelwrights, served local needs. Manufacturing was virtually nonexistent. Working farms and rural estates comprised most of the residences in sparsely populated Queens.

The Strong estate was located in Newtown, Queens, a township founded in the mid-seventeenth century in the western part of Long Island. Waverly lay on the township's rocky north coast, three miles from Newtown Village—an inland cluster of homes, a few stores, the Dutch Reformed Church, and several other houses of worship. Whether separated by a village half-acre or several country miles, Newtown's neighbors socialized and did business with one another, and their children often married. However, established wealth and pedigree crossed county lines, linking Newtown's long-settled Dutch and English families with the wider circle of old New York.

On property purchased in the early 1700s by Peter's forebears, Waverly over the years had evolved into a gracious country home surrounded by lawns, gardens, fields, and woodlands, with paths that led to the bluffs overlooking the bay. Spacious though not imposing, Waverly comfortably accommodated family members and a staff composed of a laundress, cook, waitress, two maids, several coachmen, and an elderly woman fondly nicknamed "Old Nurse," who had helped raise the Strong siblings.

Waverly's three-story main house had seventeen rooms, with a dining room, parlor, library, and drawing room on the first floor, and the majority of family and guest bedrooms on the second floor. A kitchen and pantry, along with servants' bedrooms, were located in a separate wing of the house. Of the household staff, only Old Nurse received the privilege of a bedroom in the main house with the family. It was on the third floor, down a hallway from the bedroom given to Mary and Peter on their return from their honeymoon.

With their room tucked up under the eaves, the newlyweds had a beautiful view across the bluffs to the bay. Less appealing, a low ceiling and small windows no doubt provided poor ventilation. Rosewood furniture, a Turkish rug, and a large cabinet stocked with Peter's exotic travel memorabilia gave the room a distinctly masculine flavor. Well-to-do travelers and amateur naturalists often displayed their collections, although usually in a private study or library, and P. T. Barnum had turned the display of curiosities into a lucrative business and national craze. More traditionally, the Strongs' bedroom quarters also encompassed a dressing room and—pointedly—a future nursery.

Mary probably appreciated that she and Peter had a little distance from the other family members, although the high floor might have been inconvenient and, perhaps, a bit stuffy, and Mary would have liked more space for a larger ladies' wardrobe to hold her clothes. For better or worse, however, their three third-floor rooms comprised the couple's private domain, the intimate space within the crowded world of Waverly from which Peter and Mary were launched into married life.

CHAPTER 4

A Handsome Young Matron

ONCE SETTLED IN HER NEW HOME, Mary's activities as a young wife in an affluent household most likely included—in addition to time with her husband—reading, conversation with other family members, games, strolling the grounds, and visiting or receiving friends and neighbors. Sewing—a craft at which Mary had excelled since childhood—remained a favorite activity. The author Nathaniel Hawthorne, in his 1850 novel *The Scarlet Letter*, had described sewing as a creative as well as useful act, a woman's art. His heroine, the adulteress Hester Prynne, won the reluctant admiration of her pitiless tormenters through her work as a seamstress.

Many of Mary's activities would have resembled those at Bleecker Street. However, she was no longer able to step from her front door into the bustle of Broadway or walk to a childhood friend's home. Leaving Waverly to visit Newtown Village or anywhere else required riding a horse, driving a wagon, or summoning one of the coachmen. Happily, Mary enjoyed riding, an activity approved by *Godey's Ladies' Book* as healthy and beautifying.

In exchange for her companionship and devotion, Peter was expected to protect his wife from adversity and provide for her financially. Since the couple lived at Waverly, and he had an inheritance, these responsibilities must not have seemed burdensome, at least initially. His routines most likely also stayed much as they had been—hunting, fishing, boating, and socializing with his brothers and friends. Mary accompanied him, Old Nurse later remembered, "as often as she wanted to go . . . all she had to do was to say she'd go, and she went." Peter sometimes traveled to Manhattan to check on his mother's Waverly Place properties and to visit his clubs.

One disappointment weighed on Mary. The yearning to become mistress of her own household, however modest, remained unfulfilled. Just as Mary's mother commanded the Bleecker Street household, Aletta reigned over Waverly. This was no small matter. Since a woman lacked authority in most other ways, a well-run household bestowed prestige, enhanced self-worth, and even resonated with political significance. The home was the center from which healthy, godly, and right-thinking young sons— the Republic's future citizens—emerged. Elizabeth Cady Stanton later wrote that to manage her servants, bring order to her house, and nurture the next generation, a woman needed "the strong points of character that the most successful statesman possesses."

Within a few months of her marriage, Mary was pregnant. Even more than in marriage, women were believed to fulfill their highest destiny in motherhood. Once married, they had the chance to achieve this destiny often, given society's disapproval of birth control and the absence of effective methods. Many women nevertheless dreaded pregnancy's discomforts and dangers, well aware that mother, infant, or both could die in childbirth. Mary's mother, Abby, had weathered twelve pregnancies, the deaths of two infants and one toddler, and an exhaustion that propelled her to send her older daughters to their Aunt Em's in Maine almost every summer. Married, fertile women often lived, like Abby, in a continuous cycle of pregnancy, confinement, childbirth, and recovery.

Mary entered motherhood after the successful birth of her first child at Waverly on April 5, 1854. The infant—her namesake—was nicknamed Mamie. Motherhood gave Mary an absorbing new role. She breastfed, sewed baby clothes, and tended to Mamie's good health, properly pleasing appearance, habits of obedience, and Christian upbringing. Of course, Old Nurse was available to help, maids to clean, a cook to prepare meals, and a laundress to do the wash. Still, as well-to-do young ladies such as Mary agreed, every army required a skilled general. Or, in Mary's case, perhaps a loyal lieutenant, as Aletta gently commanded Waverly.

Mary suffered a miscarriage the next year. While not unusual, a miscarriage often exacted both a physical and an emotional toll. Along with grief and disappointment, a woman might feel that she had failed in her highest calling.

After Mary recovered, she and Peter made a decision that took some imagination and daring. They abandoned their familiar world and headed to Europe, accompanied by their toddler, Mamie, and a female companion to assist them. The couple had been married two years when they embarked on their journey. For thirty-two-year-old Peter, travel meant a chance to relive adventures from his bachelor days, re-immerse himself in Old World culture, and demonstrate his erudition to Mary. For twenty-two-year-old Mary, a Grand Tour presented a thrilling opportunity to experience what she had only read about in school—the art, architecture, monuments, and music of Europe.

By the mid-1850s, many more Americans—individuals, couples, and families—were traveling abroad. Steamships now crossed the Atlantic in under ten days and aspired to great luxury, featuring saloons with gilded furniture, sumptuous menus, and bridal suites, but ocean travel remained daunting. Even on sunny days, unexpected swells flooded the deck and drenched passengers. Rough seas and gusting storms tossed those aboard bruisingly from side to side. Seasickness—more politely known as *mal de mer*, the French phrase covering up messy reality—felled men, women, and children, confining them to their cabins with basins on their laps.

The voyage also held significant dangers. Contemplating her trip home to the United States from Italy in 1850, the journalist Margaret Fuller wrote, "I read of the wreck of the *Argo* . . . There were also notices of the wreck of the *Royal Adelaid*, a fine English Steamer, and of the *John Skiddy*, one of the fine American packets."

Fuller trusted her fate to a merchant ship that sank off the coast of Fire Island. Neither she, her husband, nor their son survived. In 1854, one of the grandest ships of its day, the *Arctic*, collided with a small French steamer in dense fog off the coast of Newfoundland. Memory of the disaster lingered, but adventure continued to beckon curious, intrepid, and culture-hungry Americans.

Even on dry land, the pleasures of the nineteenth-century Grand Tour didn't necessarily make the journey easy for American tourists with little practical knowledge of the continent. Whatever languages they had studied in school, they needed to decipher a host of others; they confronted unfamiliar customs, endured the discomforts of lurching long distances by horse-drawn vehicles, ventured over unknown terrain within and between foreign lands, coped with uncertain and sometimes unsanitary living conditions, found medical help as necessary, and digested foods startlingly new to the complacent American stomach.

Still, their travels must have suited the Strongs, for Mary, Peter, and Mamie remained abroad for two years. The revolutions of 1848 had largely failed, and Napoleon III had declared himself emperor of France. But the allure of Paris was undiminished—indeed, under the new emperor's ambitious redesign of the city, it was enhanced. The Paris Exposition of 1855 presented a dazzling spectacle of more than five thousand exhibits along the Champs-Élysées. Eight hundred artists, including Ingres and Delacroix, displayed their work, and new technologies, such as the Singer sewing machine and the telegraph, demonstrated wonders of the age.

Traveling through Italy, the Strongs visited Genoa and Rome with American friends, the railroad magnate William Henry Aspinwall and his wife. Peter, a proud husband of cultivated tastes, commissioned a well-known American artist working in Rome, Paul Akers, to sculpt a marble bust of Mary in the popular neoclassical style. Praised by Nathaniel Hawthorne as a sculptor with "the faculty of putting thought and feeling into marble," Akers captured the image of an attractive woman with strong, regular features, her hair fashionably pulled back from her face, her eyes serious, a surprisingly firm set to her wide mouth. The girl who wedded Peter four years earlier seems to have grown up. A handsome young matron has taken her place, tested by the emotional experiences of bearing and raising a child, suffering a miscarriage, and traveling to places far from her circumscribed New York life.

The Strongs boarded for a time with the Aspinwalls' daughter in Florence, then moved on. Their itinerary undoubtedly included many of the other usual American destinations such as Switzerland and Germany. Back in France, they visited Mary's cousin, Mary Elizabeth Rhinelander Newbold, and her husband, Thomas, in Fontainebleau, just outside of Paris. The Newbolds' baby, Edith, was born that August, 1856, and "Pierre Remsen Strong" was a witness on her birth certificate.

On this trip far from home, Mary suffered another miscarriage.

Wrenching under any circumstances, it could only have been hard to be away from family and familiar comforts at such a time.

The couple returned to Waverly in 1857, the same year that Lucretia, Mary's favorite sister, her exuberant and loyal companion from childhood, married Richard Heckscher, a dynamic and enterprising German immigrant, and that one of her younger sisters, Frances, married Joseph Parker Norris, an earnest and industrious New Yorker. At Waverly, Elizabeth Jane Lynch's one-year-old daughter, her second child, was the newest member of the household.

Joy, however, mixed with mourning, for that same year Edward's wife died, most likely in childbirth. Susan was only twenty-three years old, a year younger than Mary, and had spent her entire, brief married life at Waverly. "I saw Edward after he lost his wife," Old Nurse remembered. "He felt very bad about it, and showed it by being very quiet and sedate, and everybody pitied him because he lost an elegant wife." Family members, friends, and servants did their best to comfort the grieving widower, even as he awoke each day among married siblings, some of whose children were close at hand.

CHAPTER 5

Weddings, Baptisms, and Funerals

By the time Mary and Peter returned from Europe, industrial progress—on proud display at the Paris Exposition—had reached even quiet Queens. Whistling across the landscape, belching white clouds of steam, speeding along newly opened railroad tracks, trains carried Queens businessmen to catch the Manhattan ferries. Competing newspapers reported on local gossip and national events, from babies' baptisms to the activities of the Republican Party, established in 1854. Manufacturing plants—glass works; oil, paint, and varnish factories—had started to mar the scenic rural countryside. Tourists and residents alike crowded Queens beaches and visited the county's racecourses to cheer their favorite horses.

During these years, movements for and against radical reform divided husbands and wives, laborers and owners, South and North. Women's rights advocates agitated for suffrage, abolitionists pressed for an end to slavery, and some for both. The Supreme Court's 1857 Dred Scott decision, a ruling that denied citizenship to African Americans—stating that they possessed "no rights which the white man was bound to respect"—heightened sectional hostility. In many northern households, slavery was considered an abomination, but the impending prospect of disunion and the possibility of a civil war were viewed as the greater horror.

In the summer of 1857, a hurricane assailed the S.S. *Central America*, a steamship carrying a cargo of California gold destined for the vaults of East Coast banks. Battered by the storm's fierce gales and towering waves, the ship sank off the South Carolina coast, its cargo of gold buried thousands of feet beneath the ocean's surface. The disaster shook confidence in an economy already on the brink of a depression, set off a run on the banks, and helped precipitate the Panic of 1857, a worldwide financial and banking crisis. For a time, the Panic threatened to ruin Mary's father, but both the Bank of Commerce and his career as its president survived. John later remembered what a comfort Mary was to him, affectionate and stalwart, during his dark days before the nation recovered.

At Waverly, an enclave insulated by its rural location and substantial wealth from the full impact of state and national storms, rhythms of work and domestic life continued much as usual. Peter, James, Edward, and Benjamin all kept horses and carriages at Waverly; by some counts, there were twenty-five horses, five coachmen, and a dozen carriages. Peter, who owned three horses and two carriages, now spent an increasing amount of time in Manhattan. Weekdays, after breakfast at seven, a coachman drove him to the railroad, where he boarded a train to the ferry that crossed the East River. Headquartered in a downtown office, near his cousin George Templeton Strong's law firm, Peter continued to serve as his mother's agent for her Waverly Place properties. His Manhattan trips also gave him a convenient chance to linger pleasurably at his clubs. Peter came home on some days at two in the afternoon and on others not until six p.m.

On August 4, 1859, Mary gave birth to the couple's second daughter, Alice—nicknamed Allie. When she had time between maternal duties, Mary occasionally took carriage rides with Edward, her widowed brother-in-law, or the two saddled horses and rode together to Newtown Village. Edward was a deacon in the Dutch Reformed Church, and he encouraged Mary to teach Sunday school classes there. Although pregnant again, she agreed. Philanthropic endeavors such as Sunday school teaching were considered appropriate activities for a genteel young matron. In addition, she and Edward were both said to be faithful believers and to take their religion seriously, a shared proclivity perhaps strengthened in Edward by sorrow after Susan's death.

Peter's youngest brother, Benjamin, was married on October 16, 1860. His bride—Frances, nicknamed Fanny—was a girl who hailed from a distinguished old New York family, and whose father, the Honorable Murray Hoffman, was a noted judge. Four days after the wedding, on October 20, Mary's third daughter, Edith, was born, like Allie, at Waverly, only fourteen months after her sister. Honored to be Edith's godfather, Edward held the infant at her baptism. Fanny, Benjamin's bride and—except for the baby—the newest member of the Strong clan, was named the infant's godmother.

Extremely frail after Edith's birth, coming as it did so soon after Allie's, twenty-seven-year-old Mary seemed not only weak but depressed and distant. In the following months, she failed to recover her health and spirits, remaining anxious, querulous, and fragile. Her doctor advised her to wean Edith early, but she refused, keeping her youngest daughter close, her decision probably influenced by a wish to avoid another pregnancy. Breastfeeding can reduce the chance of pregnancy and was considered a form of birth control.

After Edith's birth, the Strongs hired a governess to teach and care for Mamie. Matilda Mussehl, a German immigrant in her early twenties, had been recommended by Mary's sister, Lucretia, who had briefly employed her. Like Jane Eyre and Becky Sharpe, governesses of popular fiction, Mussehl turned out to be singularly observant about the household's inhabitants and activities, even noticing some coolness between Peter and Mary. "I can't remember ever seeing him arm-in-arm with his wife," she later stated. "I can't remember instances where they both participated in the same amusements . . . he kissed the children oftener than the wife."

Nevertheless, Peter seemed solicitous of Mary and concerned about her. In the summer of 1861, he leased a house in the fashionable town of Lenox, Massachusetts, most likely hoping that the resort's pure air and peaceful lake vistas would improve his wife's health. In the fall, to please her, he rented a house for his family of five on Twenty-first Street in Manhattan instead of returning to Waverly, signing a six-month contract. At last, eight years after her wedding, the mother of three little daughters, Mary became mistress of her own New York household, albeit only until the end of the Strongs' lease that spring.

A special pleasure for Mary, her beloved mother and father lived around the corner on Twenty-second Street, having recently moved there from Bleecker Street. Their move reflected changes in their former neighborhood and throughout the city. By 1861, many homes on and around Bleecker Street had been transformed into boarding houses to accommodate the city's newcomers from the countryside and abroad. The massive brick home at 64 Bleecker Street, once owned by James Roosevelt, was rented to Dr. Elizabeth Blackwell, the first woman in the United States to earn a medical degree. She used the building to open a medical facility for indigent women and children. Blackwell's achievements and institution represented great strides for women, but the founding of her hospital was considered by the wealthy one more blow to the once elegant Bleecker Street neighborhood. Some wealthier

New Yorkers had moved, like Mary's parents, to townhouses in the East Twenties. Others had constructed monumental marble palaces along Madison and Fifth Avenues.

War and politics now intruded on conversations in every household, as they had ever since Confederate troops fired on federally owned Fort Sumter in Charleston Harbor, South Carolina, on April 12, 1861. A few days after the attack, only weeks into his first term, the newly elected Republican president, Abraham Lincoln, had called for 75,000 volunteers to put down the South's insurrection and end the War of Rebellion. Lincoln initially summoned the volunteers for just three months of service, a sadly optimistic estimate of the Union Army's needs.

Of Aletta Strong's four sons, Edward answered the call to sign up in support of the Union cause, enlisting in the 45th Regiment of the United States Army of Volunteers. Pro-Union sentiment in Newtown ran high. An antiwar rally was disrupted by Unionists shouting, "Secession died at Newtown August 29, 1861," and hurling "anathemas against treason and traitors." As regiments began to form, some commanders set up camp to train their troops on the smooth, flat surface of Queens racetracks.

In mid-December 1861, Edward was assigned as an aide-de-camp to General John G. Foster, a commander participating in a naval offensive called the Burnside Expedition. The Union was assembling a fleet in Baltimore in anticipation of heading to North Carolina, where battles to control the coastline were underway. Edward traveled to Washington to receive his orders, then returned to New York for a few days before reporting for duty. Instead of going to Waverly, he stayed with Peter, Mary, and his three little nieces.

Christmas had always been a festive time for Mary—she well remembered her mother's lavish annual Christmas party—but war shadowed this one. Everyone worried about Edward's safety.

Ever a skilled seamstress, Mary sewed a dressing gown for the new soldier, a gift for him to take to North Carolina. He was, after all, a widower with no one else to care for him, and Edith's godfather. He also was Mary's friend. Her efforts mirrored that of countless other women who poured their patriotic fervor and love of family into producing flannel shirts, drawers, socks, mittens, slippers, and other items of clothing for their family members, friends, and other soldiers.

On December 23, Edith came down with a cough. What seemed to be a cold continued through Christmas. Several days after Christmas, Edward left for Baltimore. He was one of the two Strong brothers—James later joined the effort—among the approximately 460,000 men from New York State who fought for the Union in the Civil War.

By the time Edward left, Edith had steadily worsened and now burned with fever. Her parents took turns staying by her bedside, dread and sorrow building as they watched their little daughter suffer and toss. There was little they could do but pray. Children as young as Edith's oldest sister, seven-year-old Mamie, understood the fragility of life—even of their own lives. The family physician, Dr. Watson, visited daily, but his efforts— mostly herbal remedies, a tiny bit of morphine to quiet the terrible coughing, and compresses—were ineffective.

Edith died of influenza—a term broadly used for a respiratory infection—on January 2, 1862. A small, sad notice in *The New York Times* on January 4 read simply:

STRONG—In this city, on Thursday evening, January 2, EDITH, youngest child of Peter R. and Mary E. Strong, aged 14 months.

The funeral will take place this afternoon at 3 o'clock, from the residence of her parents, No. 50 East 21st-st.

The night after Edith's funeral, January 5, Mary, Peter, Mamie, and Allie sat together at home, grieving their loss. Mamie read aloud a chapter from the Bible. When she finished, Mary and Peter kissed the two little girls and sent them to bed.

Afterward, Peter thought about the Bible passage Mamie had read, which focused on the relationship between love and duty. It seemed to him that over the last few years a certain distance—a kind of casual disregard—had appeared in his relationship with Mary. When they were together, they no longer behaved tenderly toward one another, as they had at the start of their marriage. They also were known on occasion to speak harshly to one another. They increasingly spent time apart.

Now, in the wake of Edith's death, Peter felt it was time to repair the problems in his marriage. He wished, he said, to resume marital duties—surely a euphemism for more frequent sexual intimacy. He moved his chair closer to Mary's and addressed her awkwardly. He suggested that the Bible passage they had heard might inspire them to find a way to renew joy in their marriage. He reached out and took her hand, a simple gesture he had rarely made in recent years.

In response, and to his unspeakable shock, Mary pulled away, hurled herself at Peter's feet and sobbed, "Oh, forgive me, forgive me. You cannot conceive how guilty I have been."

For almost two years, Mary confessed, she had been having an affair with his brother Edward, to all appearances a paragon of virtue—a good-hearted widower, church deacon, godfather to baby Edith, and now a Union soldier.

PART 2

Dissolution

CHAPTER 6

Revelations

PETER SAT STUNNED AND HORRIFIED, disbelieving Mary's words. Abject, penitent, weeping, she stayed with him, answering his questions. After a time, he called for two servants to help him move a bed into the small dressing room next to the bedroom he and Mary shared. He gave the excuse that the children in their nearby room made too much noise. He would be disturbed less in the dressing room.

Peter and Mary never again shared a bedroom or bed. Yet, within a day, it was clear that neither one of them wanted to divorce, dreading its very possibility. Whatever a couple's miseries, in the mid-nineteenth-century United States legally ending a marriage was viewed as an abhorrent act, especially among members of the Strongs' social class.

"That domestic troubles should ever end in a divorce court was unthinkable; so families remained intact, whatever happened," the high-society matron Mrs. John King Van Rensselaer wrote in 1924, describing the world of her youth sixty years earlier. The institution of marriage was understood to be a contractual union sanctified by God, necessary to the well-being of civil society and to the advancement of the nation.

With marriage revered, divorce was almost impossible to obtain. Legally dissolving a marriage was so onerous that many couples, whatever their social class, took matters into their own hands and informally dissolved their own unions. An abused wife might flee her marriage, a restless husband might desert his wife and head west or—if wealthy enough—abroad. Among the well-to-do, quiet and private separation settlements allowed a husband and wife to live independent lives and to publicly save face.

While divorce laws differed from state to state, obtaining a divorce in New York State was particularly difficult. In all states, one of the spouses had to be found at fault for a marriage's failure, and faults that the law recognized varied. In the courts of New York, however, divorce would be granted on the grounds of one fault only—adultery. Whatever the underlying complexity of reasons—cruelty, desertion, revenge, or incompatibility—individuals bringing divorce actions had to accuse their spouse of being unfaithful. Legal separations "from bed and board" existed and could sometimes be obtained on grounds such as gross neglect. Nevertheless, a couple seeking a legal separation endured the same publicity and disapproval engendered by divorce, with all the added disadvantages of remaining legally married.

Colonial America had treated the act of adultery—sex with an individual other than one's spouse—as a serious crime as well as a sin, punishable by means from banishment to whipping to hanging. Fornication—sex between individuals not married to each other—also carried weighty penalties. As society grew more secular, however, and states developed their own legal codes, acts of adultery and fornication were prosecuted less often and less harshly, although differences continued to exist between North and South, East and West, as well as among states. Still, even where divorce laws were liberalized, the biblical stigma of sin endured. In part because of the shame they invoked, betrayals of the marriage vow tended to be treated discreetly. In New York, adultery generally was left as a private issue to be resolved between husbands and wives.

Private, that is, unless either party wanted a divorce. At that point, adultery necessarily burst into public view. Since proving adultery required irrefutable evidence of the most intimate kind, scandalous revelations inevitably followed. Suing for divorce in civil court advertised infidelity, as boldly as the scarlet letter in Hawthorne's famous novel.

Society, of course, had a double standard when it came to adultery. Men might be viewed as outcasts for a time, but society usually forgave them. "The most outrageous conduct by husbands and fathers was accorded no further publicity than the whisper of gossip," Van Rensselaer wrote. A man might continue in his business, might eventually be welcomed back among his friends.

And a man whose wife was the adulterer? The poor man might be pitied for having chosen such a faithless wife and indulged by his social circle in venting justifiable rage.

However, Peter's situation was different from—more extreme than—that of most such men, and he knew it. Not only had he been cuckolded, but cuckolded by his own brother. Avoiding a divorce action was essential to concealing the situation, suppressing ridicule, and protecting his own and the Strong family's name.

For Mary, avoiding divorce was even more critical than for Peter. The consequences of divorce weighed far more heavily on a woman than on a man. Whereas an adulterous—or cuckolded—man might be shamed for a time, the moral code of the mid-nineteenth century decreed that an adulteress was a "fallen woman," forever ruined, her life and reputation destroyed. "Women should be . . . far more reserved and more delicate than men," the writer William Cobbett advised readers. "Nature bids them be such . . . and therefore, when they commit this offence [adultery], they excite loathing."

"Ruined" working-class or impoverished women, if abandoned or divorced, struggled to find whatever menial work they could get. If unsuccessful, some turned to prostitution rather than starve. Most middle- and upper-class divorced women, previously dependent on their husbands for their financial well-being and woefully unprepared for the few jobs such as teaching or factory work open to them, were shunned by family and friends and forced to live in reduced circumstances. They, too, faced poverty, prayed for mercy, searched hard for work, and learned to live by whatever means they could scrape together. "In that day," Van Rensselaer wrote, "the woman who obtained a divorce was a Pariah. There was no appeal. By her action she became a social outcast."

Perhaps the greatest punishment, a wife divorced for adultery, no matter how good a mother, almost always was made to surrender custody of her children. In patriarchal America, a father not only possessed his children but was assumed to be the parent best able to care for them. By law and custom, he had full rights to keep them, unless he committed a wrong so egregious (persistent cruelty or gross debauchery, for example) that a judge ruled against him, a rare and controversial occurrence.

There were whispers of change, although hardly more than that. In the nineteenth century, children—once viewed largely in economic terms for their potential value as workers or as property to be traded on the marriage market—were coming to be valued for themselves, sentimentalized and loved, much as they are today. This emergent view of the child began to have an influence on the law or, at least, judicial interpretations of the law. A child's welfare became a factor in custody disputes. By mid-century it was legitimate to ask: which parent would serve the best interests of the child?

The answer, almost uniformly, was the customary one: the father. In 1860, the New York State legislature passed a law to make custody arrangements in divorce more equitable, but a judge invalidated the provision, stating that "the recognized paramount right of the father must prevail over the otherwise equal claims of the mother." Legislators modified the law to reflect the ruling.

Dreading divorce, in the shadow of their grief over Edith's death, the Strongs managed to negotiate an agreement. Mary, according to Peter, immediately showed "signs of the deepest humiliation, contrition, and remorse" and swore that she would humbly endure whatever fate he chose to impose on her. With Edward assigned to a naval battalion which was departing Baltimore, she ended her relationship with him, writing that "my husband knows all. Whatever may be the issue of that knowledge, my affections are again entirely his."

In response to her actions, Peter came up with a proposal that, while punitive, retained the façade of a respectable marriage: he would continue the marriage by "residing under the same roof with her . . . occupying separate apartments, having no marital relations with her, and, as far as possible, avoiding her society." It was mutually understood that he had every right to divorce her, should he ever change his mind. The arrangement salvaged respectability, but day-to-day interactions, with their restrictions and prohibitions, did nothing to alleviate resentment.

The Strongs' efforts to forge a private arrangement foundered almost immediately. Within three weeks, Mary admitted to Peter that she was several months pregnant. She may not have known her condition, or perhaps not been certain about it, previously. Whose child was it? This was an unanswerable question, at least in Peter's tormented mind.

WHILE PETER AND MARY were contemplating the survival of
their marriage, Edward Strong was far away from the domestic anguish he had helped precipitate. That January, a motley flo-
tilla of eighty assorted vessels, ranging from mighty gunboats to
rickety tugboats, had begun a secret journey south from Maryland to North Carolina to engage in the first amphibious battle of the Civil War. Edward was involved, as aide-de-camp to
General John Gray Foster, one of three generals serving under
Ambrose Burnside, senior commander. The Burnside Expedition,
as it became known, consisted of 13,000 army and navy Union
troops headed to Roanoke Island to gain control of the coastline
from Confederate forces there.

Delayed by powerful storms, the fleet arrived on February 7,
gunboats in the lead, a barrage of gunfire scattering the small
Confederate force that confronted them. "From the deck of our
vessel, we beheld a sight that was never seen on this continent in
extent or beauty," wrote an awed young private who, like Edward
Strong, had never before witnessed combat.

Under cover of bursting shells, dense smoke and columns of
flame, the ragtag fleet sailed along the island's inland waterway,
anchoring around four p.m. and unloading Union troops in the
midst of a raw, drenching rain. "We had to wade about 200 yards
through mud and water up to our knees," George Washington
Whitman, Walt Whitman's brother, reported to his family, "and
then found a spot not very dry." It was midnight before the last
soldier disembarked.

In the morning, the First Brigade, several thousand men
under General Foster, charged up the center of the island's cause-
way. Enemy fire forced them to dive for cover into the muck of the
surrounding swamplands. Then the Second and Third Brigades in

a surprise maneuver swept in from the left and right. As George Whitman wrote, "We kept on . . . the First Brigade driving the enemy. . . . It was mighty trying to a fellow's nerves as the balls was flying around pretty thick."

By late afternoon, Union forces had won the battle, seized control of a strategic location, and captured more than 2,500 prisoners. The northern press was ecstatic over the victory. "Every blow tells fearfully against the rebellion. . . . It now requires no very far-reaching prophet to predict the end of this struggle," crowed Horace Greeley, the influential editor of the *New-York Tribune*.

FOR A FEW DAYS IN MID-MARCH, the Strongs' residence on Twenty-first Street saw an unusual amount of hectic, seemingly chaotic, activity. Dr. Watson, who had attended Edith before she died, visited several times. Mary's mother, Abby, came and stayed the entire day. Lucretia stopped by but was told to go away. Peter, who had been at Newtown, returned, then departed. A nurse, Madame Barbier, arrived. Mary did not leave her bedroom. After two days of various comings and goings, an undertaker appeared and carried away a small cardboard box. It was said that Mary had suffered another miscarriage.

For several weeks afterward, Mary experienced so much pain that Mamie's governess, Matilda Mussehl, was asked to stay with her and apply poultices—warm herbal compresses—during the night. It was surely not a duty the governess had ever contemplated.

Eventually, Mary improved enough to return to daily life but appeared pale and weak. Her losses were multiple—Edith, her lover, her unborn child, her husband's affection, her self-esteem. Peter, too, was lost in a miasma of grief, but another ailment—bitterness—afflicted him even more seriously. His wife's lover had been his own brother? She had perhaps carried

Edward's child, not his? Humiliation ate at him. Despite their arrangement, Peter continued to threaten Mary with taking away the children and sending her into exile.

The Strongs also had to face and deal with practical matters. Their lease at Twenty-first Street ended in May. They didn't want to remain there, the site of so many unhappy events, nor could they return to Waverly, the site of Mary's love affair. Living at Waverly, where the costs of housing, food, and help were shared with his siblings or borne by his mother, had offered Peter financial benefits. Fully on his own, now, with the whole burden of his family's expenses ahead of him and a wayward wife in tow, Peter turned his little family into vagabonds, moving them from place to place, from one home to another, for more than a year.

From May through October 1862, the Strongs rented a house in Islip, Long Island, a pretty village on the water that Mary's sister, Lucretia, knew and recommended. She thought Mamie and Allie would have fun there, and that the sea air would be healthy for Mary. Mary's father, John, encouraged the move, thinking that Peter would enjoy the boating and fishing.

When their Islip lease ended in October, Peter worried about money. Why couldn't his father-in-law contribute to the rent? Instead of offering financial assistance, John offered accommodations. The Strongs moved into the Stevenses' townhouse on Twenty-second Street in Manhattan. Peter was often but not always there, sometimes dining and sleeping at Waverly.

Within a few months of the Strongs' living with the Stevenses—a household that included Mary's parents and three unmarried sisters—everyone's nerves were on edge. As cold weather came on, family members were increasingly trapped together in the house. There was little holiday festivity and no good news. That bleak Christmas season of 1862, a year after Edith's death, the press grimly summarized the terrible events suffered by the nation: 23,000 combined Union and Confederate dead or wounded at Shiloh; Confederate General Stonewall Jackson's defeat of the Union in the Shenandoah Valley and at Harper's Ferry; at Antietam, another 23,000 casualties.

On January 1, 1863, President Lincoln issued the Emancipation Proclamation, freeing the enslaved population of the Confederate states. With this action intended to cripple the South, more than three million enslaved men, women, and children were freed, although many didn't find out for years.

By late winter, the Strongs' marriage had further deteriorated. Peter was brusque with Mary in private and, occasionally, rude to her in public, once even at the family dinner table, a blatant transgression of manners. For Mary, remorse began to mingle with resentment. Would she never be forgiven? To Peter, she seemed less humble and contrite, ensconced under her father's protection. He was both baffled and angered by what he saw as her shameless pride.

Lucretia came to the rescue as best she could, inviting the Strongs to live with her family through the spring and summer of 1863 at Whitlock Point in Westchester County, in a sprawling and comfortable house surrounded by spacious grounds. The Heckschers planned to remain there until autumn. Lucretia's husband, Richard, welcomed his in-laws. Mamie and Allie had a swarm of cousins to play with, and Mary had her beloved Lucretia for company. Even Peter seemed less on edge in the new quarters, although Lucretia witnessed one fierce argument between the Strongs that began with a disagreement over their daughters' schooling.

Sometime that spring of 1863, Mary secretly confided to Lucretia her version of what had happened in her marriage. It gradually became clear that Lucretia wasn't the only person to receive intimate confidences in 1862 and 1863. Exactly what was said to whom, when, and under what circumstances would subsequently become central points of contention. Peter had informed John Austin Stevens as early as February 1862 about Mary's affair and pregnancy. Mary allegedly told her sister-in-law Julia, first in letters and later in person, not only that she had an affair, but also that she had undergone an abortion in March 1862, not a miscarriage. John informed his son, Austin, about the situation. Peter revealed the affair to his youngest brother, Benjamin. In March 1863, Mary supposedly told her story to Fanny, Benjamin's wife, who already knew some of it from her husband. While the various stories had similarities, they also had crucial differences. Still, none of the confidantes told anyone outside of the extended family. The tale was too terrible, the potential for social scandal too great.

On June 15, 1863, Peter's oldest brother, James, who by then had joined the war effort and was briefly on furlough, married Georgiana Berriman, daughter of a prominent family, in New York City. Peter attended the event with Mamie, not Mary, and gave the newlyweds two silver vases from Tiffany's. The celebratory occasion contrasted sharply with the debacle of Peter's broken marriage and the disaster of the nation's fratricidal war.

That July, more than 7,000 men died at Gettysburg, Pennsylvania, and more than 33,000 were wounded in the fighting. Less than two weeks after Gettysburg, violence erupted in New York City, until then so comfortably far from the seat of war, when rioting crowds, composed largely of immigrants and the poor, raged against the newly enacted draft. They aimed their anger primarily at the wealthy white men who could buy their way out of service by paying three hundred dollars—a sum far out of reach of most New Yorkers—but vented their fury on the city's Black population, considered by the rioters to be rivals for jobs and partly to blame for the loathed war. Among the acts of arson, rioting whites burned an African American orphanage to the ground. Black men were lynched from lampposts. Police and the military were called in. It took three days for the violence to be contained. The city was forced to witness, if not equipped to heal, the racial and class divisions that underlay its commercial day-to-day business.

Early that autumn, Peter and Mary finally admitted to themselves how much they now despised one another, how untenable their façade of a marriage had become. When the Heckschers, as anticipated, moved from Whitlock Point in the fall of 1863, Peter and Mary finally separated, informally but definitively. Mary, along with Mamie and Allie, moved into her parents' home on Twenty-second Street, while Peter returned to Waverly.

For a very brief period, the separation seemed moderately amicable, discreetly sustainable. The relationship remained cordial enough for Mamie and Allie to visit their father at Waverly, and for him to visit his daughters at the Stevenses' house.

However, both parties hired lawyers. Peter sought legal advice from Sanford and Woodruff, a well-respected old New York firm. Mary, with her father's and brother's advice, turned for counsel to the equally distinguished firm of Noyes and Tracy.

In November, when Mamie visited Peter at Waverly, he delayed returning her to Mary's care. Instead, he asked that more of Mamie's clothes be sent to him at Newtown. Mary didn't oblige. Then he suggested that Allie come to Waverly, even though Mamie was already overdue back at the Stevenses. Mary didn't reply. Despite Peter's increasingly heated demands to have both children at Waverly, Allie stayed in Manhattan with her mother.

With this stalemate, the Strongs' battle took a turn that drastically affected their daughters. No matter where they had lived or under what circumstances, four-year-old Allie and nine-year-old Mamie had always been together, the reliable presence of one child a comforting reality for the other. Now, even the sisters were separated, a lonely and bewildering state for the two little girls.

Sad memories that Christmas season undoubtedly heightened tension over where Allie and Mamie were to live. In addition, the Strongs' decision to separate inevitably created fresh hostilities as Mary and Peter, or their familial and legal surrogates, fought over issues that arose with the new situation: visiting schedules, places of residence, finances, the children's schooling.

Shortly after the start of the new year, on January 14, 1864, two years after Edith's funeral and Mary's confession—years of public pretense, private anguish, and indecision—Peter filed for divorce. He may have been ready to end the struggle or simply wished to scare Mary into a more accommodating position. There was no indication that he wished to remarry or woo other women, often an important reason for taking divorce action. After establishing certain basic information such as the dates of his marriage and children's births, Peter's complaint against Mary read in part that "disregarding the solemnity of her marriage vows," Mary had "at various times and places . . . committed adultery with one Edward N. Strong, and especially on the 9th day of April in the year 1860, and on various other days in the said month of April, and also on several days in the respective months of May, June, July and August of the said year 1860, the defendant did commit adultery with the said Edward N. Strong and they had frequent carnal connection together." According to the complaint, Peter did not know "on what particular days . . . or how often during the said months respectively such adultery was committed." However, he did affirm that "such adultery was committed at and within the town of Newtown."

The complaint went on to state that Mary and Edward also committed adultery in July and August 1860, at the Stevenses' house at 63 Bleecker Street; "on divers and several days" in January, February, May, and June, and the first twenty days of October, 1861, at Newtown; and from October 20 to December 14, and from December 24 to December 29, 1861, at Twenty-first Street in Manhattan.

Peter's complaint asserted that it had been less than five years since he learned of his wife's affair on January 5, 1862, an assertion required by law for a divorce action to be filed. He also averred, per the law, that he had "not co-habited with said defendant since the discovery thereof"; nor had he forgiven her for her adultery, nor consented to it, nor connived in its occurrence, nor procured a lover for her, nor created an opportunity for her to be unfaithful. The complaint also insisted that he had not been guilty of adultery. In consequence, the plaintiff demanded "that the marriage between him and the said defendant may be dissolved, and that a divorce may be adjudged . . . that the care and custody of the said children, during their minority, may . . . be awarded to the said plaintiff, and that he may have such other or further relief . . . as to the court shall seem just and reasonable."

Once the divorce papers had been filed, rumors of the couple's troubles swiftly leaked out among the other old New York families and those within their select social circle. "There is a clique of fast young married women in New York who are very much loosening the reins of good and decorous behavior," Maria Daly, the wife of an esteemed jurist, wrote in her diary. She was horrified by the "great scandal" of Mary's affair with Edward and saw it as a symptom that went beyond a single family: "Society seems to have gone mad, giving itself up to every kind of extravagance and dissipation."

Mary did not respond immediately to Peter's complaint. When she did, in late February, her legal answer was brief, taken by her counsel but not under oath. She acknowledged basic facts such as the birth dates of the children, but denied "each and every other allegation in the complaint." Furthermore, her answer stated, "the plaintiff ought not to have or maintain his action against her . . . because . . . if all the allegations in the complaint were true, the plaintiff, with full knowledge of the same, freely and entirely forgave the same and this defendant in relation therein."

Under her counsel's guidance, Mary denied committing adultery, but presented reasons why, if she *had* done so, a divorce nevertheless should not be granted. Of course, even with divorce papers filed, the Strongs still had the option to settle their differences before airing their conflict in public in court.

CHAPTER 7

Maneuvers

WHILE THE STRONGS DESCENDED into the morass of pending divorce, the national struggle over the divorce between North and South continued, with its calamitous toll of dead and wounded mounting. In March 1864, Ulysses S. Grant was put in charge of the Union Army. The ten-month siege of Petersburg, Virginia—a transportation gateway to Richmond, the Confederate capital— was launched in late spring, a bloody harbinger of the Confederacy's fall.

In the smaller, familial divorce, Edward was finally called to account, although not made to suffer consequences equal to his destructive acts. In April 1864, at Peter's request, a commission of lawyers traveled to Baltimore to question and depose Edward about his relationship with Mary. Edward not only confessed to sexual intercourse with his sister-in-law but, with a singular lack of gallantry, agreed to be a witness at a possible trial, should her confession to Peter prove inadmissible in court. The affair, Edward emphasized, "was with her full consent." Moreover, he stated, "I did not on any such occasion use any violence or physical force to compel her to submit to carnal connection." Edward reportedly was in a "reckless and desperate" state of mind, wildly declaring that his misdeeds should cast him into exile for the rest of his life, that nothing he ever did again would matter.

Cousin George, later learning of Edward's pronouncements, had little patience with them. "To be sure," he noted, Edward "did not <u>disclose</u> what had passed. She had already done so most fully. . . . three lives, shipwrecked—peace, prosperity & honorable social position destroyed."

As for the superficially idyllic world of Waverly, George noted the ironic elements of the domestic drama that happened there— evoking the place's handsome setting, its deceptively upright characters, and its secretly torrid scenes: "that wealthy elegant country home . . . its housefull [*sic*] of brothers & sisters dwelling together in unity so long . . . its rather specially staid & religious atmosphere . . . so grave, hightoned, & excellent a fellow, mourning his dead wife . . . the beautiful, stately noble-looking adulteress . . . their 'Sunday School' assignations!"

George spoke of Mary affectionately. "The only fault people found with her was that she was a little too straitlaced & stately an 'American Matron.'" He could not reconcile his vision of her with the tales of her alarming behavior.

In May, shortly after his admission of adultery, Edward returned to Waverly. Granted a brief furlough, he arrived one morning around 9:30 a.m., stayed no longer than an hour, and saw no one except his mother. He never again returned to the place where he had been born, married, and widowed, and where he had betrayed his brother.

❦

CONFRONTED WITH HIS FAITHLESSNESS, Edward retreated into the chaos of war. A few weeks after visiting Waverly, he was ordered to execute a daring maneuver. Several important Union officers had been imprisoned in Charleston, South Carolina, placed directly in their own troops' line of fire—a Confederate ploy designed to deter Union attacks.

Furious at the manipulation, Edward's superior officer, General Foster, wrote to H. W. Halleck, head of the Department of the South in Washington, D.C., proposing a parallel action. He requested that Confederate officers, currently held in relatively safe locations, should instead be brought to him: "So that I may place them under the enemy's fire as long as our officers are exposed in Charleston." Foster planned to give Edward the risky operation of transporting the Confederate officers. "I send Maj EN Strong in the steamer Mary A Boardman to Fortress Monroe to await your answer and if my request be granted to bring down the prisoners."

Edward successfully smuggled several important rebel prisoners through the front lines to embattled Charleston. In the end, a prisoner exchange took place, saving lives on both sides. Edward, now a major, was a hero. In war, as in private life, he was a man willing to take risks.

NEGOTIATIONS BETWEEN PETER AND MARY took place throughout the spring of 1864, focused on arriving at the terms of a private separation agreement. "That with the sole object of preventing such publicity," Peter later stated, he repeatedly offered to waive his right to a divorce. On one condition: "Provided only the custody of his two infant daughters were given him. . . ."

Peter presumed that a separation agreement would give him full custody of Mamie and Allie, as was his traditional paternal right, a right that he believed would be respected if he went to court. His demand for full custody of both children did not at the time seem unreasonable from a social or legal standpoint or, in his mind, a moral one. If proved, Mary was the spouse at fault, the faithless wife. In claiming full custody as a condition of settlement, he demanded control over the children's lives without consultation with Mary, whether on matters of the girls' education, place of residence, health, or any of the other issues involved in child rearing. Moreover, Peter asserted his unilateral right to control Mary's access to their daughters. His "exclusive legal right to such custody being secured," papers prepared by his lawyers stated, "he would exercise his discretion" as to whether and when Mary would be allowed to see her children. He would base his decision, the lawyers said, on the interests of the children and Mary's future conduct.

Mary rejected these terms as the basis for a separation. It was generally accepted that she was a good mother. She most likely feared that Peter's proposed decision-making power could be used arbitrarily to block her visits, punishing her cruelly and needlessly.

Letters were exchanged. A Strong family member by marriage—Judge Murray Hoffman, father of Fanny Hoffman Strong, Benjamin's wife—began to advise Peter on his negotiations with Mary. She, guided by her legal counsel as well as by her father and brother, had suggested a possible alternative plan for the girls. Perhaps Mamie and Allie could attend school in New York City, where she could see them occasionally, rather than having to visit them at Waverly (if even permitted), which would certainly be awkward. And perhaps she could have the girls with her for some part of their school vacations and be allowed to participate in their care if they were sick.

According to Peter, Mary had developed "a spirit of defiance." He believed her "behavior arose from hopes held out to her by counsel, that she might safely assume said attitude of defiance on certain technical grounds of defense." He knew that "procuring legal proofs of her guilt" could be difficult for a variety of reasons.

Confessions were often considered unreliable, and third-party witnesses could rarely produce the necessarily intimate details essential to proving that two people were having sex.

Peter barraged Mary with letters, attempting to make arrangements for Allie to come to Waverly. In late May, he bitterly chastised Mary: "You played a variety of parts, from that of deepest humility and contrition to that of the boldest self-justification and defiance. It would have been perhaps more polite for you to have persevered somewhat longer in the former role."

Relentless in her refusal to accede to Peter's demands, Mary clearly was motivated by her wish—for her own sake and her daughter's, who was so young to be separated from her—to keep Allie with her. However, she and the Stevens family also resented the injustice of bearing the full burden of shame and guilt for an affair in which Peter's brother, Edward, had participated. The honor of the Stevenses was under attack, with Mary potentially suffering the greater social and legal consequences of the alleged affair, while the Strongs seemed to be receiving the world's sympathy.

Murray Hoffman counseled Peter to take an unwavering stance in defense of his right to custody. Frustrated in his negotiations, Peter was persuaded to try a new maneuver. Overcoming his last scruple about public exposure, he appealed to the Superior Court of New York for a writ of habeas corpus, an order that legally required Mary to produce Allie in court. On Monday, June 6, the writ was delivered to a surprised John Austin Stevens at his bank, presumably sent there because he could reliably be found at his office as well as trusted to instruct his daughter to obey reason and the law.

On Wednesday, June 8, 1864, two court officers knocked on the door of the Stevens household to collect Mary and Allie for their court-ordered appearance. Neither one was there. Mary, who had suffered three miscarriages, perhaps one an abortion, and had already lost Edith to illness and Mamie to Peter, was desperate not to lose Allie. Flight was risky, the outcome unknown, but Mary had made her decision. She had taken Allie, and the two of them had disappeared.

CHAPTER 8

The Tenant
of Waverly Place

Summer passed without Peter locating the fugitives. There were sightings in Albany, Boston, and Portland, Maine, the home of Mary's Aunt Em. But even following up on clues with the help of a private detective, Peter failed to find his wife and younger daughter. The Stevens family denied all knowledge of their whereabouts.

John Austin Stevens had by now reached the apex of his career as president of New York's Bank of Commerce. In the nation's banking system, composed of state banks, the Bank of Commerce was the largest in the country, its success based in part on its esteemed president's reputation for honesty and integrity. On the topic of his daughter, however, John managed to dodge questions as smoothly as one of New York's infamous confidence men. Truthfully, perhaps, but definitely evasively, he stated that all correspondence went through Mary's lawyers, and that he never asked anyone where she had gone.

In September, both *The New York Herald* and the *Journal of Commerce* published a notice of Allie's death. It turned out to be false. Peter believed that it had been planted by Mary's brother,

Austin, in order to deceive him into dropping his efforts to find Allie, believing her dead. *The Brooklyn Eagle* pointed out the ruse's similarity to the plot of a popular sensation novel, *Lady Audley's Secret*, about a woman who faked her own death.

On a visit to his cousin George, Peter confided that Mary, soon after her confession of adultery in 1862, had also admitted to being pregnant. She had miscarried, Peter said, but the Stevenses were now circulating a darker story. They were trying to prove that Mary had undergone an abortion, and that she had done so at Peter's behest. Indeed, they were claiming that Peter had agreed to forgive Mary for the affair on the sole condition that she have the abortion. This unimaginably sinister twist shattered and depressed the diarist. "Marvelous are thy works, O Satan," George wrote after one of his talks with Peter. "No such domestic tragedy has been enacted among people of this social grade in my day."

The Stevenses' campaign to discredit Peter in this particular way was shocking, but not nearly as outlandish as it first appeared, for Peter had an established business relationship with a well-known abortionist: Electa Minerva Dailey O'Dell Potter, who was his tenant at Waverly Place. In 1861, she and her husband, Vernon, had rented the second floor at 104 Waverly Place. Then, in the spring of 1862, the Potters had moved to 124 Waverly Place, leasing the entire house until the spring of 1864, when they moved to other accommodations at 386 Sixth Avenue.

Electa Potter ran the Waverly Place houses, each one while she lived in it, as an abortion facility. Peter, who managed his mother's properties and collected rents, was seen to enter and leave both sites on different occasions and clearly knew their purpose. After all, Potter's work was no secret. At 124 Waverly Place, she hung out a sign on her door saying "woman doctor"—often a euphemism for a woman who did abortions along with other medical procedures—and posted her hours.

An attractive, smart, and entrepreneurial woman, thirty-seven-year-old Electa Potter had been born in Oneida County. She had married young, had a child, divorced her husband for adultery, then married Vernon, a widower a quarter-century her senior, with whom she had a second child. Vernon now worked hawking fruit from a stall in Washington Market, a busy outdoor produce emporium frequented by New Yorkers of all classes. He predictably left home for work at six in the morning and returned at six in the evening, leaving the house free for his wife to conduct her business.

Electa Potter and her colleague, Rachel Walsh, ran the medical practice together. Walsh handled housekeeping matters, while Potter did the bookkeeping and performed the abortions. Her patients sometimes boarded at the facility for several days before or after their procedures.

Potter not only used 124 Waverly Place as an abortion facility, but also as a base to run a charity called the Metropolitan Society for the Relief of Widows and Families of Deceased Soldiers. One newspaper called the charity an outright scam. The journalist reported that money was collected, but that most of it was never spent, or at least not spent for its nominal purpose. While the newspaper gave no details, some of the funds undoubtedly went to pay the Potters' rent, which was often in arrears. A small portion probably did underwrite the costs of caring for an occasional war widow who, like Potter's other patients, needed an abortion and boarded at her facility.

Abortion, like adultery, was against the law in New York State. Unlike adultery, however, which society continued to regard as a disgrace but no longer treated as a serious crime, views on abortion had toughened over the course of the nineteenth century. For the first third of the century, abortions before "quickening"—a child's first detectable movements in the uterus in the fourth or

fifth month of pregnancy—were performed frequently and usually ignored, dismissed as merely a woman's issue. Midwives, who
delivered babies, in the routine course of their work sometimes
performed abortions as needed or wanted. Depending on her condition, a woman might receive an abortifacient concocted from
herbs—some of them poisonous in the wrong dose—to induce an
abortion, or she might undergo a surgical procedure.

By midcentury, the relatively relaxed stance toward abortion
had begun to change. As New York strengthened its legal code,
newly enacted laws made an abortion pre-quickening by chemical
or surgical means a misdemeanor, punishable by a fine or a year
in jail, while an abortion post-quickening was designated second-
degree manslaughter. Still, abortions usually went unpunished—
unless something went wrong, and the procedure was brought to
the law's attention.

Several factors converged to subject abortions to more scrutiny.
Male doctors—medical schools, with the exception of Dr. Elizabeth Blackwell's, did not accept women until after mid-century—
had begun to take an interest in professionalizing their work and
also in monopolizing the profitable business of women's medicine. They often were far less sympathetic to a pregnant woman's
troubles than midwives or "female doctors." Moreover, as increasing numbers of middle-class and wealthy married women chose
to have abortions rather than bear a seventh or tenth or twelfth
child, society viewed the procedure with greater concern. Previously regarded as an issue primarily affecting poor, single mothers, abortion among well-to-do married women threatened not
only to affect the birth rate among the "better" classes, but also to
dilute the image of motherhood as a woman's highest ideal.

The nation's best-known abortionist was Ann Lohman, who
called herself Madame Restell. She had been imprisoned for a
year in 1847, prosecuted by a lawyer named John McKeon. Restell

would thereafter be continually hounded by anti-abortion crusaders until her suicide in the 1870s. Nevertheless, her business in the 1860s was brisk enough, and her clients wealthy enough, that she could afford to build herself a splendid Fifth Avenue mansion.

Electa Potter was neither famous nor rich, but she apparently ran her business relatively smoothly, encountering few problems with either her clients or the police—with one serious exception. In the spring of 1863, a middle-class, recently widowed woman from Brooklyn, Elizabeth Adams, sought an abortion and died soon afterward. Potter was said to be genuinely devastated. A doctor, John Dennis, who sometimes referred patients to Potter, had issued a death certificate with a diagnosis of congested lungs, and Adams was buried. It was uncertain whether her abortion indeed had caused her death, and the matter seemed to be, as it were, successfully buried with her body. Unfortunately for Potter, however, Adams's death soon became linked to the question of whether or not Peter Strong had enabled—indeed forced—his wife to abort her pregnancy.

While Peter insisted that Mary had experienced a natural miscarriage in the spring of 1862, not undergone an abortion, the Stevenses claimed that Peter had collaborated with Potter in facilitating or committing just such a criminal deed. With the negotiations for a separation agreement at an impasse, Peter's in-laws began to wonder whether threatening him with imprisonment for a criminal abortion might be enough to make him abandon his divorce plan. And if so, could Electa Potter be convinced or coerced into giving testimony against Peter?

In October 1864, the Stevenses' lawyers interrogated Electa Potter. They intended to steer her into testifying that Mary's miscarriage had indeed been "artificially produced," and that Peter "had been concerned in producing it," giving Mary instruments and specific instructions supplied by Potter. It was understood that Potter's role in such an abortion might be overlooked if she implicated Peter.

Potter refused to cooperate. She swore that she had never met Mary and knew Peter only as a rent collector. She also stated that Mary's brother, Austin, had tried to bribe her to say otherwise.

Potter's sturdy defense of Peter only provoked the Stevenses into further efforts to pressure her. Why had she been allowed—on very favorable terms—to move from 104 to 124 Waverly Place in the spring of 1862, a time that coincided exactly with Mary's abortion? Just how frequently did Peter visit Potter? In the course of investigating Potter, the Stevenses learned about Elizabeth Adams's death and decided to use the incident for their own purposes. They alerted Abraham Oakey Hall—New York's powerful and politically ambitious district attorney—to the two alleged crimes: Adams's death and Mary's abortion.

With the stakes ever higher, Peter left the staid law firm of Sanford and Woodruff, hiring as his champions instead a team of three lawyers recommended by his cousin George: Henry Cram, Murray Hoffman, and Edmund Robinson. After the death of her principal lawyer, William Curtis Noyes, Mary also changed attorneys. In her absence but surely with her approval, her father hired Elbridge T. Gerry, Jr., whose grandfather, a signer of the Declaration of Independence, had invented the eponymous tactic of gerrymandering, and John McKeon, who had prosecuted the abortionist Madame Restell in the 1840s. Both men had useful political connections. John Graham, arguably the city's most famous criminal attorney, also joined the team representing Mary.

Abraham Oakey Hall moved forward with his investigations and convened a grand jury to look into Peter's and Potter's role in ending Mary's pregnancy. The grand jury—later criticized by Peter and his allies as corrupt and biased—met twice over the next several months without returning any indictments. A parallel inquiry into Adams's death proceeded simultaneously and produced results. Early in February 1865, police arrested Potter for homicide in the Adams case. She was imprisoned overnight in New York's infamous Tombs, a damp, grim, and foreboding fortress.

Peter believed that Mary's brother, Austin, engineered the arrest to force Potter into a deal: a lesser charge in the Adams matter in exchange for testifying against Peter in the case of Mary's abortion. To remove Potter from temptation, Peter quickly arranged for her bail.

But Oakey Hall was not finished with either Peter or Potter. He convened a third grand jury. This time, after reportedly impassioned—and, of course, secret—testimony from Mary's sister Lucretia, jurors in late February 1865 indicted both of the accused for "manslaughter in the second degree for the murder of Mary Strong's unborn infant."

CHAPTER 9

Criminal Charges

PETER NOW FACED TWO TRIALS in two different courts. He was a plaintiff in a divorce suit, a civil matter to be tried in New York's Superior Court, and a defendant in a manslaughter case, a criminal matter to be tried in the Court of General Sessions. He and Electa Potter hired different lawyers to handle the manslaughter charges against them, and their cases went forward separately.

As if Peter weren't already seriously compromised, the Stevenses subjected him to yet another blow. Mary's attorneys prepared a much belated "Supplemental Answer" in response to Peter's divorce complaint—in effect, countersuing him. The charge? Committing adultery with Electa Potter, conducting an affair with her from September 1861 to the present day, at 104 Waverly Place, 124 Waverly Place, and 386 Sixth Avenue, as well as at "various hotels and divers other places." On the basis of this accusation, the Supplemental Answer demanded that *Mary* be the one granted a divorce, custody of the children, reasonable support for herself and the children, and reimbursement of all legal costs.

The Stevenses had found—some would say "bribed"—two witnesses to testify to Peter's infidelity. One was Potter's former partner, Rachel Walsh. The other was Walsh's friend, Sarah Bixby Massey, who had previously lived at 104 Waverly Place. Neither woman was considered an impeccable witness, but the accusation against Peter nevertheless was a clever move. Peter now had to worry about a jury's being convinced of Mary's innocence and his guilt. Moreover, if a jury found both of them guilty of adultery, divorce would be flatly denied under New York law.

Peter contested every allegation in the Supplemental Answer. Under his lawyers' guidance, he began composing an affidavit to present that March in the Superior Court of New York, where his divorce suit was scheduled to begin. The affidavit's purpose was to request a postponement, allowing him time to clear his name of the criminal charge of manslaughter as well as to dispute the adultery accusation.

On the night of March 6, jets of red, white, and blue fireworks burst over Manhattan, the evening sky exploding with brilliant light. The city hummed with high spirits and festivities in honor of President Abraham Lincoln's second inauguration. Celebrants watched the fireworks and waved from doorways, windows, and rooftops; cheering crowds packed the streets.

"All this extravagant, exuberant rejoicing frightens me," George Templeton Strong wrote with chilling prescience. "It seems a manifest omen of mishap."

Equally gloomy, Peter's affidavit, presented in court a few days later, recounted his own disastrous troubles from 1862 through the winter of 1865—at least from his point of view. He told how his wife had admitted to adultery, and how he did not begin his divorce action until he had exhausted "all means of securing the custody of his two daughters by negotiations and concessions." He described how his in-laws had contrived to ruin him completely, slandering his character and destroying his credibility so that no sane jury could ever trust him. He averred that the Stevens family—notably,

Mary's father and brother—had thus far tried to discourage him from pursuing divorce "without any defense on the merits . . . but by oppressive and vexatious efforts . . . to deter him . . . by the abduction of his child . . . and by attempting to injure his character and prejudice his cause in the eyes of the public. . . ."

The document contained Peter's ringing declaration that the accusation against him for adultery with Potter was "untrue and without the color of truth," and that he had "never been unfaithful to his wife, either before or after his discovery of her infidelity to him." Concerning the criminal charge of manslaughter for Peter's role in Mary's abortion, the affidavit asserted that he had "pleaded not guilty to the said indictment. . . . And . . . further says that he is innocent of the charge contained in the said indictment."

Peter's request for a delay was granted, his divorce trial postponed for two months. Commenting on Peter's affidavit, with its revelations of adultery, abortion, abduction, and counteraccusations of adultery, a *Brooklyn Eagle* reporter noted that few people "can fully realize the fact that the incidents of everyday life are stranger than the most sensational pages of the novelist."

Maria Daly, the judge's wife who critiqued society in her diary, agreed with the journalist's assessment. She mirrored the outrage of many in her social circle, complaining especially that the salacious tale had been allowed to go public. "Poor Peter Strong . . . is much to be pitied, and has, I believe, done what he could to keep his grief a secret, but his wife and her relations seem utterly shameless." She considered the scandal all the greater because Mary and "her paramour" were church members, and "all this wickedness went on coming or going to evening church. It is most horrible." The behavior of Mary's parents seemed brazen at best. "They go everywhere and even entertain company at home instead of bending with true show of humility to this terrible chastisement until at least this scandal is somewhat forgotten."

Daly's opinion was shared by several of Peter's friends, but George Templeton Strong was not among them. "Some of Pete Strong's injudicious friends are trying to make him consent against the advice of his counsel to have his divorce suit tried before a Referee or submitted to arbitration," he wrote. "They may succeed, for Pete is nervous, vacillating, weak. It would be a fatal mistake, but it's no concern of mine, thank God."

Court business had come to consume Peter's life. The district attorney in the Court of General Sessions and Mary's lawyers in the Superior Court, along with Peter's counsel in both courts, predictably jockeyed for position, making motions, objections, and countermotions. They squabbled over what documents should be included, which witnesses should be summoned, and what decisions should go forward. Attorneys failed to appear in court for reasons ranging from family commitments to conflicts on the court calendar; reluctant witnesses offered excuses, were subpoenaed, reluctantly appeared, or mysteriously disappeared; different judges heard different motions on different days and offered different opinions.

In the Court of General Sessions, Peter's lead lawyer—Henry Cram, cousin George's colleague—moved to dismiss the manslaughter charge, alleging that District Attorney Oakey Hall had corrupted the grand jury process into an instrument of malign personal animus wielded by the influential Stevenses. The motion was quashed.

Next, turning to the Superior Court, Cram moved to dismiss the countercharge of adultery against Peter. He argued that Mary's Supplemental Answer, which accused Peter and Potter of a long-running affair, had been submitted too late to be valid. He did not succeed here, either. Its issues, the judge ruled, overlapped with and were integral to those presented in Peter's original complaint against Mary. The judge ruled that all the adultery charges would be addressed simultaneously during the forthcoming divorce trial.

In April, momentous and terrible events forced Peter Strong's struggles from everyone's mind, except perhaps from Peter's.

"LEE and his ARMY HAVE SURRENDERED! *Gloria in Excelcis DEO*," George Templeton Strong exulted on April 10, the day after Robert E. Lee and Ulysses S. Grant met to negotiate terms at the village of Appomattox Court House, Virginia.

Horror followed six days later: "9 A.M. Lincoln & Seward assassinated last night!!!" George wrote on April 15. He and the nation later learned that Seward, stabbed by a coconspirator of John Wilkes Booth, survived his wounds.

In May, for reasons unrelated to the Union's triumph or the nation's tragedy, the Superior Court postponed the Strong divorce trial a second time, until June.

In the Court of General Sessions, Henry Cram made a second attempt to quash the manslaughter indictment against Peter, this time for lack of sufficient evidence. The indictment stood. Peter's criminal trial on the manslaughter charge for Mary's abortion was set for October. In the meantime, his divorce suit in Superior Court was moved from June to November.

While the Strongs' legal dramas dragged on, the nation surged forward into a new age. Vice-President Andrew Johnson became the nation's seventeenth president. Jefferson Davis, president of the Confederacy, was captured in Georgia on May 10. The Thirteenth Amendment, abolishing slavery in the United States, enacted by Congress earlier in the year, wended its way toward passage by three-fourths of the states.

The criminal case against Peter reached the Court of General Sessions on October 16, an icy day in mid-autumn. The prosecution again moved for postponement, this time on the grounds that doctors had forbidden the most important prosecution witness, Mary's sister Lucretia, to leave the house. At eight months pregnant, Lucretia was considered to be in a delicate condition. "It would be unsafe and dangerous for her to appear at the trial," the prosecution explained, adding that "the incidental excitement would be persistently dangerous to her life."

Cram vigorously objected on Peter's behalf. His client wished to proceed immediately. Lucretia's condition might have been anticipated; her absence should not excuse further delay. The presiding judge that day, John T. Hoffman—called Recorder, an esoteric title sometimes used in the court system—agreed with Cram's opinion and responded with outrage to the prosecution's motion to postpone. "The case," Recorder Hoffman said, "has appeared in the papers, and has been so frequently before the courts either on a motion for trial or to postpone, that it has become a public scandal." He scheduled the criminal trial for the following week and stipulated that it would not be postponed again.

Lucretia's delicate condition could backfire, George Templeton Strong mused that night. News had leaked that the grand jury's indictment against Peter was based largely on a secret conversation between the sisters several years earlier. Such intimate confidences, George felt, could now be called into question. Because any court appearance by Lucretia would be at "the utmost personal risk," her testimony would be "conclusive proof of the strongest personal feeling. This fact would be damaging to a witness called to prove admissions made in conversation some three years ago!" He expressed pity for "poor Pete" and the ordeals he was experiencing "all because he asked a most beautiful girl, the daughter of one of our best N.Y. families, whom any man might be proud to wed—to marry him twelve years ago." Just where that beautiful girl was—who she had become, or where she had fled—he did not speculate.

The criminal trial—*The People v. Peter R. Strong*—opened on

October 25, 1865. The assistant district attorney began with a dramatic summary.

> In the latter part of February, 1862, it was charged that
> Mrs. Strong was pregnant with a child six months old,
> and the testimony . . . would show that Mr. Strong visited
> Mrs. Potter and wanted some instruments with which
> to procure an abortion on his wife. . . . The abortion was
> performed, the child was destroyed, and it was born dead.
> Some might ask what motive had the defendant in doing
> that? We replied . . . the motive was the serious charge
> which he had made against his wife—that she was preg-
> nant with a child, the fruit of an adulterous intercourse
> with his own brother, or of an outrage committed by
> him upon her.

Unwieldy in her late-term pregnancy, Lucretia waited in a back room of the courthouse until called. An even more critical witness than Lucretia was to be summoned before her: Madam Barbier, the nurse who tended Mary from the last day of her 1862 preg-nancy through her convalescence the following week. Barbier's testimony was expected to set the scene of Peter's crime and pro-vide crucial proof of its occurrence. Barbier had claimed in earlier interviews that Peter, on hiring her, had told her in advance that Mary's baby would be born dead. How could Peter have known the child's fate unless the death was preplanned?

The court summoned Barbier. Silence. A surprised mur-mur. She was called again and did not respond. The prosecution assured the judge that Barbier had formally been subpoenaed. The judge dispatched a court officer to the delinquent witness's home. A servant greeted the officer at Barbier's front door and informed him that Madame Barbier was home but couldn't be seen.

"The officer brushed past the servant," a reporter wrote, and was rushing upstairs when he was suddenly confronted by another woman who, brandishing a bundle of 'duds' [clothes] in her hand, threatened to 'wipe his face' if he didn't make himself scarce. The result was a precipitous retreat."

The officer returned to court. Questioned by Recorder Hoffman, prosecutors revealed with embarrassed apologies that, by mistake, a subpoena for Barbier had not been issued. Insisting that the nurse was essential to their case, they called for the now-routine delay, certain it would routinely be granted.

Cram rejected their excuses and appealed to the judge: the prosecution had run out the clock; it was imperative that the criminal matter be resolved. The date for the divorce suit approached. *Laches* had occurred, a doctrine that allowed either party in a case to be penalized, even to have a case dismissed, if that party had caused an unnecessary and frivolous delay in proceedings.

The exasperated judge agreed that the trial had gone awry. Recorder Hoffman was a man of stature and influence, widely considered a lawyer and judge of distinction. Moreover, as a descendant of one of the oldest New York families, he was equal in social standing both to the Stevenses and the Strongs. And he was fed up.

Without that witness, "the case could not proceed," he said, echoing the prosecution's argument that Madame Barbier's presence was essential, but doing so to an altogether different purpose. Since there was "no evidence in the case upon which a verdict of guilty could be rendered," Recorder Hoffman instructed the jurors that it was their "duty to render one of not guilty."

Such an instruction might have appeared cavalier in any court other than that of New York State. Despite increasing surveillance, hundreds of abortions were performed each year in New York City, most never reported. Moreover, with New York City riddled with all kinds of crime, fewer than a third of the criminal cases tried before juries ended in convictions. Many juries failed to reach any verdict at all.

Jurors in Peter's manslaughter case obediently complied with the judge's clear directive. Peter was acquitted, not on the basis of what was proved but on the basis of what was not.

The trial had lasted less than a day.

George Templeton Strong professed himself bewildered. If the prosecution had planned to press the case against Peter, why hadn't they subpoenaed their witness, Madame Barbier, and ensured she was there? And if they hadn't planned to press their case, why had they brought Lucretia Heckscher into court, given her condition?

Despite his acquittal on the manslaughter charge, Peter still faced formidable obstacles to obtaining a divorce and winning custody of his children. The question of Peter's role in Mary's abortion would linger, as would the issue of his alleged adultery with Electa Potter. Both would shadow the divorce suit that November—after almost four years, now only one month away.

The divorce trial would raise issues of concern to many Americans: equity in the judicial treatment of men and women; the rights of mothers to their children; the near impossibility of obtaining a divorce; attitudes toward marriages that failed. But for many in the social class to which Mary and Peter belonged, the pressing question was: how could such tawdry secrets have been allowed to emerge?

Other related questions troubled those who asked them. New York and the nation had endured cataclysmic grief and turmoil during the war years. Still, were some rules of genteel society— surely discretion would suffice in the absence of moral rectitude and righteous behavior—nevertheless considered inviolable, no matter what else happened or changed? Moreover, between the seemingly dissolute and lawless behavior of the poor in places like the infamous Five Points neighborhood, and the apparent potential for the newly wealthy in their Fifth Avenue mansions to behave in equally immoral and lawless ways, was there any place for those who abided by the rules and revered the ways of old New York? And in a nation altered by the war in ways that could not yet be foreseen, did it matter?

George Templeton Strong acknowledged the significance of battles to come in changing the social landscape of his city. "I look on this case with dismay," George wrote. "It seems to me one of those great public scandals that have sometimes been the forerunners or portents of . . . revolution & calamity to the community in which they occurred."

PART 3

Attack

CHAPTER 10

A Civil Judge and Jury

WEEK 1
Trial Day 1
Thursday, November 23
Jury Selection

THE *STRONG V. STRONG* divorce trial opened on Thursday, November 23, 1865, as a storm battered the city with high winds and sheets of rain. Journalists, friends, family members, and curiosity-seekers juggled umbrellas and jostled elbows, trying to gain entrance to the proceedings. Because of "the social relations and the position of the parties, and the singular charges and counter charges," *The New York Times* reported, "no case before our courts for many years has attracted greater attention." The elite nature of the embattled parties, the accusations of adultery, abortion, and child abduction made for multiple headlines and the public's voyeuristic fascination.

Although rare, divorce was certainly not unheard of in America. True, many couples preferred more discreet, or simply more expeditious, solutions to their problems. Nevertheless, an Ohio newspaper announced that "there were twelve divorce cases before the Cuyahoga Common Pleas on Saturday." A Massachusetts newspaper compared "the infamous Harris divorce case in New London, a month or two ago" to the Strong case, "now on trial at New York." Lawyers advertised their services to unhappy husbands and wives in the classified section of newspapers. "Divorces—Private Consultations on the subject as to this and other states. Decrees legally obtained," one notice advised, referring to the fact that most states had more liberal laws than New York. There also had been high-profile divorce suits in the past. *Forrest v. Forrest*, perhaps the most notorious, began in 1851, when the renowned Shakespearean actor Edwin Forrest sued his wife, Catherine, for divorce on the grounds of adultery, and she countersued him for the same offense. She was declared innocent and won her divorce, but the case had recently reappeared in the news, with Edwin appealing the original decision.

The Forrest case, however, couldn't compare in important ways to *Strong v. Strong*. While Edwin Forrest was internationally famous, fame was exactly what families like the Stevenses and Strongs had always wished to avoid. The status of an actor, even a renowned one, was a far cry from that of an elite New Yorker from a well-established family.

The venue for *Strong v. Strong*, Manhattan's Superior Court, was all too familiar to Peter Strong—his lawyers had filed motion after motion there about his divorce suit in the last two years. A city court, it was created in 1828 to try civil cases such as contract and property disputes, thereby easing the Supreme Court's overcrowded case load. Surprisingly, neither the Superior Court nor its criminal counterpart, the county's Court of General Sessions—also familiar to Peter from his manslaughter trial—had a permanent place to meet. The former city almshouse had served for a time as home to many of the courts, but it burned down in the mid-1850s, and for several years afterward judges held trials in a nearby firehouse. One judge indignantly resigned in protest, claiming the uncomfortable conditions ruined his health.

In 1861, the powerful politician William M. ("Boss") Tweed, who controlled the city's Democratic Party from his headquarters in Tammany Hall, spearheaded construction of an ambitious new courthouse to be located in City Hall Park, an open patch of trees and paths in Manhattan's downtown business district and the site of New York's imposing City Hall. Admired by some for his support of immigrants and the poor, Tweed was loathed by others for his alleged boondoggles and rigged elections. Mired in debt and graft, the splendid courthouse he envisioned would remain unfinished for twenty years. Some trials in the meanwhile were being held in a three-story brownstone building, also located in City Hall Park, that was partly occupied by the Office of the Tax Collector. When taxes were due, law-abiding citizens thronged the building's narrow halls and stairways, frantically trying to pay what they owed. Judges were rumored to have been kicked down the stairs by impatient taxpayers.

On the Strong trial's first day, *The New York Times* reported, the courtroom assigned to it was "densely packed with the friends of both parties and many members of the bar." No one was comfortable. When the windows were closed, it turned hot and steamy; when opened, it became icy. The sashes were raised, then lowered. Up and down, up and down. From freezing to stuffy and back again. Over the next several weeks, journalists, participants, spectators, and supporters crowded into the courtroom suffering from red noses and colds.

Peter Remsen Strong, the plaintiff, sat with his three lawyers at one end of a long, curved table in the front of the courtroom. Now forty-two years old, he seemed serious and self-contained, no longer the jovial clubman and country squire. He would be a daily presence at the trial. His friend and cousin, George Templeton Strong, also attended on the trial's first day to show support for "poor Pete." George anticipated that his beleaguered relative would have to suffer silently through a torrent of "vitriol" from Mary's lawyers.

"The defense goes into the battle defiantly," George wrote in his diary that night, especially disdainful of Lucretia Heckscher's forthcoming deposition on behalf of her sister. Lucretia reportedly had sworn to statements by Mary, "of course as inadmissible as they are preposterous—that Edward Strong ravished her, vi et armis, and kept ravishing her . . . for about two years without a word from her to her husband or anyone else, until her ravisher went to N. Carolina."

Vi et armis, by force and arms, meant rape, generally defined at the time as "unlawful carnal knowledge of a woman, forcibly and against her will." It was an accusation that neither the press nor the Stevenses had openly broached. Proving rape was difficult without evidence that a victim suffered physical injuries in the attack or that she raised a "hue and cry" against her attacker. Even with these as proof, society usually viewed a raped woman as suspect and sullied. Ruined. This was especially true if an alleged rape extended beyond an initial event to further encounters, as these were assumed to indicate a consensual relationship. Whether or not Edward had sexually assaulted Mary, the question likely mattered only to Mary and the Stevens family.

Mary's father, John, and her brother, Austin, both attended the trial on its first day, as they would every day thereafter. They sat alongside Mary's three lawyers, with the defendant's entourage positioned warily at the opposite end of the same long, curved table from the plaintiff's counsel. At seventy years old, John looked sallow and haggard, his expression a mask of contempt for the proceedings. Thirty-eight-year-old Austin, youthful in appearance, was now a prominent banker and civic leader, active on the boards of august institutions such as the Chamber of Commerce and the New-York Historical Society.

Notably absent from the courtroom that first day were three of the four figures central to the divorce suit: Mary Strong, Edward Strong, and Electa Potter. As almost everyone in the room knew, Mary, the thirty-two-year-old defendant, and her daughter Allie had disappeared in June 1864, seventeen months earlier. Detectives had thus far failed to track them down. Nevertheless, Mary's spectral presence haunted the courtroom. Where was she now? Had she kept her little one safe? Had she indeed committed the dreadful offenses of which she was accused? Was she a victim? A seductress? Both roles were nineteenth-century stock characters in the popular sensation novels of the day, images that journalists resorted to when more nuanced information was unavailable, or when thrill-seeking readers craved more drama.

Edward, too, was absent from the courtroom, appearing there neither as spectator nor witness. After serving with distinction during the war, he was living quietly in Darien, Connecticut, where he and his brother Benjamin owned land. Edward presented legal counsel on both sides with a perplexing challenge. His testimony could damage Mary by confirming their affair. However, his testimony also could leave him vulnerable to accusations of fornication or even rape. Moreover, since he was implicated in a near-biblical tale of fraternal betrayal, his testimony threatened to disgrace the honor of the entire Strong family and raise undesired questions in a juror's mind. Was the family complicit in the illicit affair at Waverly? Why had no one seen what was happening and spoken up? How could such immorality have existed in such a respectable clan? Edward's testimony seemed unlikely to benefit anyone.

Electa Potter, like Mary and Edward, did not attend court that first day. However, she would appear intermittently and quietly among the spectators in the weeks to come. Surprisingly, the press rarely commented on either her presence or absence. It was equally intriguing that Peter's counsel chose not to introduce an affidavit that she had given several weeks earlier. Although Potter firmly denied being Peter's lover, her denial was explosive and explicit. She insisted that she had never told the two women who accused her of adultery—Rebecca Walsh, her former associate, and Sarah Bixby Massey, Walsh's friend—that "Strong was much excited by liquor or passion or that he kissed her or that he was a very passionate man . . . or that she had her thumb on Strong . . . or that Strong said to her that he did not care anything about his wife." Her denial of intimacy seemed rather too impassioned and intimate, too suggestive, for the plaintiff's counsel to risk putting her on the stand. Who knew what she might say?

The lead counsel on Peter's team of three lawyers, Henry Cram, had also represented him at his criminal trial in the Court of General Sessions. Only a few years older than Peter and an esteemed colleague in George Templeton Strong's law office, Cram proudly traced his ancestry to the Pilgrim fathers. Although George long ago had mocked Cram for his "ultra foppery in person and manner," the two had developed a close bond of mutual respect over the years. For Cram—married seventeen years and the father of both daughters and sons—defending a member of the extended Strong family was as much a matter of personal honor as defending a member of his own.

The oldest member of Peter's legal team was seventy-four-year-old Murray Hoffman—no relation to Recorder John T. Hoffman, the judge in Peter's criminal case. A former Superior Court judge, Murray Hoffman brought impressive credentials to the cause. Moreover, he had an even greater emotional stake in the suit than Cram's because Hoffman's daughter, Fanny, was married to Peter's brother Benjamin. Five years earlier, she had been named godmother to Edith. At the child's baptism, she had stood next to Edward, the baby's godfather, innocent of the fact that her brother-in-law had a secret and illicit relationship with Mary.

Hoffman had been deeply involved in Peter's case for some time. He had communicated extensively with Mary's counsel and advised Peter on terminating negotiations with his wife.

Peter's third lawyer, Edmund Randolph Robinson, was in his late twenties, a namesake of Edmund Randolph, George Washington's attorney general and second secretary of state. Randolph, Robinson's great-grandfather, had been forced to resign in the midst of a political imbroglio, but the prestige of his name endured.

However impressive Peter's team, Mary's had something that his lacked—fire. Her attorneys, hired by her father, were as formidable in legal skill as her husband's, but they were willing to scrap like street urchins. The junior member of the group, twenty-eight-year-old Elbridge T. Gerry, Jr., was socially the best pedigreed of the three. Aggressive and articulate, young Gerry was tackling his first major case.

Twice Gerry's age, John McKeon had broad experience as an elected representative to Congress in the 1830s, New York County district attorney in the 1840s, and United States Attorney for the Southern District of New York in the 1850s. He was known for pursuing what he believed to be right with implacable determination.

McKeon shared responsibility as Mary's lead counsel with John Graham, one of the city's most famous criminal lawyers. Noted for tenacity, irascibility, and volubility, Graham had successfully defended high-profile clients such as General Daniel Sickles, who shot to death Philip Barton Key, the man Sickles suspected of being his wife's lover.

Tried in 1859, the Sickles case, like the Strong suit, involved prominent members of society. General Sickles at the time was

a well-known congressman from a wealthy New York family;
the victim, district attorney of Washington, D.C., and the son
of the man who wrote "The Star-Spangled Banner." However,
there were important differences between the two cases, notably
of course that one was a divorce suit and the other a murder trial.
Equally significant to many in the circle of New York City's elite,
Sickles was not really one of their own, his behavior having exiled
him from their embrace. He was famously disreputable, dissolute,
and—especially unseemly—a politician.

Graham's three-day opening argument on behalf of the general had swamped the jury with quotations from the Bible, the
law, and Shakespeare. In the end, Sickles was acquitted as a
"wronged husband," a verdict that earned Graham the general's
lifelong friendship, and that established a precedent for setting
murderous husbands free.

With Cram, Hoffman, and Robinson on the plaintiff's side,
and McKeon, Gerry, and Graham on the defendant's, scuffling
began immediately with jury selection. The pool consisted entirely
of white males. Although women were allowed to be trial witnesses, they were not permitted to serve on juries, and African
Americans were generally eliminated from juries by property
qualifications where the law did not already bar them. None of
the jury pool was equal in wealth or status to members of either
the Strong or the Stevens family. However, it represented a seg-
ment of America's comfortable urban middle class: merchants,
tradesmen, small-scale manufacturers, and clerks. There were no
factory laborers or farmers.

The first potential juror, a bookseller, announced that he had
read about the case and formed an opinion on it. On the other
hand, he admitted, he couldn't remember what that opinion was.
Cram declared him a competent juror. Graham snapped that a
man who forgot an opinion was wholly incompetent and, in fact,

less acceptable than someone who had a bias but at least remembered it. The court dismissed the abashed bookseller.

Another potential juror, a pattern maker, also protested that his memory was poor; he worried that he might forget some of the evidence. When the audience burst into laughter at this woeful confession, Graham sharply accused the opposing counsel of bringing "a set of gigglers into the courtroom" to distract everyone from the seriousness of the issues at hand. The absent-minded juror also was dismissed.

By the end of the day, twelve men had been impaneled for the jury. The jury foreman, Edward Draper, was a quiet, seemingly good-natured man who owned a dry goods store. Another juror, a butcher and distiller named Job Long, admitted to feeling ill but wanted to serve anyway. Charles Berry, a dealer in butter and cheese, feared that his business would suffer in his absence. Nathaniel Betts was a shoe seller; John Worstell, who considered himself something of an expert because he had sat on juries before, called himself an agent, or middleman between retailers and wholesalers; Wilkes Gay was a clerk; John J. Sigler made moldings; I. N. Sickels, like the forgetful gentleman previously dismissed, was a pattern maker.

The rest of the jurors listed their occupations simply as *merchant*. Francis Burke had such a sorrowful countenance that it made him seem hopeless and despondent from the start. James Rufus Smith, while sharp-eyed and clearly bright, was so whippet-thin that Cram fretted he wouldn't survive a long trial. Yet another merchant, John Willets, seemed ready to argue every point with the lawyers as well as with his fellow jurors. If the twelfth juror, Robert Mackie, had any distinguishing characteristics, they were not mentioned by the lawyers or the press.

The judge in charge of the proceedings was fifty-five-year-old Samuel B. Garvin. Over six feet tall, with a girth to match his height, he was a commanding figure, married, the father of one son and three daughters. He was a native of New York State, a former district attorney of Oneida County, a Mason and a member of the Fraternal Order of Odd Fellows. Perhaps more to the point, Garvin was a rising star among Boss Tweed's Democrats. In this, he wasn't alone among his cohorts. Superior Court judges, elected for a term of six years, were a colorful and frequently corrupt lot, many associated with Tammany Hall's infamous political ring. Nevertheless, despite the controversial nature of some of his associates, Garvin was known as a fair and able jurist.

Strong v. Strong was categorized by the press as a cross-suit: Peter and Mary each accused the other of adultery, requested a divorce, and asked for custody of the children. In summary, the issues to be tried by the jury included the following:

Did Mary, the defendant, commit adultery with Edward Strong?

Was Peter, the plaintiff, ignorant of such adultery, if committed, until January 5, 1862, and was such adultery committed without his consent, connivance, privity, or procurement?

Had more than five years elapsed between the plaintiff's discovery of the adultery and his filing of the divorce action?

Had the plaintiff, with knowledge of the adultery, forgiven the offense by actual cohabitation with the defendant, and was there proof of such forgiveness?

Did the plaintiff commit adultery with Electa M. Potter, as alleged by the defendant in her Supplemental Answer?

The jury, presided over by Judge Garvin, was ultimately responsible for deciding which spouse, if either, had been unfaithful. Under New York State law, one party had to be demonstrably guilty of adultery, and the other party clearly innocent, in order for a divorce to be granted. And, as noted earlier, if jurors found both Mary and Peter guilty, divorce would be denied.

There were several other grounds for denying a divorce. Since unhappy couples could be granted a divorce only for adultery, a husband and wife sometimes colluded to create the appearance of infidelity. Collusion or connivance was a reason to deny divorce. So, too, was forgiveness or condonation, if either partner could prove that a reconciliation had occurred.

With divorces so difficult to obtain, couples sometimes petitioned the court to permit a legal separation "from bed and board" for "lesser" grounds such as cruelty or desertion. Spouses who reached mutual agreement could also arrange a private out-of-court separation—a solution that the Strongs had tried and failed to negotiate. However, the freedom to legally remarry depended on obtaining a divorce decree, at least for the party judged innocent. The guilty party generally was barred from remarrying during the innocent party's lifetime. Divorce in many ways served an angry spouse with a potentially satisfying outlet for exacting revenge.

Judge Garvin dismissed the court at five p.m. The *Strong v. Strong* divorce trial's first day had been successful; the jury had been impaneled.

Bright stars that night promised sunshine the next morning.

CHAPTER 11

Opening for the Plaintiff

WEEK 1
Trial Day 2
Friday, November 24
Plaintiff's Attorney: Henry Cram

HENRY CRAM BEGAN HIS OPENING on behalf of Peter Strong, the plaintiff, conventionally enough: "Gentlemen of the Jury: This is an action for divorce. The plaintiff is the husband, the defendant his wife. . . ." Then he produced a surprise. "But the real parties are two little girls, my clients; and on the other side is not a poor, foolish woman, but a rich and powerful family, who have taken a misguided course, and have threatened to crush and ruin my client."

Cram's strategy—boldly discounting his real client, the plaintiff—was astute. Although acquitted, Peter had been indicted for manslaughter in a criminal abortion, and he had been accused of adultery. He had also, according to his own statements, been cuckolded by his own brother while living under the same roof. He was hardly a sympathetic figure. Cram's first few sentences managed simultaneously to capture the jury's attention and divert it from Peter.

Cram also avoided any temptation to portray Mary as a seductress. Lawyers could depict poor and working-class women as bawdy from the get-go. The image of middle- and upper-class women, on the other hand, had to conform with society's expectations. Members of the weaker but more virtuous sex, gentlewomen could be led astray but were usually portrayed as passive victims in their actions.

Aware of the challenges confronting him, Cram chose a safe route. He presented the judge and jury with a different cast of characters altogether: the innocents, Mamie and Allie, versus the haughty, entitled, and aggressive Stevenses. The real battle, as Cram framed the story, was on behalf of the children, with the Stevens family—subsequently defined as John and Austin rather than Mary—as the antagonist. The Stevens men, in deference to the customs of New York society, should have buried their family scandal instead of provoking Peter into a public trial.

Cram's opening made for effective theater, though neither of the Strongs' daughters was in the courtroom. Eleven-year-old Mamie was at Waverly, where she'd been living with her father, grandmother Aletta, and assorted aunts, uncles, and cousins for two years. Six-year-old Allie was gone, spirited away by Mary. Rumors circulated that they had escaped abroad. Despite the girls' absence, Cram's opening had fixed jurors' attention exactly where he intended: on two hapless lambs.

Cram went on to tell an eloquently rendered version of Peter's shabby, sorrowful tale. He began as far back as the death in 1838 of Peter's father, James, who "left his property to [his] widow, providing that there should be a home for all the children." Now seventy-six years old, blind, and partially paralyzed, Aletta had "lived at Newtown ever since with her children." He anticipated but dismissed the defense counsel's claim that familial closeness had facilitated seduction. "This has been considered a crime— that in this America it is unsafe for people to live together in a common home, and I shall leave it to you to determine if it was ill-judged or wicked."

Cram stressed that the marriage between Peter and Mary started as a true love match, a relationship "of mutual desire and mutual affection . . . they were happy, for they really had this love, I believe at that time." In emphasizing the Strongs' youthful romantic love, thus making adultery a betrayal not only of the marriage contract but also of the heart, Cram appealed to jurors' sentimental side.

Peter and Mary, according to Cram, not only shared a bond of true love but also yearned for a simple home life in the bucolic haven of Waverly. Peter might not have recognized himself in Cram's description: "Plaintiff had quiet domestic habits, was not fond of fashionable life, and cared only for his home." Cram added, in a less than candid statement, that "the residence of the plaintiff and defendant at the mother's house was of mutual desire."

Waverly was appealing for practical reasons as well, Cram argued, since it was all Peter could afford. On the yearly income of $4,000 left him by his father, he "could not live in the city, for he had no income which would permit him to keep up such an establishment as the family of his wife would desire." The arrogant Stevenses, Cram implied, expected Peter to spend beyond his modest, albeit respectable, means.

Cram's narrative traced the life of Mary and Peter up through Mamie's birth, their European Grand Tour, and the death of Edward Strong's wife, Susan. As the grief-stricken widower coped with his loss, his sorrowing thoughts turned first to religion as a consolation. Then, Cram indicated with a touch of irony, they "turned also to the wife of my client." In the spring of 1860, "incest crept into that circle despite the watch-guards and protections that stood sentinel at the portals of that family home. Edward and Mary grew intimate. . . ."

Calling the relationship between Edward and Mary *incest* was a theatrical flourish but an inaccurate statement. Just as the laws governing marriage and divorce varied from state to state, so, too, did definitions of incest. In New York, no law at the time banned intercourse between brothers-in-law and sisters-in-law. Depending on the two individuals' marital status, the act constituted adultery, fornication, or both. Not incest. However, Cram skipped over this fact, stressing only that Mary's affair was so repugnant that "Peter did not suspect anything wrong—who could or would ever suspect so dreadful a crime?"

Equally horrifying, the affair took place while Mary was pregnant, while she bore "poor dead Edith under her heart." Since civilized husbands customarily refrained from intercourse during the late stages of a wife's pregnancy, Cram expected jurors to understand that in this way, too, the affair transgressed the limits of common decency.

Despite Peter's continued devotion to his wife, the couple's relationship inevitably began to change, Cram told the jury, and "an estrangement grew up." Still, Peter remained ignorant of his wife's affair until, soon after Edward went to war in December 1861, the Strong's daughter Edith tragically died. Having refrained from invoking religious taboos and punishments, Cram now introduced them. "When her lover left her," Cram said of Mary, "God took one of her children away."

He lingered with a dramatist's exquisite flair on the scene of Mary's confession the night after Edith's funeral, recounting how Peter and Mary sat together with Mamie and Allie for a time, and then, after the children left the room, how Peter took his wife's hand and confided his hope for a brighter future. At that

point, Cram continued, "the wife seemed most strangely and violently agitated, and rising from her chair, flung herself at his feet,
and implored him to forgive her for her long neglect and indif-
ference . . . and . . . said 'O, forgive me, forgive me; you could not
conceive how guilty I have been.'" When Peter responded that
"her excitement led her to exaggerate her neglect," she answered,
according to Cram, "'But you do not understand me; I have been
more guilty than you can imagine.'"

While slow to suspect the truth, Peter began to experience
a growing sense of dread. "Defendant finally succeeded in convincing plaintiff of her guilt," Cram said. "Plaintiff sat stupefied
and overwhelmed. He felt no anger, only shame and loathing.
There are losses to which bereavement by death are compara-
tively a gain."

Mary at last rose from the floor and walked to the bedroom
door. When Peter asked her where she was going, she answered,
Cram said: "'To mingle with other lost creatures like myself.'"

Was the phrasing Mary's, Peter's, or Cram's own? It resonated
with the cadences of nineteenth-century fiction, drenched in
the trope of the "fallen" woman. Jurors may not have read Hawthorne's *The Scarlet Letter*, Elizabeth Gaskell's *Ruth*, or any of the
popular sensation novels with which their wives were probably
familiar, but the theme was well known.

Cram explained that Peter summoned Mary back, and they
spoke for a while longer. Then, as she turned again to leave the
room, Mary paused and made a request. She "urged plaintiff to go
to bed with her, saying, 'If you do not now, you never will again.'"
Instead, Peter asked for separate beds to be prepared, and he has
"never since been with her."

With this statement, Cram ended the fateful scene. Having
presented unusually intimate information about sleeping arrangements and sexual relations, he moved on to the aftermath of

Mary's confession. No man, he asserted, could have been kinder and more reasonable than the plaintiff under the circumstances. Caring only for the welfare of his two daughters and his elderly mother, Cram explained, the plaintiff chose to avoid publicity and conceal the horrific and humiliating events. Rather than divorce his wife, he retained the façade of marriage by living with her under the same roof while abjuring marital relations. They revealed their true situation only to family members.

Cram recapped the facts about the Strongs' nomadic living conditions over the next few years until they definitively separated in October 1863. Mary and the girls returned to her parents' home, and Peter to Waverly.

And this event, according to Cram, was the crucial turning point in the Strongs' marriage, more so even than Mary's confession. This was the moment when Peter made his fatal mistake. Once he and Mary parted, Peter generously permitted Mamie and Allie to live with their mother, while only visiting their father. Had Peter been less kind and lenient, had he been more stalwart in defending his paternal rights, Cram asserted, the Strongs' marriage would never have reached the point of divorce and public scandal. Had Peter "done as any other man would, and demanded his children, there would have been no problem." Instead, Peter's unusual flexibility and generosity encouraged a spirit of "hostility and defiance" in Mary and in the wealthy, arrogant Stevens family. When Peter invited Allie to join her sister, Mamie, at Waverly, Mary "shut the door" on her husband, Cram said, "claiming the right to his child." In response to a habeas corpus in June 1864, Mary "kidnapped and ran away with the child."

Cram wanted jurors to recognize that the emotional blow Mary inflicted on Peter constituted an assault on masculine prerogatives, on paternal privilege—the foundation of the social order. By challenging Peter's paternal rights, members of the Stevens family weakened the very pillars of patriarchy. The "theft" of Alice, a more severe offense than infidelity, was unendurable.

Up to this part of his narrative, Cram's presentation was chronological, culminating in his impassioned argument for Peter's right to custody. However, the last hour of Cram's three-hour opening statement turned strangely garbled, vague with hints about lies and deceit to come, warnings about disreputable defense witnesses bribed to make dark accusations. Cram's murkiness undoubtedly was deliberate. He wanted jurors to understand that the Stevenses conspired to ruin Peter's reputation. At the same time, he also wished to obscure the alleged conspiracy's lurid details, lest any juror accept them as fact.

Cram introduced this part of his argument with a seemingly innocuous topic—real estate. He indicated that Peter oversaw and managed two Waverly Place houses owned by his mother; that Mrs. Electa Potter, a tenant, along with her colleague, Rachel Walsh, had run a medical partnership from there, and that Mrs. Potter received a rent reduction after falling into arrears. Cram explained neither the reason for the rent concession nor the nature of the "medical partnership."

"At this time," Cram continued, without drawing conclusions, Mary's brother, Austin, "attempted to induce Mrs. Potter to swear that Peter had committed an abortion." The Stevenses then used their corrupt cohorts to have Peter indicted for manslaughter. After numerous postponements, a trial finally took place, and Peter was acquitted. Peter's foes had never expected to have the criminal case actually reach the point of trial, Cram alleged. "They simply intended to terrify him."

Cram explained that a new and different accusation against Peter followed, also orchestrated by the Stevenses. Rachel Walsh, along with her friend, Sarah Bixby Massey—two disreputable women "who would do anything for pay"—swore that Mrs. Potter "boasted to them" that she had committed adultery with Peter. According to Cram, Austin had paid the women well for their claim, and the evidence would prove that they lied.

Cram managed to be so oblique that many observers and some jurors might have been completely confused by his tale. On one point, however, Cram was absolutely clear: the Stevenses, and more specifically Austin, had been behind any accusations against Peter, whether for abortion or adultery. They had set out to destroy the plaintiff's reputation and thereby cause him to abandon or lose his divorce suit. Because of their falsehoods, Cram now felt it was essential "to say a word about Peter's history and character." In the past, it had been "without stain or blemish."

After saying his very brief "word" in defense of his client— faint praise though it was—Cram returned to his "true clients," Mamie and Allie.

"I come here taking in each hand a little child, seeking to obtain security for their future." Addressing the jury directly, he asked, "Shall they go to an unstained father, free from this infamous, false charge, or shall they go to their guilty mother . . . with the black cloak of her disgrace around them?"

Cram's opening had accomplished several goals. He painted Peter as a man of good character. He also combatted in advance several points the defense would raise: whether Peter, in living at Waverly, had failed to support his wife in a suitable manner; whether he had failed to meet the companionate as well as financial obligations of a husband and provider; whether he had cohabited with and forgiven Mary for a period before suing for divorce. Each of these topics, elaborated, could help establish sympathy for Mary or introduce reasons for denying a divorce. In addition, Cram successfully skipped over Peter's criminal trial, referring to it only to highlight his client's acquittal, and he made a powerful plea for Peter's custody of the girls. He had firmly dismissed Peter's alleged adultery as the Stevenses' malicious fabrication.

Lawyerly hostility ended the divorce trial's second day as an apparent misplacement of depositions ignited a quarrel between Cram and McKeon. After a mild rebuke from Judge Garvin, court adjourned for the weekend.

CHAPTER 12

The Governess

Trial Days 3, 4
Monday, November 27; Tuesday, November 28
Plaintiff's Witness: Matilda Mussehl

THE LAST WEEK OF NOVEMBER, war loomed between Mexico and France. Andrew Johnson, the new president of the United States, known to be sympathetic to the South, assured Mississippians that if they diligently complied with the law and gave protection to all freedmen, federal troops would soon be withdrawn from their state. New York City police made arrests for reckless horseback riding down city streets. Macy's announced a clearance sale of laces, blankets, corsets, hoop skirts, and kid gloves. The steamship *Niagara*, carrying two hundred passengers, collided with another vessel on the Mississippi River. One hundred African American soldiers on the ship's deck drowned. Most cabin passengers and crew survived.

And the Strong divorce trial? From New York to California, newspaper articles—some a paragraph long, others half a page or more—reported on its progress. *The New York Times* predicted "Singular Revelations of Life in the Country." The *Tribune* echoed with "Painful Revelations of a Domestic Spiritual Tragedy." A curious public anticipated a vivid glimpse of life usually hidden behind walls of brick and propriety, about to be opened up to view like the front of a child's Victorian dollhouse, its floors, rooms, and staircases all visible, peopled with husbands and wives, sons and daughters, siblings and servants, mothers and lovers.

On Monday, November 27, the third day of the trial began with unfinished business. A defense witness jailed overnight for resisting a subpoena, the husband of Sarah Bixby Massey, was released on $100 bail. John Graham, one of Mary's lawyers, caused further delay when he complained that an article in *The New York Herald* was misleading and demanded its correction. "Mr. Strong does *not* swear that he was innocent of adultery, but swears that he *denied* the charge of adultery—a very different thing."

Henry Cram rumbled, "It's not customary for counsel to reply to an opening in this way."

Judge Garvin reassured Graham that he "need be under no fear of our misapprehension. The case will now go on."

Although especially rich in opportunities for speculation and gossip, the Strong divorce wasn't the only court case drawing avid attention during this time. Trials held so much general interest that *Harper's New Monthly Magazine* had published the satirical article "In the Witness Box" a few months before. Among the caricatures were The Dull Witness, The Respectable Married Witness, The Confident Witness, The Witness Who Doubts His Own Handwriting, The Deaf Witness, The Knowing Witness, and The Irrelevant Witness. The Interesting Witness was described as a "modest, demure, timid creature [who] . . . betrays herself under a severe cross-examination."

Matilda Mussehl, the Strong children's former governess and Cram's first witness, fit this description perfectly. She approached the witness stand hesitantly, her appearance neat and crisp, her demeanor modest and timid. Now twenty-eight years old, she had been hired by Mary in October 1860, primarily to tutor and look after six-year-old Mamie at the time when Mary was preoccupied with breastfeeding newborn Edith and tending to one-year-old Allie.

In her daily routine, Mussehl had typically eaten meals with her young charge, and, when not educating Mamie (French, singing, dancing, and drawing were among the skills she taught) or amusing her (hide-and-seek and, for girls, string games like cat's-cradle were favorites in many homes) helped Old Nurse and the servants with household tasks. In the United States, as elsewhere in literature and life, the role of governess was *sui generis*, that of an outsider embedded inside, neither family member nor ordinary domestic staff. The position provided an inimitable vantage point for observing a household's activities.

Mary had used an allowance for household expenses to pay Mussehl a monthly wage of fifteen dollars, on top of room and board. The amount was almost double a domestic servant's wage and, although less than a schoolteacher's, enough for Mussehl to buy a simple dress and pair of shoes and still have money to send to her mother in New Jersey.

Mussehl had lived with the Strong family for eighteen months—first at Waverly, then at the resort town of Lenox, Massachusetts, in the summer of 1861, and lastly at 50 East Twenty-first Street in the winter of 1861–62. A few months after Edith's death, in April 1862, Mussehl left the family's employment.

On the witness stand, Mussehl spoke slowly, with just a trace of a German accent, her words seemingly drawn from her against her will, her voice pitched so low that the court reporter often had to repeat what she said. Henry Cram's examination of her, calm and methodical, established a pattern he would follow with his other witnesses, largely focused on Mary's interactions with Edward.

"At the house in Newtown, did you see Mr. Edward Strong," Cram asked.

"Yes, sir."

"State when you first went there if you noticed anything in his conduct in his relations with the defendant, Mrs. Strong."

"I object to that," John Graham said.

The judge allowed the question.

"I noticed them together," Mussehl answered.

"When you speak of seeing them together . . . give us the facts as nearly as you can recollect," Judge Garvin requested.

"They used to be most continually together."

"I object to that. 'Used to be' tells nothing," Graham interrupted.

"Confine yourself to the facts," the Judge told her.

"During the whole summer, I used to notice them together," Mussehl said.

"Now that is a violation of the instructions," Graham chided.

The judge again urged specificity.

"I saw them walking together, always, and being as much together as they could be."

Prodded by Cram, Mussehl eventually admitted that Mary and Edward seemed to be "always together . . . riding and walking . . . on horseback, in carriages and sleighs; would be gone three or four hours, from morning until dinner time; this was very often the case."

Elaborating further, Mussehl recalled that Mary sometimes seemed to signal Edward by coughing as she passed his bedroom door. Immediately after, he would fling his door open and follow Mary downstairs to the parlor or outside, wherever she was going.

Asked to identify a diagram of Waverly, Mussehl indicated not only the sprawling size of the three-story house—in addition to its seventeen rooms, a separate wing for cooking and servants' bedrooms—but also the number of family members who resided there, sometimes as many as fifteen, including siblings, spouses, and children. Edward's bedroom, she noted, was on the second floor; Peter and Mary's bedroom, with a separate dressing room and nursery, on the third. Reviewing a diagram of the Twenty-first Street house, she indicated that it, too, had three floors but fewer rooms, suitable for Peter and Mary's family of five.

At Newtown, Cram asked, had she ever seen Mary in Edward's second-floor bedroom?

"I remember seeing her leave the room once, and knew her to be in the room for three hours on another occasion," Mussehl said, adding that she knew Mary "to be there often."

One afternoon at Waverly, she recalled, she and several servants were sitting on the second-floor staircase sorting laundry, a task that took about three hours, since at least 150 pieces needed folding. As evening came on, and the gaslights were lit, the women heard Peter's carriage coming up the drive. Suddenly, as the carriage approached, the door to Edward's room opened, and Mary rushed out, her face flushed and excited. Mary hastened upstairs to her own bedroom and closed the door behind her.

Another curious incident took place at Twenty-first Street, Mussehl testified. One morning, an acquaintance knocked on the front door. Alice O'Grady, one of the servants, answered it. Busy polishing silver, O'Grady asked Mussehl to find Mary and announce the unexpected caller. Although Mary's bedroom door was open, the mistress of the household was not inside. So Mussehl mounted the stairs to look for Edward, then a guest on the third floor. His bedroom door, too, was open, but he was nowhere in sight. Next, Mussehl tried the closed door to her own third-floor bedroom. She found it locked, although she had left it unlocked when she went downstairs earlier that day.

After returning to the parlor, she told the caller that her mistress could not be found. Then she remounted the stairs. Now, through open doors, she saw Mary in her bedroom, and Edward in his. When she came to her own bedroom door, she found it closed and unlocked. Entering the room, she saw it was "disordered."

"What part of it was disordered?" Cram asked.

"The bed."

"In what way?"

"It looked as if it had been occupied."

"What did you do after you saw this?"

"I went right down again, and met Mrs. Strong with an ink-stand in her hand, which she was carrying to my room," Mussehl said. "When I went back to my room it was arranged again." Her answer suggested, albeit obliquely, that the inkstand—a useful item for a governess—served as an excuse for Mary to revisit and straighten Mussehl's room.

Questioned about other incidents involving bedrooms, Mussehl recalled that Mary and Peter had always shared a bed at Newtown, and, initially, at Twenty-first Street, too. However, after Edith died, a bed was moved into the adjacent dressing room, and Peter slept there rather than with his wife. Mussehl seemed to know only one reason for the change. "Mrs. Strong told me that Mr. Strong changed his bed on account of the noise the children were making." Beds and bedrooms would become one of Henry Cram's recurring themes.

John Graham, famed for his theatrical short temper, began his cross-examination routinely enough, asking Mussehl about her employment since leaving the Strongs. She had served as a tutor for several different families, she replied, and currently resided with her mother in Hoboken, New Jersey. She was visited there by Peter and Cram, who interrogated her about the relationship between Mary and Edward. She was not paid to testify, she said, and in fact preferred not to do so. Instead, she had recommended that Cram contact Alice O'Grady. But he had subpoenaed her anyway.

She testified that, while living with the Strongs, she had told no one—not Peter, nor Mary, nor Aletta Strong—about witnessing anything suspicious in Mary's relationship with Edward. That is, not until she was ready to leave the Strongs' employment. At that point, it seemed, Mussehl's discretion vanished. "When I left," she admitted, "I told Mrs. Strong that the servants knew about it." It was clear that Mussehl meant the affair, but unclear whether her warning was intended in kindness or malice.

Why did she leave? Graham continued.

"I left of my own accord, and she paid me. She wanted me to stay and that made some unpleasant talk. We did not separate exactly good friends."

While Cram had concentrated on the interaction between Edward and Mary, Graham in his cross-examination at this point took a very different approach. He focused not on the alleged affair but on Peter's behavior toward Mary, on whether tenderness existed between husband and wife. Mussehl commented that she had rarely observed tender or intimate moments between them. Peter seemed more demonstrative with the children, kissing them more often than he did Mary.

Not surprisingly, Cram objected to this line of questioning, but Graham asserted his reasons with characteristic ferocity. "A wife can't be thrown aside like a dirty dog; if a man neglects his wife—fails to pay her those attentions which the nature of woman requires—he connives at her downfall and helps set the trap at which the feet of his wife are caught."

Graham then turned back to the Strongs' houses. After reviewing the diagrams of Waverly and 50 East Twenty-first Street, Mussehl described the bedroom that Mary and Peter shared at Waverly. The room had "a Turkish carpet, a writing table, a bureau and chairs; there were pictures, but no guns, pistols, javelins, etc. The ceiling of the room was low." Throughout the trial, the lawyers would use different opinions about the Strongs' Waverly bedroom to suggest Peter's sensitivity, or lack thereof, to his wife's feelings and needs.

Pressed to talk about the time that she found the door to her room locked instead of unlocked, Mussehl noticeably wavered. "I can't swear that the door was locked at this particular time; I suppose I tried it, but I don't remember. I won't swear that there was any fastening on it. I knew no one had a right to be in my room, but I did not ask who was there."

Graham moved on to Edith's death and funeral. Mussehl recalled how the loss of his child devastated Peter. "Mr. Strong was very grieved by Edith's death . . . he had her likeness taken after death. Her decease worked upon him very much; it appeared to be his continuing thought." As for Mary's response, Mussehl denied hearing rumors about the bereaved mother's attempt to commit suicide through an overdose of laudanum. A powerful brew of morphine and alcohol, laudanum was a common household remedy for ailments such as headaches and menstrual pain.

In March 1862, about two months after Edith's death, Mussehl remembered being called upon to sleep with Mary for three or four nights and to care for her by applying poultices, which were likely warm and saturated with herbs. She did so because "Mrs. Strong was ill; she had a miscarriage."

"Up to that time," Graham asked, "What had been the character of Mrs. Strong's health? Was it good or bad?"

"Mrs. Strong's health had been pretty good."

"After that event, and down to the time of your leaving, how did her health appear compared to what it had been before?"

"Not as good."

The question, Cram interjected, was irrelevant. Graham nevertheless pressed the matter by repeating the question in a different way, this time deliberately introducing the more controversial version of events by asking "as to whether the ill health was the result of 'the abortion.'"

Judge Garvin allowed the question since it targeted Mary's physical health.

"After that event," Mussehl answered, "Mrs. Strong's health was not as good as before."

Judge Garvin adjourned court at four p.m., the usual hour.

DENSE HAZE CLOUDED THE CITY and sky on the trial's fourth day, foretelling snow but failing to deter visitors to the courtroom. Graham continued his cross-examination, asking about the time Mary allegedly rushed from Edward's room at the sound of Peter's carriage. Mussehl's memory seemed as hazy as the weather. "The noise, perhaps, could be heard in the house, but I don't know; don't remember whether it was cold or not, or whether the doors were open, or the windows up . . . I don't remember that I saw the carriage. I can't swear it was Peter's carriage because I didn't see it. . . ."

"What was the conduct of Mr. Strong [to Mrs. Strong] up to the time of Edith's death?" Graham asked.

"He was kind to her."

"What was the conduct after the death?"

"Very different. He was cold to her. He used to stay in another room . . . I never saw him speak affectionately after that."

Graham asked about a summer evening Mary and Peter spent at Lenox with friends, but Mussehl denied all knowledge of it.

"I was not present at Lenox when there was a gathering and a poem called 'Parisina' was read, nor when anything else by Lord Byron or anyone else was read."

Published in 1816, "Parisina" was a lengthy poem by Byron, one of Peter's favorite poets, that retold the story of a fifteenth-century Italian duke who discovered his wife's affair with his bastard son. As with Mary's failing health and the couple's bedroom arrangements, Peter's taste in art and literature, and its impact on his wife would become issues that resonated throughout the trial. However, since Mussehl denied being present at the poem's reading, Graham did not pursue the topic further.

Cram's redirect was brief, with only a few additional questions. Then he dismissed his first witness. In calling Mussehl, he had hoped to conjure in jurors' minds suggestive scenes of suspicious encounters that illustrated Mary's faithlessness. He succeeded to a point, only to have Graham cast doubt on Mussehl's memory and on her motives for testifying. She and Mary, jurors would remember, did not part "exactly good friends."

Henry Cram apologized that his next witness, Julia Strong Bedell, was unavoidably delayed.

CHAPTER 13

The Bishop's Wife

CRAM'S NEXT SCHEDULED WITNESS was Peter's oldest sibling, forty-four-year-old Julia Strong Bedell. Long considered an invalid, she suffered from an unspecified malady which made climbing even a single flight of stairs difficult and painful. Her life had been hard in other ways as well. Married in 1845 to the Episcopal cleric Gregory Thurston Bedell, she and her husband had sorrowfully remained childless after three babies died in infancy. Her reputation for long-suffering kindness and fortitude had earned her the ironic sobriquet "the Beata" from cousin George.

Julia had stayed close to her family at Waverly even after her husband was appointed Bishop of Ohio in 1859, and the couple moved west. Since then, she had traveled east by railroad no less than seventeen times to visit her mother and siblings. Although now in New York—she, to testify at the trial; her husband, to accompany her and also to attend a convention—neither Julia nor the bishop was present in the courtroom. Cram, dapper and unruffled as ever, mildly reassured the court that Julia was delayed but expected within fifteen minutes. To save time, he offered to begin reading Julia's hundred-page deposition to the jury.

Graham irately objected to Cram's seemingly innocuous suggestion on two counts: first, the deposition had been improperly processed; second, it could in no way substitute for the witness herself. "In nine cases out of ten," Graham fulminated, "the appearance and manner of a witness on the stand serve as a window for the jury to look at his heart."

Why was she absent?, he continued. "Is there anything in this woman's character that she can't come here? Is she too good . . . too sensitive or delicate to be brought into this sanctuary of justice? I want her here." Graham's rhetorical questions disparaged Julia without directly attacking her. Insulting a bishop's wife was, after all, a delicate business.

The lawyers haggled and conferred until Cram reluctantly yielded and instead produced Sarah Hutchinson, known as Old Nurse. Hired in the 1820s at twenty-four years old by Peter's parents, she had nurtured, celebrated, and mourned a multitude of Strongs through their births, marriages, and deaths. At once fussy and forceful, subservient and bossy, the Nurse in Shakespeare's *Romeo and Juliet* might have been Hutchinson's ancestor.

Hutchinson's near-total deafness and extreme near-sightedness required the lawyers to stand unusually close to her and virtually shout their questions. Their best efforts made no difference. She either didn't hear objections or ignored them. "She seemed to enjoy the scene, and talked back quite as loudly and imparted quite as much zest to her replies as was allowed in court," a reporter commented.

"Tell us what you know about Edward and Mrs. Strong," Cram began.

"Well, I remember . . ."

"Hold on!" John McKeon interrupted on behalf of the defense.
"I left my room and . . ."

"Hold on!"

Much to observers' amusement, Old Nurse talked over him.
"I came down one day about seven or eight o'clock, and one of
the women"—

"Hold on," McKeon futilely objected a third time.

In the habit of referring to Mary as "Mrs. Peter," Old Nurse
evoked a suggestive scene. Early one morning, having overheard
some noises that provoked her curiosity, Old Nurse intentionally set out to eavesdrop. "I went into the pantry and thought I'd
listen," she testified, shamelessly admitting her snooping. "Mr.
Edward's door opened a little at a time, and Mrs. Peter peeped
out a little at a time, cautiously, and then she ran up the stairs.
She wore a calico wrapper; she used to wear it in the bedroom
and nursery."

What respectable woman would wear a wrapper, or dressing
gown, in her brother-in-law's bedroom? The question was unspo-
ken. Beneath a daytime or evening dress, its tight-fitted bodice a
chore to unbutton, a woman customarily wore formidable layers:
knickers, stockings, a chemise and corset, ample petticoats and, in
some cases, a steel frame to support a hoop skirt. Beneath a wrapper, on the other hand, she wore nightclothes. Or undergarments.
Or, perhaps, nothing. A wrapper was worn in the most intimate
circumstances. Old Nurse had introduced a sensuous mental picture into the courtroom, and she wasn't quite done.

"I saw Mrs. Peter in the same hall once or twice after that;
she looked frightened, her hair was flying, and I was agoing to
say, Mrs. Peter, what's the matter." Loose, flowing hair—natural,
not some stylized and artificial arrangement of plaits, buns, or
curls—implied freedom from social norms, private moments of

rest, childlike play, or sexual abandon. Old Nurse, with spite or obliviousness, had indicted Mary for unorthodox, if not illicit, behavior.

In his cross-examination, McKeon tried to dilute Old Nurse's testimony by asking about Waverly's residents and their movements within the household, whether others besides Mary were apt to visit one another casually and without ceremony.

"The children who were married were there with their wives," Old Nurse acknowledged. "They visited around the rooms, and Mrs. Peter went from room to room." Servants as well as family members had few restrictions. "We sat in the hall a great deal of the time; we all went where we wished to about the house; I used to go into the rooms when I wanted to."

Asked about Edward, she replied, "I haven't seen Edward since the war closed; he came home once for about an hour to see his mother . . . we were all glad to see him home safe from the war." Her affection for him motivated a sharp defense. "I know they say a great many things about Mr. Edward, but I don't believe one half the things they say about him, not one half."

As Cram helped Old Nurse down from the witness stand, McKeon stopped them with one more question: "When did you tell Peter what you saw"?

"I never did tell Peter what I did see . . . I was afeared to tell him."

Court broke for a forty-minute lunch break. When it resumed, Julia Bedell still had not appeared. Expressing his superficially sincere apologies, Cram received permission to read her deposition aloud, despite continued defense objections. Julia's testimony had been taken under oath before a court-appointed commission in her home state of Ohio; then a transcript had been sent to the New York judge and attorneys handling the suit. Like some novels, Julia's deposition recounted a story within a story, the tale of an affair as retold (Graham would subsequently argue) by a biased, secondhand narrator.

In the spring of 1862, Julia had testified, she opened two letters from Mary. Each nondescript in appearance, sent by regular mail, written in Mary's handwriting with ordinary ink, sealed with black wax, they turned out to be extraordinary confessions of Mary's infidelity. Stunned of course, Julia wrote back, posing an explosive question.

"Who was the tempter?" she asked.

"I was the tempter," Mary allegedly replied. "And afterward there was no time when Edward would consent to break the bonds, though I sometimes made the effort." Mary wrote that she sometimes felt remorseful about the affair, but that at other times she yielded to temptation without feeling troubled.

Julia admitted to destroying the letters, an act which she claimed was mutually agreed upon. She apologized to the Ohio commission for not being able to produce them but only to recall their substance.

At Peter's instigation, Julia continued, she met alone with Mary twice in 1862, the first time in August at Waverly for less than an hour. Highly agitated, Mary described the unstable state of her marriage and Peter's decree that he "would live with her—although he had a right to separate from her, and take the children away—occupying different rooms, and, if necessary, sitting at different tables, meeting only when the exigencies of housekeeping required it." Nevertheless, Peter remained uncertain as to how long he could tolerate this existence. "Any day he might feel it his duty to take the children away and live away from her."

Julia's second meeting with Mary took place in October 1862, at the home of one of the Bedells' friends, and lasted more than two hours. Julia testified to engaging her sister-in-law in a religious conversation, during which Mary expressed belief that

God would forgive her sin, although she admitted to wavering between feelings of peacefulness and doubt. Afterward, to help Mary in the important work of repentance, Julia read to her from the Bible, concluding with the passage, "'Though your sins be as scarlet, they shall be as white as snow."

These might not have been the exact words of the passage, Julia once again apologized in her deposition, but they conveyed its substance.

During their second meeting, Julia also asked Mary, "What could have induced your falling into sin," and she remembered listening without interruption as Mary told how the affair began.

"Though [Mary] had lived in the same house with Edward for many years," Julia stated, "she had never felt anything improper until one evening her hand touched his, and a thrill of emotion went through her frame, and she was irresistibly drawn to attract his attention, which she easily did; he reciprocated her regard, and after a little they went down together in the course of sin."

Julia added that Mary and Edward found it "easy to arrange interviews, as Peter went regularly to New York, having business, while Edward had none, and spent his time in walking, driving, etc." Mary confessed to going "occasionally to Edward's room, and on one occasion Peter knocked at the door, asking a question, which Edward answered without opening the door."

If it seemed odd to strangers that no one observed anything suspicious between Mary and Edward or intervened, Julia believed that habits of honor and innocence excused the family's obtuseness. "The reason why the family discovered nothing," she explained, "was that they were entirely unsuspicious and did not notice their intimacy."

As for the reason Mary gave for being vulnerable to sin? She was convinced that Peter's affections toward her had cooled. He was angry at her father, John Austin Stevens, for refusing to pay a promised allowance and threw this failure up to her often. Moreover, Peter held her up to ridicule, sometimes in front of others, telling her that she had married too young and should go back to school to improve herself.

Julia rejected this unsympathetic picture of her brother. "I never could forget his love at the time of [your] engagement," she recalled admonishing Mary during their meeting.

Mary also spoke of wanting to live at Waverly again and to convince Peter's mother of her repentance. She yearned to do anything to avoid divorce.

Except, according to Julia, a dark and threatening caveat followed this expression of contrition, one that contradicted Mary's declarations of repentance. "Peter is very much mistaken," Mary allegedly warned, "if he thinks I will take care of the children unless he lives with me, I can tell him I will not. I will send them back to his mother's."

Shock after shock followed. Here, at this second meeting, Mary told Julia that "she had destroyed the life of her unborn child, and for several moments neither of us spoke; she said 'Do you think it very wrong, Julia?' She felt bitter at the time because she did not know whether Edward or Peter was the father of the child."

Thus, according to Julia, an abortion indeed had occurred, but responsibility for the decision to commit the crime as well as its execution rested squarely with Mary.

Shaken to the core by the conversation, Julia invited Mary to kneel and pray beside her. When they arose, evidencing the polite manners and forgiving nature of a good minister's wife, Julia "gave her some refreshments."

Julia and Mary exchanged more letters in 1863. "I destroyed them myself," Julia told the members of the Ohio commission, "in pursuance of an understanding between Mary, Peter and myself, in order to prevent a premature disclosure of the crime."

The first part of Julia's deposition was concluded. Judge Garvin charged the jury to return to the jury box the next day at ten a.m., an hour earlier than usual.

DESPITE JULIA'S INFLAMMATORY REVELATIONS, the nation, or at least the press, seemed bored with the Strongs' marital catastrophe by the trial's fifth day. "The Court-room was not as densely packed at the opening as usual," one journalist reported. "The case drags along," another wrote. The reading of Julia's long deposition, compared to live testimony, was unavoidably dull.

Julia nevertheless remained absent, and the reading continued. Cross-examined by the Ohio commission, Julia admitted in her deposition that the Strong family, after all, was not completely oblivious to hints of an inappropriate relationship between Mary and Edward. "My mother is blind and has been for 12 years past." Julia stated. "She more than once spoke to me of Edward's intimacy with Mary and wondered that Peter did not see it. I don't know that she ever spoke to any of them about it, or that Peter was apprised by any of the family of the observation." Julia, however, approached the issue with Edward, speaking to him about "his undue attention to Mary." At what point she did so, and whether admonishing him had any impact, she did not say.

Forced to confront Peter's complicity in Mary's abortion, she adamantly denied his involvement. "Nothing was ever said of Peter's having made the abortion and the destruction of said infant a condition of forgiveness, or of . . . being the highest proof of devotion," she insisted.

At the end of her sworn testimony, Julia repeated the following, ensuring it would be remembered. "I wish to state also that

Mary said to me 'I am the tempter,' and again, 'if Peter thinks I will take care of the children without he lives in the house with me, he is very much mistaken.'"

Graham, having interrupted Cram's courtroom reading of the deposition numerous times, exploded at its conclusion. Always a showman, Graham here seemed authentically outraged that Julia presented, at times word for word, what she claimed was Mary's own confession. Yet where was Julia now? Nowhere to be seen in the courtroom, nor were any letters—presumably the only solid evidence of Mary's adultery. Some had been destroyed, and the plaintiff's counsel had failed to produce the rest. With Julia conveniently unavailable to be examined in person under oath, the jury—Graham thundered—had heard a completely unverifiable, deliberately selective, and clearly biased secondhand version of what Mary had said and done.

Graham objected not only to Julia's absence from the courtroom but also to her behavior toward Mary and its implications for jury consideration. If her two meetings with Mary in 1862 went as she claimed, he warned jurors, they were a travesty of ethical behavior. By using a "pretense of religious sympathy" and quoting biblical texts to the effect that Mary's sins "should be made white as snow," Julia had drawn Mary "into the most beautiful trap ever baited." She had "artfully turned the conversation upon the points that would benefit her brother's case," while Mary, "instead of thinking she was confessing to a witness, was confessing to God . . . and confessions made in the course of religious discipline cannot be admitted in this or any other court."

None of Graham's sweeping objections—to Julia's absence, to her recollection of letters previously destroyed, or to her religious manipulations—swayed the court. Her deposition before the Ohio Commission was admitted in its entirety. Nevertheless, Graham had successfully managed to raise questions about the deposition's legitimacy and to some extent had tarnished Julia's image—presenting her as hypocritical and duplicitous—as she had tarnished Mary's.

One newspaper commentator wholeheartedly agreed with Graham. A particularly disgusting part of the story, he noted, "was played by the wife of a Rev. Mr. Bedell, who appears to have visited the afflicted wife in her sorrow and desperation and under the guise of a religious consolation wrung from her a confession of guilt. The evidence discloses that none can hate as fiercely as man and wife, and none prove so false to each another as women."

CHAPTER 14

Eyes and Ears Everywhere

WEEK 2

Day 5 (cont.)
Wednesday, November 29 (cont.)
Plaintiff's Witnesses: Marie Tondre, Ellen McArdle, Benjamin
*   Lynch*

BECAUSE THERE HAD BEEN more than a year between Peter's divorce filing and trial, Cram had worried about losing witnesses, particularly household staff. Seemingly invisible but with eyes and ears everywhere, valued for their discretion but feared for their insiders' knowledge, servants often provided crucial testimony in a trial.

Unlike in England, however, where butlers, maids, cooks, and housekeepers might stay with a family for a lifetime, domestic workers in the United States (apart from those enslaved in the years before and during the war) were a generally transient population. Like others in the growing country, many were on the move—headed to California for a new adventure, to a nearby town to reside with relatives, or to a different household for better wages. Demand for servants in the upwardly mobile society outpaced supply.

The arduous work, early morning to late night, ranged from a cook's responsibility for planning and preparing three multi-course meals a day for family and staff to a housemaid's lighting of predawn fires, cleaning the rooms from parlor to bedchamber, doing chores such as emptying slop pots, shining silver and brass, washing laundry, and often serving and cleaning up after the evening meal.

By the 1850s, dozens of household manuals had been published on ideal methods of housekeeping, with titles such as Catherine Beecher's *Treatise on Domestic Economy* and Sarah Josepha Hale's *The Good Housekeeper*. Most were targeted to the housewife herself, but one of the most popular, *The House Servant's Directory*, was directed specifically at domestic employees, with rules for the optimal performance of their duties. Written in the 1820s by Robert Roberts, an African American butler to an affluent Boston family, the *Directory* covered everyday tasks such as extinguishing oil lamps, issues of etiquette such as addressing fellow servants, and esoteric challenges such as washing gold embroidery. It was a standard in many nineteenth-century homes, and proceeds from the book made its author wealthy. Roberts, who died in 1860, devoted his later years to the abolitionist cause.

Given the demands of their jobs, high-spirited young men and women in domestic service often preferred to work in cities, where, in the little time they had for themselves, they could easily meet friends and enjoy entertainments and exhibitions at places like New York's Niblo's Garden or Barnum's Museum. Daily newspaper columns filled with classified advertisements for amusements lured audiences to spectacles, dramas, farces, and minstrel or variety shows featuring dances, ballads, costumes, and jokes. "The Greatest Triumph of the Season—Tumultuous Applause—Immense Excitement" proclaimed an ad for Thorpe and Overin's "Minstrels of all Nations," onstage at the Temple of Music during the Strong trial's second week. Nearby, the American Theater boasted "The laughable Farce entitled *The Quiet Family*." Little Effie Parkhurst, soon to be famous for temperance songs such as "Father's a Drunkard and Mother is Dead," was featured in a concert at the Broadway Atheneum. City life was harsher but more fun than remaining isolated in a country home like Waverly.

Despite obstacles in finding scattered witnesses, Cram had managed to assemble a varied group of the Strongs' former employees to testify at the trial: Marie Tondre, the children's French nurse; Ellen McArdle, the Irish chambermaid; and Benjamin Lynch, the African American coachman. Tracking them down had been a matter of footwork, advertisements, and sometimes luck.

Tondre had bumped into Peter by accident one afternoon the previous spring in Madison Square Park, and they talked for ten minutes. "He did not ask me what I knew," she testified. "He told me what I was to prove." Afterward, Peter's lawyers had visited and interrogated her, preparing her to testify, then subpoenaed her for the trial.

An immigrant from France, Tondre began working for the Strongs at Islip in the late fall of 1862, almost a year after Edith's death. Eighteen years old at the time, Tondre stayed for nine months, her main responsibility the care of Mamie and Allie. In that, she seems to have replaced Matilda Mussehl, although lacking a governess's title and authority. After two months at Islip, Tondre moved with the Strongs to the Stevenses, and then to the Heckshers. She subsequently worked for two different families, with a brief period of unemployment between jobs.

Cram began the questioning by asking Tondre to describe the Strongs' sleeping arrangements in each of their households. Some jurors by now might have intuited the reason for Cram's intrusive attention to bedrooms. If the Strongs resumed sharing a bed, might their intimacy imply Peter's condonation, or forgiveness, of Mary's alleged infidelity? Beds in Islip, however, had remained decisively separate, with Mary's bedroom on the second floor, in the front; Peter's, next to it. At the Stevenses and Heckschers, Tondre said, Peter stayed overnight only occasionally, and then also in a separate room.

In his cross-examination, Graham wanted to know more about the Strongs' relationship and social life at Islip. Were Mary and Peter isolated from the company of others, kind to one another, in good health and spirits? Tondre spoke of cordial visits by family members from both sides. As for the couple's relationship, she echoed Mussehl in stating that she never saw Peter and Mary "walk arm in arm" and "saw them talk together very seldom," but had not noticed any overt hostility between them. As the children's caregiver, Tondre thought both parents seemed very fond of their daughters and recalled that Peter sometimes took them riding. Otherwise, he was often away during the day to hunt or shoot or visit Waverly, and he spent some evenings socializing at the local seaside hotels. He rarely went to the city.

Tondre thought that Mary's health at Islip "was pretty good, but not as good as it might be." While neighbors visited occasionally, Mary rarely returned the favor.

At the Stevenses in 1863, Tondre found that everyone seemed on good terms. Although Peter never addressed his wife directly, Tondre seemed unperturbed by this lack. He appeared to be friendly with other members of the family, and they ate meals together.

"Then it was a regular family group?" Graham asked, attempting to make the group sound as unremarkable as any other family. The routine of sitting down together to dine often signified family cohesiveness and could, like shared bedrooms, perhaps suggest a reconciliation.

"Well now, this woman is not familiar with the English language," Cram intervened, "She is very intelligent, but still, she is French . . ."

Graham rephrased. "Was it a family gathering?"

"It was," Tondre replied in her charming French accent.

She thought that Mary's health improved at the Heckschers' home, and that Peter seemed to get along well with his sister-in-law Lucretia and her husband. Lucretia's subsequent testimony on the latter point, her description of angry arguments with Peter, would call Tondre's accuracy and powers of observation into question.

Graham returned to the topic of Islip, asking a question in sharp contrast to the relatively benign ones preceding it: "Did you ever see a box in Mr. Strong's bureau containing instruments?" This was the trial's first mention of such a container or its unspeakable contents, the instruments that Peter allegedly had procured from Electa Potter.

"I did not."

"Are you positive of that?"

"I am." Her firm reply denied Graham the chance to introduce the abortion, at least for the moment. Tondre was dismissed, and the next witness summoned.

Born in Ireland and about five years older than Tondre, Ellen McArdle worked for the Strongs as a chambermaid and laundress at Twenty-first Street for six months, starting shortly before Edith died. Like Mussehl and Tondre, she had since worked in several different households, and Cram had to place a classified newspaper ad to find her, offering payment for information on her whereabouts. She, too, had been subpoenaed rather than appearing voluntarily.

As household manuals made clear, chambermaids (like all domestic help) were expected to be perfectionists, subject to the strict routines of the household in which they worked. Many homes had their own distinct way of doing things. "In some families," one 496-page manual disparaged, "it is the custom of the chambermaids to have all the bedrooms on hand at once, first going round and making all the beds, then sweeping all the rooms, then dusting them all, and lastly performing a tour with the fresh water and clean towels. This is a most inconvenient practice, as it keeps all the chambers unfinished." The writer recommended tackling one bedroom at a time and cleaning it thoroughly before moving on.

In examining McArdle, Cram again expressed interest in the question of separate beds. McArdle well knew who slept where. She made up Peter's bed "every morning but one Sunday, when I went to church early in the morning, and another person tended to it. I made up Mrs. Strong's bed every day." Sleeping arrangements changed the night of Edith's funeral, with Peter moving to a small bedroom behind the one previously shared with his wife.

Under Graham's questioning McArdle also remembered Edward's dining one evening at Twenty-first Street with Mary, Peter, and the children, and she thought that he visited a second time but recalled few details. Except, of course, about performing her usual tasks: "It was my duty to attend to the rooms. I was called to make a bed for him by Mrs. Strong; it was in the evening."

Twenty-three-year-old Benjamin Lynch, the third Strong employee to testify, had worked for the family for years rather than months, serving as one of Peter's coachmen—his favorite— from 1859 to 1863. The *Tribune* didn't mention his race, but the *Herald*, noted for its lively descriptions, called him "a gentleman of color" and extolled his "bright, intelligent eyes and smart appearance" and the "commendable coolness" of his walk.

Lynch was born and raised in Maryland, a slave state that had remained in the Union, until he was about twelve years old. How Lynch came to New York, whether enslaved or free, alone or with family, after a terrifying escape or routine journey, remained unexplored in court.

In many households, a coachman such as Lynch did double duty by helping with chores such as serving at the table. But a coachman's primary work was prestigious and challenging. It demanded knowledge of horses; expert care in their feeding and grooming; and fastidious attention to ornament and equipment—uniform crisp and spotless, bridle and harness gleaming, carriage free of the previous day's mud and debris, shining like the sun and ready for passengers. Most important, the position required skill in driving, the true coachman's hands said to be as sensitive as those of a musician—"so delicate and gentle," one horseman wrote, "that the mere weight of the reins is felt on the bit, and the directions are indicated by a turn of the wrist rather than by a pull; the horses are guided and encouraged."

Even before Lynch was sworn in, John McKeon tried to puncture his dignity, perhaps given the unpleasant task because the lawyer was known for his abolitionist sympathies, so that derogatory comments would seem to be motivated by fact rather than race. Had not Lynch been in the State Prison once, McKeon queried and then answered his own question. "We are credibly informed that he was," McKeon stated, "and if that be true, we must object to his testimony." Judge Garvin advised McKeon that he needed to produce court records proving Lynch's conviction of a crime. Otherwise, Lynch had the right to decline questions that tended to be degrading. McKeon had no such documentation, and the witness was sworn in.

Responding to Cram's usual bedroom query, Lynch recalled that in Islip he helped Peter push a large wardrobe against the connecting door to Mary's room. "It was there until I left," he said. He was familiar with both spouses' bedrooms, since he left Peter's polished boots in his bedroom every morning, and Mary's boots at her door.

"Have you ever seen Mr. Strong in Mrs. Strong's room when she was there?"

"No, sir."

His point made, Cram asked no further questions.

McKeon, in his cross-examination, again pressed the witness about his past. "What offense sent you to the prison?"

"That I decline . . . I don't answer because I don't wish to. My own judgement tells me I need not answer."

And, as Graham had with Marie Tondre, McKeon questioned Lynch about a mysterious box.

"I had access to Mr. Strong's room, and know where he kept his cigars; they were in one of the drawers of the bureau; don't know what else there was in the drawer; didn't see anything in a box nor in the drawer." The answer seemed to confirm Lynch's reliability as a witness. An employee who knew where his employer stored a treasured cache of cigars surely knew all.

A question about a coachman's work at Waverly produced new insights into that affluent household. Every family member at Waverly had horses, Lynch stated, usually more than one. Even "old Mrs. Strong had two horses and two carriages . . . there were altogether fifteen or sixteen carriages and about twenty-five horses at the stables at Waverly; they had four coachmen, five at one time." He often drove Peter to Manhattan, frequently to Peter's club or business, but not every day. He never dropped him at the corner of Waverly Place—where, presumably, Peter might have been visiting Electa Potter.

Lynch's services as coachman were needed less often at Islip, as Peter always took the railway or horse cars from there to the city. Peter's spare time was spent fishing, boating, shooting, and, sometimes in the evenings, socializing at the village hotels. Lynch recalled taking Mary, Mamie, and Allie for occasional pleasure outings around the village or to the seaside, but not Peter with the children. In delicate health, Mary sometimes entertained family members such as her sisters, but she rarely received any calls from neighboring ladies and never made calls herself.

In response to Cram's brief redirect, Lynch mentioned that Peter owned a saddlehorse that Mary rode once or twice. None of the newspapers reported the context for Cram's question or Lynch's answer, but McKeon was interested enough to follow up with another question about the horse. It led Lynch to refer to an incident: "The horse was fractious. We had to put boots on him. I recollect he threw Mrs. Strong."

In their testimony, Tondre and Lynch had agreed on several points: Mary's fragile health at Islip and, apart from visiting family, her tendency to seclusion; Peter's social and recreational activity there. They had offered few salacious details such as those supplied by Old Nurse and Matilda Mussehl. Instead, their testimony, coupled with that of McArdle, amounted to a sad confirmation of the irreparable breach between husband and wife, starkly symbolized by their separate beds.

CHAPTER 15

The Judge's Daughter

WEEK 2
Trial Days 5 (cont.), 6
Wednesday, November 29 (cont.); Thursday, November 30
Plaintiff's Witnesses: Fanny Hoffman Strong, James Mariner,
Charles Sanford

LATE AFTERNOON GLOOM seeped through the courthouse's windows. The courtroom was claustrophobic; the benches were crowded; the wintery smell of wool clothing pervaded every corner. The jury had already heard testimony from four witnesses— Julia, via her deposition, and the three employees. Who could blame a juror who was briefly tempted to "rest his eyes," or a spectator who dozed in the last row of seats? This complicated trial day was still unfinished. The fifth witness, thirty-three-year-old Fanny Hoffman Strong, was the daughter of former Superior Court judge Murray Hoffman, the elder sage of Peter's legal team. Judge Hoffman sat at the front of the courtroom, observing his pretty and self-confident daughter with paternal pride.

"I was married in October 1860," Fanny testified. "My husband is Benjamin Strong, brother of Peter. . . . I live at Newtown, and have done so since November 1860."

Listening to Fanny, Peter might have recalled the summer day when she and Edward, named Edith's godmother and godfather, stood side by side at the infant's baptism, the ceremony performed by Bishop Bedell. The irony of that moment, its deceptive familial closeness, in retrospect could not have escaped Peter.

Cram intended Fanny to be his most important witness, his secret weapon. Unlike Julia, who had destroyed certain letters, Fanny possessed other letters considered crucial to making Peter's case. But this revelation would have to wait for the right moment. Cram had other matters he wanted to pursue first, in effect setting the stage. He reviewed basic biographical facts with the witness, then asked for her observations about Mary's interaction with Edward.

"At Waverly I saw Edward and Mrs. Peter Strong very much together," Fanny said. "They were too much together. They rode and walked and drove together." She thought that Mary instigated the meetings. "Mrs. Strong decidedly sought the society of Edward," she stated. "I saw her make signs to him to follow her; she beckoned to him." Mary also spent time in Edward's bedroom. "I saw her open Edward's door and come out three or four times; he was in there at the time."

Fanny painted a flattering picture of her brother-in-law, Peter. He was a man of "domestic habits," and "very affectionate to his wife and children; he was kind and attentive to them." His routines were regular. "He was very seldom away from home at night . . . once or twice, when he went on an excursion." He provided for his wife "liberally" and ensured that Mary was always "handsomely dressed."

The three rooms given to Mary and Peter at Waverly—their bedroom, dressing room, and the children's room—also were handsome, Fanny noted. Especially the couple's bedroom. One of the best in the house, with rosewood furniture and a "fine exposure" overlooking the bay. In fact, Mary lacked for nothing. Although not a rider himself, Peter bought her "a very fine riding horse." She did not mention that the horse, if Benjamin Lynch had been correct, tried to throw Mary. Emphasizing Peter's generosity rather than any possible thoughtlessness, Fanny stated that the horse "proved rather gay for her . . . [so] he bought a more quiet one."

In addition, the Strongs were solicitous of Mary's family. They warmly welcomed the Stevenses, and Mary's mother and sisters visited often.

Cram nudged Fanny into more dramatic testimony, questioning her about a meeting with Mary in March 1863. At the time, Mary was living with her parents on Twenty-second Street, while Fanny, Benjamin, her mother-in-law, and other Strong family members were residing for several weeks at Julian's Hotel on Twenty-third Street in Manhattan. Fanny didn't state exactly who was at the hotel or why, but James's wedding to Georgiana Berriman of New York was planned for June. With James away at war, his family may have wished to be close to his bride-to-be and share in the wedding excitement.

To everyone's surprise, Mary visited her in-laws at the hotel— entirely unexpectedly, according to Fanny. She remained alone with Mary while the rest of the family speedily made excuses and left on errands. Fanny then went on to have a serious conversation with her sister-in-law, one which she recounted for jurors almost verbatim, much as Julia had done in front of the Ohio commission.

"Fanny, I suppose you know all," Mary allegedly told her at their meeting.

"No," Fanny recalled answering. "I know something terrible has happened."

Mary's next words, Fanny said, stunned her.

"Yes, it is terrible, so much so that Peter can get a divorce from me if he chooses . . . I have lived for eighteen months as Edward Strong's wife . . . I have sinned grievously but I hope to be forgiven."

Abruptly, on that memorable note, Cram ended the direct examination, addressing the judge with a request. "I trust your Honor will not sit longer tonight. I am very weary and the heat here is terrible."

Caught by surprise but determined to erase the last scene from jurors' minds, Graham energetically objected. He wanted immediately "to grasp this evidence by the throat . . . to go into its very bowels and show what it's made of. . . . Can't we go on now with the cross-examination?"

McKeon, equally insistent but less bombastic, interjected that "we would like to go on now, Sir. The jury hear this and go away with an impression. . . ." Neither lawyer wanted Fanny's version of Mary's confession, uncontested and uppermost in jurors' minds, to end the day.

But it was after four p.m., the early dusk of late November, and Judge Garvin saw no reason to continue. "The plaintiff is not done with the witness, and of course the defense must wait," he ruled. "If the counsel feels sick, I must grant him the courtesy of an adjournment."

CRAM INTRODUCED HIS TWO MOST critical and concrete pieces of evidence the next morning—two letters, allegedly written by Mary. After receiving them from Peter, Cram had sent them on to Benjamin, who shared them with his wife, most likely at the lawyer's request. Since Fanny had seen the letters before the trial, she could legitimately identify them at the trial. Intentionally or not, Cram had arranged an effective tableau: the "good" woman peering down at the "fallen" woman's words, appraising them.

The first letter, dated January 6, 1862, was to Peter; the second was labeled "copy of a letter written in 1862." As soon as Fanny identified them, Graham seized them. He turned them over, minutely examined them, commented on differences in handwriting, and questioned whether the same person indeed had written both letters. The letter to Peter was scribbled in haste, Cram explained, accounting for any differences in appearance.

Graham raised two more objections. Since the first letter omitted the name *Edward Strong*, who could say if it referred to the current case? Moreover, husbands had been known to coerce confessions from their wives. After all, "a husband could throttle anything he wanted from his wife," Graham said. Precedent existed for excluding such documents.

Objections noted but dismissed by the judge, Cram read the first letter.

> *The following is freely given to an injured husband by a loving wife, to prove that if at any future time he should be driven by the power of his wretchedness to a course of reckless misery and despair, that my faithlessness has been the whole cause of it. On the evening of January 5, I made, in the bitterness of my soul, a full . . . confession of a course of guilt which had stained my life, and extended over a period of nearly two years.*
>
> *God's merciful judgment has snapped the cord of iniquity, and His strength has enabled me to confess the crime to him I had wronged, and relieved my conscience of the heavy weight of concealment.*
>
> *If my husband sinks beneath the blow, and is driven to destruction, I wish to bear the blame; I wish it to be known to all, that he may be excused and shielded from reproach.*
>
> *May God avert the dreadful issue—send peace to his heart—grant to me a sincere repentance and forgive me.*
>
> *Mary E. Strong*
> *Jan. 6, 1862*

Listening closely, Peter leaned forward, elbows bent on the table in front of him, head in his hands, hiding tears. Cram paused, allowing the moment to resonate before moving to the next letter.

Graham barked his objection. The document was marked *copy*. Where was the proof of its delivery? The judge deemed delivery irrelevant, and Cram read:

> *Edward N. Strong:*
> *A judgment of God has arrested me in my career of sin,*
> *and thrown down the barrier of concealment. My husband*
> *knows all. Whatever may be the issue of that knowledge, my*
> *affections are again entirely his. I [illegible] bitterly.*
> *Mary E. Strong*

This time without a pause, Cram resumed his questions. He turned to the topic of religion, a natural enough transition after jurors had listened to Mary's appeals to God. However, his focus seemed less about holiness and more about opportunities for intimacy. Fanny confirmed that Mary was religious, a member of Newtown's Dutch Reformed church and a Sunday school teacher, and that Edward, a church deacon, also taught there. He and Mary went to services together every Sunday at nine a.m., usually in Edward's wagon, while Peter didn't go until ten a.m., if at all.

Jurors might not have known that Edward's "wagon" was a stylish two-seater, drawn by two horses, a perfect vehicle for a couple to snatch a few quiet moments to talk between themselves. The jury didn't need to know the details to infer the implications.

Fanny saw other manifestations of closeness between Peter's wife and brother. For example, Mary gave Edward a special gift when he returned briefly on furlough at Christmas, 1861. "I rec-

ollect her making him a present . . . a dressing gown; she told me
she had made it for him the day he left." It was not only a very
personal gift, but it also took Mary's attention away from Fanny.
"She was very busy making the gown . . . and excused herself for
not being ready to receive me. . . . I have never made presents to
the gentlemen of the family, nor they to me."

When Graham's chance to cross-examine Fanny finally
arrived, he wanted to know about Edward's current whereabouts.
On leaving the army in the spring, Fanny replied, Edward moved
from Baltimore to Darien, Connecticut, where he owned land.
Fanny and Benjamin, who managed his brother's business affairs
during the war, visited him there. "I saw [Edward] two weeks
ago," she said. "He was fishing, riding, driving, and walking; he
was at a boarding house . . . he used his own name." She was not
friendly toward Edward, although civil. She shook hands and
asked how he was. "He was not happy; he was quiet."

Questioned further about Edward's demeanor and life in
Darien, she elaborated. "He was as attractive as ever," she admitted, but dismissed any hint that he might be enjoying himself
or, an unseemly thought, flirting. "Edward did not speak of the
Darien society," she said, "nor of the success of his attractions; no
allusion to his irresistibility among the ladies."

As for family relationships, Fanny indicated that Benjamin's
correspondence with Edward had grown terse, all business,
no affectionate exchanges. The rest of the family was warmer.
During wartime, Aletta Strong had sent Edward Christmas
presents—usually treats of food—and probably would continue
to do so. Julia had visited him recently, and Elizabeth wrote to
him frequently.

Graham switched from the present to the past. In April 1864,
Fanny said, Edward was deposed in Baltimore in connection with
Peter's divorce suit. Benjamin attended and was away from home

two days. About six weeks later, Edward visited Waverly for an hour one morning. He spent the time with his mother. Neither Peter nor Mary was there that day. To Fanny's knowledge, "Peter has never spoken against him, nor threatened his life, nor spoke of shedding his blood, nor has he spoken well of him."

In the years before the scandal broke, Peter generally was an even-tempered man, Fanny recalled. Although "his disposition was occasionally disturbed . . . don't know that he was morose; he never spent days in an unpleasant mind; he was not sour; he was occasionally ruffled and out of humor." She didn't say how long his "ruffled" moods lasted.

Fanny's account of Mary's relationship with the Strong women amounted to a set of denials. Fanny never heard "Mrs. Bedell speak ill of her, nor of her being 'fashionable' nor 'fancy' . . . there was not the least ill feeling against Mary, no one spoke unfavorably of her as a proud, overbearing woman, never heard any attack upon her character."

"I have heard the family speak of her as changeable," Fanny reluctantly admitted, but "never heard them suggest that she was better born or that she came from a proud and pretending family."

If Mary had complaints about the bedroom at Waverly being too warm or too cold, Fanny did not remember them. In her opinion, she reiterated, the bedroom Mary and Peter shared "had the best furnishings in the house." True, there was a cabinet of oddities such as a dagger—but no weapons of war like firearms and shells, "nothing unpleasant to look at or unsuited to the delicacy of a lady." No javelins or mummies or stuffed animals and birds. Beautiful paintings hung on the wall, "nothing cruel or ferocious in man or beast." They were "pictures of animals—dogs, I believe, landscapes, etc."

Graham placed one of the portraits from the Strongs' bedroom in front of Fanny for identification and displayed it for jurors to see. Depicting neither a dog nor a landscape, it was a reproduction of a famous painting, popular among nineteenth-century tourists to Rome, of the beautiful and tragic Beatrice Cenci. According to a tale dramatized by the poet Shelley in a five-act play, Beatrice's father, a cruel sixteenth-century aristocrat, had plotted to seduce her, and she took revenge by having him assassinated. Liquid-eyed and sweet-faced, garbed in a white robe, her head swathed in white cloth, awaiting execution, Beatrice gazed pleadingly from the picture frame.

Mary's counsel had already pointed out Peter's love of the transgressive Romantic poets: Keats, Byron, Shelley. And here was a painting suffused with forbidden themes of passion and incest. Were these appropriate for a lady's bedroom? "I understand it is a copy from Guido Reni," Fanny commented demurely, discounting the painting. "There's nothing but the head of a woman."

When Graham asked about Peter's purchasing a "fine bay horse" for his wife, Fanny denied knowing that the animal not only tried to throw Mary but also to overturn a wagon she was driving—forcing her "to get out of the wagon to save her neck." Fanny claimed not to recall Mary's eventual refusal to use Peter's "unsafe horse." The second horse Peter purchased for his wife, Fanny again assured the courtroom, caused no problems whatsoever.

Did Edward "look like a man whose touch would send a thrill of emotion through a woman's frame," Graham abruptly demanded. Fanny, just as abruptly, answered that Edward "never looked like that." She thus sought to allay any impression of him as a dangerous man, a seducer of women. In fact, she testified, she hadn't told Peter what she observed about Mary and Edward because it all seemed innocent. "Didn't think much of it at the time." Although Mary and Edward were often together, Fanny "still thought them pure."

Graham returned to Fanny's meeting with Mary at Julian's Hotel in 1863. Fanny had earlier implied that she "did not call and invite [Mary] to come . . . I did not know she was coming at this time." Under cross-examination, as it turned out, that statement was not strictly accurate. She and Mary had never been intimate, but Fanny had nevertheless reached out to her, eager to hear her story. "[Benjamin] had had a talk with Peter and was quite excited, so that I knew something had happened; he didn't tell me what it was. I at once communicated with Mary Strong."

According to Fanny, Mary hoped above all to be allowed to see her children and had vowed, "I would go away—I would live with my aunt or anywhere, if I may only be permitted to see my children." Although Mary wept as she spoke, Fanny later felt no guilt about sharing what her sister-in-law confessed. "I did not promise not to tell what she said," Fanny testified. "She started the conversation."

Some jurors or observers might have experienced Fanny's attitude as rather hard-hearted. Judge Hoffman, her father, evidenced no such concern but warmly congratulated his daughter at the conclusion of her testimony on her poise and deportment as a witness.

The day ended with brief testimony from James Mariner, an officer of the court, who asserted that he had served Mary a writ of habeas corpus in June 1864, and from Charles Sanford, the lawyer who, along with Murray Hoffman, had advised Peter on issuing the writ. It had ordered Mary to appear with Allie in court. Peter's lawyers presumably thought that, once there, the recalcitrant Mary might be made more reasonable about custody arrangements.

Asked whether Mary obeyed the writ, Graham replied, "She did not. She obeyed a higher law, and I honor her for it."

"A higher law? I'd like to have that as evidence," Cram said. "We obey the present law."

Fanny's testimony, like Julia's, had drawn its strength largely from Mary's confessions—firsthand, if jurors accepted the authenticity of Mary's letters; secondhand or hearsay, if they didn't believe the letters were authentic.

Fanny and Julia, Mary's sisters-in-law, were the only family members on the Strong side summoned to testify. The evident reason? Mary confided in both women. However, a deeper rationale resided in their demeanor and rectitude. Well-dressed and well-spoken, Fanny and Julia both embodied the image of the proper matron. In representing the ideal of the loving wife who carried out her duties in support of her husband, they provided a sharp contrast to the missing Mary.

Moreover, Fanny and Julia did not—as women, could not—serve in distinguished positions nor even on a jury, but the reputation of the important men in their lives—Judge Hoffman, Bishop Bedell—imbued them with vicarious authority, empowering them to discuss the most shocking subjects and level the most damning accusations while still preserving a genteel aura. In calling them, Cram had gambled that they could safely impugn Mary—a lady herself, albeit an errant one—without creating a backlash of sympathy from the jury.

CHAPTER 16

A Fishing Expedition

WEEK 2

Trial Day 7

Friday, December 1

Plaintiff's Witness: Robert B. Roosevelt

DAY 7 BEGAN WITH CRAM introducing the will of James Strong, Peter's father, into evidence and, at Graham's request, reading it aloud. Whatever relevance the lawyers attributed to it, the will confirmed what the Strong family already knew. Aletta Strong, genial and frail, of fading memory and failed sight, yet a force of nature and a matriarchal powerhouse, was firmly in control of her six children's finances. Until she remarried (unlikely at her advanced years) or died, James Strong's entire estate was hers to do with as she wished. The will did ask her to provide for her children so long as they remained in her home, and, if she so desired, to distribute an equal and reasonable share of the estate's income to each of them on coming of age.

Aletta was one of five executors—the other four were male relatives and friends trusted to be her allies and advisors should she need them. Strong's will was unusual in leaving money matters so firmly in the hands of his wife. However, the will was appropriate, for Aletta was descended from two long-settled and prosperous New York State families. Having brought substantial land and wealth to her marriage, she was entitled to what remained of that original bounty, if not more, on her husband's death.

After the will's reading, Cram called Robert Roosevelt, the day's first and only witness. Among long-settled and prosperous New York State families, there was no more estimable surname than his. One of his Roosevelt ancestors had come to America from the Netherlands in the mid-1600s. Since then, the Roosevelts had intermarried with other well-pedigreed families, acquiring real estate that extended east and north across Manhattan into Long Island and the Hudson River Valley, and developing business interests that encompassed railroads, manufacturing, and banking. The Roosevelts were politically influential as well, although they didn't agree among themselves on most matters of politics. If Peter wished to highlight his old New York connections, he could not do better than to ask a Roosevelt to testify on his behalf.

A few years younger than Peter, thirty-six-year-old Robert was a lawyer whose father, businessman Cornelius Van Schaack Roosevelt, was one of the richest men in New York State. Although Peter never maintained an active law practice, he kept an office in the same downtown building as Robert did. More important, the two men were personal friends who had known one another for twenty-five years.

Cram's interrogation revealed little about the Strongs that was new. Robert Roosevelt knew Mary as well as Peter and visited them at Waverly and Islip. The Strongs' shared bedroom at Waverly, according to Roosevelt, held a number of handsome paintings, including the reproduction of Beatrice Cenci's portrait, and an original oil depicting Waverly, painted by the artist Jasper Francis Cropsey. The room also held a cabinet of oddities from Peter's travels, Roosevelt confirmed, among them a little mummified foot, no larger than a hand. He did not seem to find anything offensive in the decor.

In Islip, Roosevelt testified, husband and wife slept in separate rooms, where a weighty piece of furniture—perhaps a large washstand, he suggested—blocked the passageway between their rooms. The couple spoke very little to one another at dinner, behaving in a distantly polite manner, although Mary did join the men for an hour or so in the parlor after dinner. Roosevelt did not comment on the fact that Mary's joining them was unusual. Protocol generally dictated that men retired on their own after dinner to enjoy masculine conversation and a nightly brandy.

Cram's direct examination, straightforward and dry, gave not a hint of the entertaining cross-examination to follow. Roosevelt, as it happened, was an avid sportsman and an occasional author. Well-aware of this fact, McKeon instantly raised the topic of Roosevelt's recent book, *Superior Fishing*, an account of a twenty-day Lake Superior fishing excursion in the summer of 1863 that the author took with Peter. The trip occurred a few months before the Strongs separated for good. Roosevelt acknowledged that the character of "Don Pedro" in the book was based on the plaintiff, although, he added with a twinkle, the portrayal could not be construed as entirely accurate.

McKeon, showing not a whit of glee beneath his lawyerly countenance, asked Roosevelt to read aloud a section describing the Peter-like character.

> Don Pedro is descended from one of what we in our young country call the old and highly-respectable families, and having been nurtured among the refinements and luxuries of life, is one of the most gentlemanly men imaginable. . . .
> Never having taken an active share in the world's affairs, his abilities, which are far above the average, have lain dormant, or run to criticizing art or committing

poetry, and he is very apt to discuss very small matters with a minuteness and persistency that important ones scarcely merit.

He had traveled Europe, of course; had shot quail and taken trout in Long Island, fired at crocodiles on the Nile and jackals in the desert, and although probably the greatest exposure of his life had been damp sheets at a country inn, and his severest hardship the finding of his claret sour . . . he was now seized with a sporting mania, and determined to rough it in the woods.

As described in the book, when the men arrived in Cleveland to meet their boat, the first hurdle they encountered centered on the amount and type of liquor to take with them. Roosevelt suggested a case of Don Pedro's favorite brandy. Don Pedro, however, not only worried about running out but also about sharing such expensive spirits with their guides, "when they would probably prefer a coarser article." Every possible alternative in quantity, type, and quality was considered and debated in detail. Decisions plagued Don Pedro even while ordering at a local store, until Roosevelt finally dragged him away "leaving the clerk, bottle in hand, looking the image of despair at the avalanche of inquiries that had burst upon him."

The next hurdle involved selecting a stateroom on the boat.

He at once devoted his entire attention to it, flitting from place to place in the forward and after cabins . . . pointing out defects here, suggesting changes there . . . describing his foreign experiences and the prime necessity of comfortable quarters, turning down the sheets, peering into cracks . . . casting a suspicious eye upon the blankets . . . and finally resolved to take [a stateroom] which could not be examined at the time for want of the key, but which the steward, who had been a respectful and sympathetic listener, assured him had none of the defects he had pointed out.

Other matters of concern on the journey entailed the lack of white sugar, clouds of mosquitoes, and how to cook a good ham.

Smiles and muffled laughter in the courtroom indicated that everyone, with the exception of Peter, enjoyed hearing about Don Pedro's idiosyncrasies.

"In this way we went on," Roosevelt continued, "and I passed three weeks of unalloyed happiness."

"Well, Sir," McKeon said, satisfied that Don Pedro had captivated the courtroom, "we will now return to the subject matter."

Roosevelt denied hearing anything about the Strongs' marital troubles until the habeas corpus was issued. Then he spoke to Peter about them only once. In that conversation, Peter "said that . . . it had been proposed by one side or the other that . . . [Mary] was to take one child, and he the other, alternating, and each was to see either child whenever they wished, but he was to preserve the absolute legal right" to control the children's upbringing and take them away "when he thought proper."

On that last point, according to Roosevelt, negotiations broke down. Mary found Peter's claim of "absolute right" to the two children wholly unacceptable, whether Peter ever exercised that right or not, and whatever the law and custom might ordain.

McKeon next asked Roosevelt about Electa Potter, perhaps hoping that Peter had revealed a clandestine affair to his friend. Roosevelt denied knowing about anything other than a business relationship as landlord and tenant between Peter and Potter.

McKeon pounced, reading aloud a note that Peter wrote Potter in March 1863. Surely it indicated unusual tolerance on a landlord's part toward a delinquent tenant?

> *Dear Madam—A five-dollar bill on the Bank of America,*
> *which I took this morning in payment for your rent, is*
> *pronounced a counterfeit, and a one-dollar Treasury note*
> *was also refused. . . . I will bring them with me for you to*
> *exchange when I call on Friday or Saturday. Yours very truly,*
> *P. R. Strong*

Hadn't Peter also quite generously reduced Mrs. Potter's rent for no apparent reason, McKeon inquired. Roosevelt responded that Peter had done so but without favoritism, as "he did reduce the rent of his tenants at one time, and hers among the rest."

In his redirect, Cram tried to correct the impression that Don Pedro and Peter were one and the same. Roosevelt obliged by stressing that Don Pedro was never intended to be an accurate representation of his friend Peter, not at all. In writing his book, the author had wished "primarily to describe the Superior Region." As for the rest, "it was merely an indulgence in the realms of imagination, to the best of my ability."

Roosevelt was Cram's last witness. In only one week's time, the lawyer had presented a veritable parade of good citizens, ten in all: genteel ladies, hard-working servants, honest bureaucrats, and one notable high-society gentleman. In trials of the time, reputation was no small matter. A witness's credibility counted almost as much as substantive proof, and an individual's standing and reputation in the community were considered valid evidence of his or her credibility. Honorable and sincere, Cram's witnesses had served as a kind of group character reference on

Peter's behalf. Moreover, they had agreed in their assessment of Mary and Edward's suspicious intimacy and in their description of Mary and Peter's separate beds.

"This is all, your honor," Cram said, "and with this rests our case."

Stepping from the witness box, Robert Roosevelt probably doubted—if he thought about it at all—that anyone amused by Don Pedro would go on to read *Superior Fishing*. Yet there was much in the book of interest beyond its comedic Don Pedro anecdotes—information for serious sportsmen and naturalists about species and their habitats, effective techniques and equipment for catching different types of fish, even a section on cooking fish, whether in the wild or at home. Roosevelt also included a warning that he wanted to be widely heard about species preservation. As the nation expanded, its citizens had heedlessly engaged not just in overfishing its rivers, lakes, and seacoasts, but in the needless slaughter of many different species, mammals, birds, and fish, and the destruction of their habitats.

A sportsman, Roosevelt wrote, who "fishes only for quantity, and from a vain-glorious spirit of boastful rivalry is, indeed, a ruthless thing; he spares neither fish, flesh, nor fowl, whether he can use them for food, or must leave them to putrify, and regardless of the means or implements he employs."

Few in the courtroom that afternoon could have imagined the influence Roosevelt would soon exert in attempting to preserve "the beautiful lakes and rivers, ensconced in the wild woods and amid the green hills of our unopened country." In 1868, Roosevelt established the New York State Fish Commission, its mission largely to protect the state's fish population, and he served as the organization's commissioner. Three years later, as a one-term congressman in 1871, he introduced a bill establishing the United

States Fishery Commission, an organization with a similar purpose on a national scale. He is often credited with instilling a passion for conservation in his nephew, Theodore Roosevelt, seven years old at the time of the Strong trial and a future president of the United States.

PART 4

Counterattack

CHAPTER 17

Opening for the Defendant

WEEK 3

Trial Days 8, 9

Monday, December 4; Wednesday, December 6

Defendant's Attorneys: Elbridge Gerry, John McKeon

JURORS, JOURNALISTS, AND SPECTATORS were primed to hear the defense counsel's opening statement that Monday morning. Instead, Gerry presented a motion to dismiss the entire suit. The reason? The plaintiff's counsel had offered no definitive proof of adultery. The standard for proof, Gerry opined, should be the same for civil matters as for criminal ones. In other words, jurors should find for the plaintiff only if persuaded beyond a reasonable doubt that the defendant, and only the defendant, had been unfaithful. But was there any convincing proof of that?

"There is no proof directly of any act of adultery," Gerry alleged. "There is not even proof of a single act of familiarity between Mrs. Strong and Edward—nothing except that she rode, walked and drove with him openly, and the testimony of some of the plaintiff's hired menials that she was seen coming out of Edward's room in the daytime. . . ."

Gerry adamantly rejected the reliability of written and oral confessions, citing the eighteenth-century legal authority William Blackstone that "'they are the weakest and most suspicious of all testimony: ever liable to be obtained by artifice, false hopes, promises of favor, or menaces; seldom remembered accurately or reported with due precision.'" Confessions were useful only as corroborating evidence, Gerry insisted. First, evidence had to show that an offense or crime actually had occurred. For this reason, two documents allegedly written by Mary Strong—her confession and her letter to Edward Strong—were insufficient proof. They were composed with Peter Strong "in the same house at the same time, and the law presumes he obtained them (if she ever wrote them) by threats and force."

With a certain slipperiness of logic, Gerry then suggested that, *had* adultery occurred, it might well have been committed with Peter's connivance and procurement. Active cooperation was not required under the law. Knowledge and passive acquiescence would have been enough. "Every husband is to be considered as the guardian of his own honor," he advised the jury. If a husband "by a gross and palpable neglect . . . exposed his wife to the temptation under which she has fallen, such a husband may be held to have been immediately instrumental in his own dishonor." The family's apparent awareness of the affair, "the common subject of conversation among servants and friends," made Peter's supposed ignorance of it that much more suspect.

As for the matter of forgiveness, Gerry quoted the statute that divorce could be denied if "forgiveness be proven by . . . the voluntary cohabitation of the parties" and asserted that the term "voluntary cohabitation" did not necessarily mean sexual intercourse. Instead, he suggested that "where parties continue to dwell together in the same house and appear in public as husband and wife . . . that the case comes within the words of the statute, 'voluntary cohabitation.'"

After expounding on confessions, connivance, and forgiveness, Gerry pivoted to the subject of the plaintiff's witnesses. Had they indeed provided credible proof that adultery took place? He disparaged their testimony one by one, beginning with Matilda Mussehl.

"A woman in her own husband's house, surrounded by women . . . is seen coming out of her brother-in-law's room flushed and excited. Is this evidence of physical pollution? If so, there isn't a woman in the City of New York safe."

The old family nurse was equally unreliable. She saw Mary come out of Edward's room one morning.

"Peter was in the house at the time, and if Mary was in Edward's room all night, Peter must have known it."

While he complimented Fanny Strong on her "unusual intelligence," he scathingly discounted her testimony, especially the incident of the dressing gown.

"I would like to know how many men in this court-room have not received dressing-gowns from married women, and if the present of such articles are to be considered evidence of adultery, the sooner the women of New York know it the better."

Fanny's meetings with Mary, according to Gerry, were arranged by Peter and his counsel, with the help of Julia Bedell. They were a product of the plaintiff's malice and his family's manipulations.

He was even harsher in dealing with Julia Bedell's testimony, lingering on her interviews with Mary, labeling the bishop's wife a "clerical detective." He claimed not to care whether Julia in her testimony "stated what is false or misstated what is true," only that her "errors" were reprehensible. She had not only lured a much younger woman, clearly distraught, into inadmissible confidences, she also deliberately destroyed private letters, then shared their alleged contents from her faulty memory. "She had no right," Gerry said.

He followed this assertion with an uncomfortable question posed to the courtroom at large, a query with implications that must have shocked Julia's family and friends. He first noted that Julia, in probing Mary for information, had repeated Mary's statement about experiencing a "thrill of emotion," at Edward's touch. "Would a pure woman, the wife of a Bishop, remember such expressions," Gerry then inquired, a barb aimed at pious Julia's salacious curiosity.

When Gerry concluded his four-hour-long motion, Judge Garvin made short work of it. It evinced excellent research and information, Garvin acknowledged, but added that in his opinion he had "no power to take this from the hands of the jury."

With Gerry's motion denied, McKeon began his opening statement after a thirty-minute recess. He spoke directly to "the fathers, brothers, and sons" in the jury, appealing to them as men who respected and protected the beloved women in their lives, and assured them that they would soon see how Mary, not Peter, was the "shamefully wronged" party. He acknowledged awareness of the case's high drama—exceeding "any romance written"—and highlighted this point in his abbreviated, carefully orchestrated, telling of the tale. "A fine girl, 19 years of age, religiously educated and from one of the most respectable families in the city, was delivered to this man [the plaintiff], and in a few years was returned to her father ruined and by whom—by his own brother."

In many respects what McKeon would say over the next two days duplicated what Gerry had already argued. But where Gerry focused on the insufficiency or failure of evidence, McKeon focused on the injustices done to Mary and on Peter's motives for committing them.

First, McKeon denied that the Stevens family bore responsibility for bringing the suit to court. Judge Hoffman, Fanny's esteemed father and the senior member of Peter's team, "dragged this case into the superior court, where he [Judge Hoffman] thought the shadow of his influence would still remain. . . ." Hoffman had insisted that "the children should be left to the sole charge and custody of Mr. Strong." When Mary proposed reasonable terms, Peter, influenced by Judge Hoffman, "entirely rejected the propositions and notice of suit was served."

Mary's family, McKeon emphasized, had rallied around her. He presented this as a virtue, rather than, as others had claimed, a shocking violation of respectable norms. Aware that Mary's brother, Austin, would be severely criticized for his role in pursuing—some would say, "bribing"—witnesses, McKeon praised him. "He has done nothing for which he can blush. He has done whatever has been done by advice of counsel—and I take my share of it."

Greed was Peter's motive for seeking divorce, McKeon declaimed, simple greed. Dissatisfied with his inheritance, angered by John Austin Stevens's refusal of an additional allowance, Peter conspired to be done with Mary and find a rich woman to marry. "It's the avarice of the man which prompts the whole of the case. They say he can't live on $4,000 a year. Why, he certainly can't live on it as they did at Waverly, with 25 horses and 15 carriages."

McKeon noted that Peter's mother, brothers, and sisters all had known about the affair, but none of them had interfered to stop it. Indeed, they had continued to visit Edward, helped him conduct business, sent him presents. Were these the actions of a family innocent about the immoral activities in their midst?

At four p.m., after listening to McKeon rail against the Strong family's wealth and Peter's greed, words designed to rankle in a working man's heart, Judge Garvin adjourned the court.

⌐ee⌐

"THE REAL OBJECT OF MR. STRONG is to be divorced that he may remarry, although he pretends he wants to get his children."

McKeon relaunched his attack on Wednesday morning, claiming that Peter's demeanor was altogether false. "He has endeavored to impress you with tears, and his eyes roll like those of a player in fine frenzy." Rather than protecting his wife and children, however, Peter had done the precise opposite, thrusting scandal on them in order to "attain his darling object and get married again."

McKeon's story of the Strongs' marriage diverged radically, of course, from Cram's. He told jurors that Peter, as a rich and carefree youth, had spent several years abroad, steeping himself in "all the habits and luxuries and vices" of the Old World. On his return, he failed to go to work but instead wooed a "pure, unstained, religious and accomplished" woman. He did so with one purpose in mind: "He sought her for her father's money."

McKeon continued, alleging that Peter was "mean, and he took her to his mother's . . . What kind of a home was that . . . we find the grossest corruption rankling there." Having put her in a house "where she might be tempted . . . she fell."

McKeon asserted that Peter, through his actions, had "connived at his wife's fall, and this being proved, it is the duty of the court to deny the divorce." While Peter claimed ignorance of his wife's supposed affair, his claim was absurd at best. If "the old blind mother saw it," the husband certainly should have done so.

Like Gerry, McKeon reviewed the witnesses' testimony against Mary and sharply criticized it. Matilda Mussehl and Old Nurse described a few innocuous scenes, subject to interpretation. Any letters of confession attributed to Mary might well have been coerced or cajoled, dictated or forged. As for the other letters, the ones that were destroyed and thus could not be examined, Mary had called Mrs. Bedell's description of them untrue. "I don't charge [Mrs. Bedell] with perjury," McKeon asserted, "but I do say that her treacherous memory is the sacrificial knife with which the throat of my client's reputation is to be cut. Why didn't they keep the letters? They were evidence that was most desirable, and yet we find them gone."

Time was up. Garvin dismissed the jury that afternoon with a reminder that the next day, December 7, court would not convene. President Andrew Johnson had set the first Thursday in December aside as Thanksgiving Day. The reminder was useful, since Thanksgiving at that point was a moveable holiday. Traditionally only observed in some states and not on the same date, it had been ordained a national holiday by Lincoln in 1863 and celebrated the last Thursday in November. Johnson had shifted the date again.

Those gathered in the courtroom could not yet know it, but the current day—Wednesday, December 6—was the one that, though never institutionalized as a holiday, would have a lasting impact on the nation's future. For on that day, the Thirteenth Amendment to the United States Constitution was ratified. Passed by Congress earlier in the year, the amendment required approval by three-fourths of the states. Of the then thirty-six states, Georgia had become the twenty-seventh state to ratify it, completing the process.

The amendment formally abolished slavery, stating:

> Neither slavery nor involuntary servitude, except as a
> punishment for crime whereof the party shall have been
> duly convicted, shall exist within the United States, or
> any place subject to their jurisdiction.

CHAPTER 18

A Resolute Old Man

WEEKS 3, 4
Trial Days 10, 11
Friday, December 8; Monday, December 11
Defendant's Witnesses: John Cotton, John Austin Stevens

CHURCH BELLS TOLLED across the city on Thursday, December 7, calling New Yorkers to Thanksgiving services. Worshippers battled their way through shards of sleet. Everyone gave thanks that the war was over; many, as well, that slavery had been abolished. Aromas of roasting turkeys and fresh-baked pumpkin and apple pies spiced the air of households that could afford the meal. Thousands of families, rich and poor, mourned a father, husband, brother, or son who died in the fighting. Others shared their table with a family member or friend maimed in the carnage.

At a school in Five Points, one of the city's poorest neighborhoods, children gave a concert for charitable donors, the youngsters warbling favorites such as the lively (if incongruous, given the urban locale) "Over the River and through the Woods" and "A Farmer I Shall Be." Afterward the children were asked if anyone had a relative who died in the war. Two-thirds of them raised a hand.

Despite gratitude and prayers for national unity, no one forgot the differences that continued to ravage families, races, regions, political parties, and congressmen within each political party. "Complete unity of sentiment in regard to public measures," one minister pontificated, was going to be elusive. Nevertheless, progress was being made, he insisted, resorting to a grim metaphor. "A serpent with one head and many tails will glide through a thicket much easier than another serpent with many heads and one tail."

On Friday morning, December 8, John McKeon continued his opening statement for the defense. Whereas Cram's opening on behalf of the plaintiff had focused on a heartfelt telling of the Strongs' story from Peter's point of view, McKeon's opening on behalf of Mary focused on bluntly attacking Peter. The lawyer began this portion of his statement with a tally of Peter Strong's misdeeds, largely targeting the plaintiff's relationship with Electa Potter. Although a court had acquitted Peter of manslaughter, McKeon aimed to imprint chilling images in jurors' and journalists' minds: Peter delivering steel instruments and instructions to his wife, intent on forcing her to abort her pregnancy; Peter visiting his lover—the abortionist—who had him "under her thumb." Peter was painted as a brutal villain in this version of the tale.

It also fell to McKeon to bolster Mary's image as a genteel and respectable woman who had somehow allowed herself to be coaxed into sin. He ended with an appeal directly to the jurors, comparing Mary to a little wounded dove who was in their hands. Were they going to further harm her, or help her to heal?

Undoubtedly to the relief of many, McKeon finally called his first defense witness, the Reverend John Cotton Smith, pastor of the fashionable First Church of the Ascension on Fifth Avenue, who briefly and mildly testified that Mary became his parishioner in 1862 and attended church regularly. McKeon wished to use Smith to reinforce Mary's piety. Cram, however, craftily changed direction in his cross-examination. Smith, it turned out, had succeeded Julia's husband, Gregory Thurston Bedell, as head of the First Church.

"I knew Mrs. Bedell intimately," Smith acknowledged.

"What is her character for truth?" Cram inquired.

"I object," interrupted McKeon.

Jurors surely remembered that Julia had accused Mary of being a "seducer," and that John Graham had sharply attacked her testimony.

"[Mrs. Bedell] has been accused of . . . infamous things," Cram snapped, "and I want to show by this witness that she is a woman of the purest character."

The Court ruled out Cram's question, but he had made his point.

The morning was cold; the crowded courtroom, again over-heated. Spectators stirred on the wood benches, either from dis-comfort or expectation. The next witness was Mary's father, John Austin Stevens.

John remained a formidable presence, tall, gray-haired, ele-gant, and austere. Although wealthy, with a fortune of about three hundred thousand dollars, which would be worth more than five million dollars today, he had never lived extravagantly. He was too much an exemplar of old New York to approve of showiness, even as newer New Yorkers such as Cornelius Van-derbilt and August Belmont luxuriated in marble mansions, hav-ing built fortunes worth millions of dollars then and hundreds of millions today.

Before scandal struck, the stability of John's family circle had seemed assured. His wife, Abby, was devoted; his brothers and sisters, close; his children and grandchildren, affectionate. In his civic and business life, he had encountered challenges from reces-sions to wars, and he could look back with pride on his remarkable achievements. As president of New York's Bank of Commerce for many years, he had overseen its expansion into the nation's largest bank. During the war, he was instrumental in transforming a welter of state banks, each issuing its own currency, into a federal system with a single national currency. As head of the Bank of Commerce, he had assumed de facto leadership of the new system.

However, the anguish of hearing Peter Strong's accusations against Mary had upended John's world. Such stories would have been shocking to hear about anyone—but about Mary? She was the most studious of his daughters, religious, a Sunday school teacher. Her love and faith had helped him endure his own hard times—she had visited him almost daily during the nation's devastating 1857 bank failures.

He had decided not to abandon or disown his daughter. Few among society's inner circle of old New Yorkers could accept that decision. Most condemned the steadfastness with which he and his son, Austin, stood by Mary. No one understood how John could have allowed the scandal to reach open court.

In fact, John not only loved his daughter but nursed his own grievances against his son-in-law. Peter, in his opinion, had failed to live up to the customary role of a husband in many ways. He had dodged manly responsibilities; avoided becoming head of his own household; refused Mary a home of her own; never worked to earn an income sufficient to support a woman of her class; and was too busy with hunting and fishing and visiting his clubs to pay husbandly attentions to his wife. Given his feelings about his son-in-law, John surely wondered how Mary alone could be blamed for the debacle at the Strong family homestead. He surely asked himself whether Mamie and Allie, his granddaughters, would be better cared for at Waverly, where the Strong family saw how Edward betrayed his brother and destroyed Mary.

John at first stood to give his testimony, steadily refusing to make eye contact either with Peter or the jurors. Then he suddenly sat down, just as suddenly rose again. This restless motion, up and down every few minutes, was the only sign of agitation that he showed during his testimony. Otherwise, he spoke in a cool and collected manner, his voice quiet, a voice that forced listeners to lean forward in their chairs.

Questioned by McKeon, John testified that he first learned about his daughter's marital troubles at a meeting requested by Peter. On a dreary Sunday morning, February 1, 1862, the two men met at the Twenty-first Street house where baby Edith had died a month earlier. Mary was at church, and John found Peter waiting for him in the back parlor. They sat in chairs by the fire.

John listened to Peter in silence, becoming ever more aghast. He initially thought Peter completely deranged and spoke to him soothingly. "I told him 'Mr. Strong, dismiss such idle fancies from your mind; you have mourned too much for the loss of your Edith.'"

Peter finally stopped trying to convince him, curtly advising: "'Ask Mary. . . . She will soon be home.'"

Alone, John remembered, he waited in the front parlor until he heard the outside door open. Then he rose to greet his daughter in the hallway. Wrapped tightly in her winter cloak, she shivered, not from cold but from anxiety. He drew her into the parlor and placed her next to him on the sofa. He saw that she was "pale, excessively agitated and entirely overwhelmed." He, too, was in shock, he told the jurors, so much so that he was unable to recall for the courtroom, "one word from me to her or from her to me. I don't think one word took place; I got up and left almost immediately."

That morning, John said, was the only time father and daughter ever broached the subject of her affair. His subsequent negotiations with Peter happened without his asking Mary anything more about her actions. He talked about these with his wife, Abby; his other daughters, especially Lucretia; and his son, Austin, but never again with Mary.

John met with Peter twice more that February. The first time, only three or four days after their initial meeting, seemed reassuring. Peter called Mary a noble and fine woman, John stated, and declared that he would not cast her off. Instead, he would continue to live with her and allow her to oversee their children's upbringing and education. "[Peter] said the past should be buried up . . . the substance of what he said was that 'we were to take no steps against each other'; he was bound; and I was bound."

John believed that Peter's motive in proposing this arrangement was in part concealment and in part—though the word was not explicitly used—forgiveness. Relieved, he told his son-in-law that Mary's confession had been "an act of Christian heroism," and that Peter's own behavior under the circumstances was "equally creditable."

The third meeting, two weeks later at the Stevens household, had a far more dire tone, presumably because Peter had learned of Mary's pregnancy. According to John, Peter warned that the proposed arrangement with Mary might collapse "'if the child is born alive . . . You cannot expect me to live with a child about whose parent I have any doubt.'" Ruminating on a dark future, he wished that "'the child may not be born alive, or Mary may die; her health, you know, is very delicate; or I may die, or my brother Edward may die, and that may settle all.'" Peter then abruptly got up and left the room.

John explained to the jury that in subsequent talks with his son-in-law, he severely chastised Peter for his failings as a husband, telling him that "he must have seen the attentions of Edward to his wife; that it was his duty to have checked them . . . that there were duties and attentions which belonged to a husband . . . that he could not have been entirely unaware of what everyone else had seen."

John acknowledged that he especially resented Peter's long-ago decision to reside at Waverly. "I told him that he never ought to have denied Mary a home, that she earnestly entreated him for a separate establishment, however humble, that it had always been refused, that he saw she was very unhappy at his mother's house." Even the couple's Waverly bedroom, John testified, lacked amenities suitable for a lady. There was not enough heat, nor were there enough trunks to hold Mary's wardrobe. "The windows were not such as you could lift up and down. The ceiling at the eaves was low." Not only uncomfortable, the room was also distasteful, with a cabinet of masculine memorabilia, "the gathering of [Peter's] Eastern traveling . . . a good many dresses such as the Armenians wear, also some weapons, some clubs and daggers."

John denied ever promising the couple an allowance of ten thousand dollars, or countenancing Peter's living in idleness. While he admitted to being a man of some fortune, John stressed that he had necessarily been prudent with his finances. He had, after all, raised nine children—eight of them, daughters. He stated proudly and a little indignantly that he had never even owned a carriage.

McKeon, not wanting his star witness—a banker!—to sound miserly, asked John to describe the ways in which he had helped the couple. John explained that he had intermittently sent Mary money to use as she wished, including when she was traveling in Europe, and he had invited Peter, Mary, and the children to live with him after their Islip lease ended. They stayed at the Stevenses' home for a period of seven months. John dryly confided that the wine on the table alone had cost him a fortune.

John testified that the relationship between Mary and Peter

noticeably deteriorated during the months that they stayed with him. "Mr. Strong was not so agreeable to his wife at table; he was less attentive to her; his manner became . . . more harsh . . . he was most insulting to his wife in his manner, and to us all, and to our servants."

John thought that matters improved for a time after the Strongs moved to Whitlock Point in the spring of 1863. But by that fall, the Strongs' relationship had again turned bitter. When they left Whitlock Point in October 1863 they separated for good. Peter returned to Waverly; Mary and the girls, to the Stevenses' home on Twenty-second Street.

It was at this point, John explained, that both sides hired lawyers and began to negotiate terms for a permanent separation or, as Peter threatened, a possible divorce. Numerous letters were exchanged about present and future arrangements, some involving the children.

McKeon handed him a sheaf of about a dozen letters. John examined each one carefully, as though seeing it for the first time, peering through a large round bankers' magnifying glass, holding its wooden handle. The letters, he testified, were in Peter's handwriting. McKeon read one aloud, dated November 11, 1863, in which Peter requested that Mamie visit him at Waverly.

McKeon asked John whether the child afterward was returned, as expected, to her mother's care?

"Mamie has, I think, been under the control of her father since."

John described other letters. In one, Peter stated his intention to send a wagon for Allie. When McKeon asked what happened when the wagon arrived, John answered that Allie and her mother were not home. A letter from Peter at Christmas requested that Allie join Mamie at Waverly on New Year's Day, 1864. Allie remained in Manhattan with Mary. Peter filed for divorce in January, but the letters continued through the winter and spring.

The fifteenth letter, sent on May 26, 1864, contained Peter's response to a proposal from Mary's lawyers for formalizing mutual access to the girls.

McKeon read Peter's letter to Mary aloud:

> *In my last communication I endeavored to express myself*
> *with regard to the unconditional nature of my demand for*
> *Alice . . . I now repeat the determination which I uttered to*
> *your father a year ago to 'make no terms about either of my*
> *children.' God knows my love for Alice, but if I am doomed*
> *never to see her until I make such 'pledges' as you propose, she*
> *and I will meet no more on earth. I consider any proposition*
> *based upon an assumption of equality between us in this*
> *matter as preposterous, if not insulting. . . .*

In his cross-examination, Cram expressed no interest in anything provocative or ill-conceived that Peter might have said or done. The lawyer focused instead entirely on Mary's wrongdoings. He began by asking John to elaborate on her reaction following Peter's revelation of her infidelity. John had initially testified, "I don't think one word took place" when he met her on that bleak February morning. But, under Cram's questioning, he remembered that in fact a brief exchange had taken place. He recalled asking, "Mary, what story is this that Peter Strong has been telling me about you and Edward?"

And he recalled her stark answer: "'It's true father, every word.'"

It must have been agonizing for him to repeat that statement in the courtroom.

The hour approached four. After a few more questions, court adjourned until Monday morning.

THERE WAS STANDING ROOM ONLY in the courtroom on Monday, December 11, at the start of the trial's fourth week. As a nationally known figure of some import, John not only aroused wide curiosity but had already delivered dramatic testimony and was expected to produce more. When Cram resumed his cross-examination, the banker acknowledged giving Mary $4,500 over the course of her marriage. However, he considered this amount, paid to her and not to her husband, an advance against her inheritance. He had paid her nothing since her disappearance.

Cram turned to the topic of money paid to witnesses. Two women, Rachel Walsh and Sarah Bixby Massey, had accused Peter of infidelity with Electa Potter, their accusations supposedly based on confidences that Potter shared with them. One of the women, Mrs. Massey, was currently being kept in style, along with her husband, at a local hotel.

"I will prove you bribed this woman Massey," Cram threatened, his first genuinely harsh remark to the banker. Seeming bewildered, John not only denied paying money to Mrs. Massey, but denied knowing who she was. He did, however, admit that his counsel had housed several witnesses waiting to give testimony at an establishment called Earle's Hotel. His counsel managed all such matters, he noted; he did not follow any of the details. He believed that five thousand dollars altogether may have been paid to his lawyers for their fees and whatever other expenses they deemed necessary.

He acknowledged being served a writ of habeas corpus for Allie in early June 1864. Afterward, Mary and Allie had vanished. "I do not know where they went, or where they have been since, or where they are now," John stated, not bothering to hide his measured defiance. "I never made any effort to find out where [Mary] was. It was not for me to turn myself into a detective. . . . I did not intend to aid you in bringing her back with the child she took."

Cram interrogated him, as he did everyone, on the question of the Strongs' bedroom arrangements and received the same answer: separate beds.

On concluding his testimony, the banker addressed the jury and judge with utmost civility and irony: "I thank your Honor for your kindness and courtesy. Gentleman of the jury, I wish you all happiness and health."

JOHN AUSTIN STEVENS testified for the better part of two days, bridging the trial's third and fourth weeks. Lawyers for both sides treated him politely, respecting his age and position.

In his testimony, John accomplished several significant goals. Under cross-examination, he acknowledged Mary's admission of guilt—"It's true, father, every word"—but interjected mitigating factors, notably Peter's failure to fulfill his duties as a husband. Peter had been so neglectful of his wife that he allowed another man, his brother, to assume a husband's role. How could Peter have been so blind?

Or was he? John also insinuated that Peter and his family may have colluded in the affair by permitting it to go on under their noses.

John's performance was powerful, impressive. Even George Templeton Strong, who never liked him, was moved by "the hard, resolute, strong-willed old man." He was "master of himself, and fought Cram's questioning with dogged pluck." John admirably sought, the diarist believed, to be "rigorously honest."

CHAPTER 19

Delicate Health

WEEK 4

Trial Days 11 (cont.), 12

Monday, December 11 (cont.); Tuesday, December 12

Defendant's Witnesses: Richard Heckscher, The Reverend
*   Anderson, Joseph P. Norris, James D. Trask, Anthony*
*   E. Scheide*

"HER HEALTH WAS VERY FEEBLE; she fainted constantly, was deadly pale and very thin," said Richard Heckscher, the husband of Mary's sister Lucretia. Called to testify immediately after his father-in-law, Richard described his grave concerns about Mary's physical state in the spring of 1863. She had changed dramatically for the worse from the glowing young mother he met in 1857 when he married Lucretia.

At forty-four years old, Richard was balding, strikingly good-looking, tall and slim, with deep-set eyes, a long nose, and a narrow, chiseled face. The son of a German banking family, he had immigrated to the United States twenty years previously and become the successful cofounder of several coal mining companies in Pennsylvania. He was noted for a forceful presence in the business world combined with a warm-hearted and generous nature in private life. His handsome face reflected the worry he felt about Mary.

He spoke clearly and authoritatively with a slight German accent as McKeon began the questioning. In April 1863, Richard testified, he initiated a private meeting with Peter, hoping to head off the mounting threat of divorce. The two men met at the residential St. Denis Hotel in Manhattan, where the Heckschers were then renting rooms. Richard had expected a relatively restrained encounter, but Peter erupted, complaining that "he had tried to live with his wife and found it impossible, that instead of finding her humiliated and subdued, she was just as proud as ever and spoke to him as if he were the guilty party and not she."

According to Richard, Peter also railed against his father-in-law for reneging on a promised dowry in the past and waffling on a financial settlement in the present. "[Peter] told me that Mr. Stevens . . . was not a man of his word; that Mr. Stevens told him that he would rent a house for him wherein to take his wife and that he did not do so; that he would make him 'bite the dust before long.'"

Richard appealed to Peter to abjure divorce for his children's sake. Peter answered that both his brother-in-law, Bishop Bedell, and his mother, Aletta, assured him that "he was justified in considering his own happiness before that of anyone else." Peter failed to understand "why he should suffer" when Mary was living "contented and happy with her family." According to Richard, Peter then repeated several times, "'She ought to die. Why does she not die?'"

Taken aback, Richard recalled saying that he hoped Peter "would not move a hand to bring that about."

As jurors by this point already knew, the Heckschers invited the Strongs to move in with them that spring at Whitlock Point. Richard remembered that Peter and Mary seemed to get along well at first, but separated when they left Whitlock Point in the late fall.

Richard Heckscher's testimony was far briefer than that of his father-in-law but largely supported it, including a description of the Strongs' bedroom at Waverly. "I saw arrows and bows and a dagger and a mummy's foot," Richard stated. However, he introduced a new and compelling element in response to an explosive question from McKeon. The lawyer asked whether Richard ever feared that Peter might murder his wife.

"I knew that he had tried to," Richard answered.

"That's a most outrageous answer!" Cram objected.

"It's a very proper answer," McKeon responded, repeating the question, trying to force Richard to elaborate. This time, however, the witness's reply was more ambiguous.

"I can only say what I knew he had done. I cannot give an answer to the question. I do not know."

Cram's cursory cross-examination focused on having the witness clarify a few biographical facts. Then McKeon, in his redirect, stubbornly returned to the topic of murder, although framing the question differently. "Had you heard of any attempt to destroy Mrs. Strong on the part of Mr. Strong?" he asked.

"I object," Cram said, predictably.

"Yes," Heckscher crisply spoke over Cram's objection. "I heard it from my wife."

McKeon dropped the subject, leaving jurors with the impression that Peter perhaps had at some point attacked Mary with deadly intent. Was the incident with the "fractious horse," perhaps, a calculated attempt to harm her? In fact, as Lucretia's deposition would soon make clear, Richard's insinuation of murder was related to the dangers posed by abortion.

The Reverend Anderson, minister of the Dutch Reformed Church at Newtown, testified next, explaining that Peter sometimes attended services with his family, though not a church member. Edward, on the other hand, had been very active as deacon.

Anderson had often noticed Edward and Mary together, driving away after church. "The family would be gone; I supposed Peter had gone home." No proceedings had been taken against Edward in the wake of the allegations against him. Away at war, he could no longer serve as deacon, but he remained a church member.

Like his brother-in-law Richard Heckscher, the next witness— Joseph Parker Norris—had worried about Mary's health. In 1862, she was "very delicate," Joseph said. In the years after, she was "very miserable."

Forty-one-year-old Joseph had married Mary's younger sister Frances in 1857, the same year that Richard married Lucretia. Like Richard, Joseph worked for a living and was currently employed at a new federal agency called the Internal Revenue Service. Established by President Lincoln, the Service collected income taxes to help fund the war effort, and Joseph, an investigator, evaluated tax returns for accuracy and looked into any discrepancies. He expected the job to end shortly, as the Service was expected to be disbanded after the war.

He testified that he had been quite friendly for many years with Peter, who invited him to his downtown office in May 1863 and told him about the Strongs' troubles. Joseph admitted to being so distraught by the news that he wept. Surprisingly, Peter at that point didn't seem to want to divorce, Joseph said, and in fact defended his wife as the best guardian of Mamie and Allie.

Despite his previously warm feelings for Peter, Joseph willingly recounted instances of Peter's neglectful and abusive behavior toward Mary. Again, the tale of the unruly horse galloped into the courtroom. Although Peter had a perfectly nice carriage, on one occasion he drove his then pregnant wife in a rickety wagon hitched to a temperamental, kicking horse. Joseph drove her home in his own wagon, "she refusing to go with Peter on account of the fractiousness of the horse."

Joseph described other instances of mistreatment. Once, at the Stevens home on Bleecker Street, Mary made some remark for which Peter chastised her sharply and publicly, telling her, "don't make such a _____ fool of yourself." A more serious incident took place at the Twenty-second Street house, after Mary's parents had moved there. The altercation was "in reference to the miscarriage. . . . She charged [Peter] with having caused the death of her child, and he said, 'Did you send for me to listen to this disgusting conversation' and then said, 'you're a disgusting strumpet and whore.' I told him she was a woman and should not be spoken to so."

Under cross-examination, Joseph testified that he had seen Mary the previous January in Portland, Maine, where she was using the name Mrs. Strong and residing with "two respectable old ladies." Friends and family in the courtroom might have wondered why, if Mary had been living openly under her married name with her Aunt Em, Peter had failed to find her.

Court adjourned after a curious day. In the testimony of Richard Heckscher and Joseph Norris, jurors might have noticed certain sad parallels between the plaintiff and defendant. It seemed that husband and wife had both tried to plead their separate cases in person with their in-laws—Peter, with Richard and Joseph; Mary, with Julia and Fanny—before allowing their divorce suit to reach the formidable courts of law and public opinion.

TUESDAY INITIATED A DISCUSSION of medical issues. The question of Mary's health, of such concern to Richard and Joseph, resonated with wider significance. According to theories of the time, a woman's womb both reflected and affected the well-being of her brain, nerves, and other physical organs. The uterus, indeed, was said to dominate a woman's life. When she was sad or worried, her womb, too, was disturbed. She might, for example, experience menstrual irregularity. When her womb was disturbed, her emotions or other bodily functions might suffer.

The problem, as the nineteenth century understood matters, was that even the healthiest womb by its very nature constituted a problem, for women menstruated monthly except when pregnant, breastfeeding, or experiencing certain illnesses. While assuredly a natural process, menstruation was equated with a recurring bout of illness, with its loss of blood, weakness, vulnerability, pallor, even pain. Whereas men could forge ahead with their daily lives, go about their business, handle work, function as rational beings, it seemed that women were hampered not only by pregnancy and childbirth but by menstruation. Their health waxed and waned monthly.

Indeed, male sexuality also was viewed warily to some extent; too many sexual climaxes were presumed dangerous to a man's general good health, weakening his body and mind through the ejaculation of semen, a vital bodily fluid. Men, however, were believed to have control over their unruly masculine sexual impulses—exercise, cold baths, self-discipline, and a healthful diet helped curb them. Every woman, on the other hand, was considered to be at the mercy of her womb and her biological sex.

In an ongoing debate, doctors questioned whether diseases of a woman's reproductive system could produce not only mental depression but also insanity, a potential defense in some criminal cases. Dr. James D. Trask, a doctor who had attended Mary at Edith's birth and for several years afterward, was called upon to discourse on the topic and its relevance to the Strong divorce case.

"There was some disorder of the uterine system," he explained in reference to Mary's health. "Mrs. Strong was the subject of menorrhagia. . . . Menorrhagia means an extensive flow of blood or excessive menstruation." He believed that Mary's nursing Edith for too long a time—against his advice—caused the condition.

According to Trask, menorrhagia would certainly produce depression, although its extent would depend on circumstances and temperament. Edith's death assuredly put Mary at great risk. "A lady suffering from depression of spirits from menorrhagia after watching over a sick child would necessarily become more despondent." Mary's counsel hoped that Trask's theories would both frame Mary sympathetically and excuse certain of her behaviors. Any actions Mary took in the wake of Edith's death—including, perhaps, confessing to an affair and agreeing to an abortion—could be attributable not only to terrible grief but to a uterine disorder.

Even more serious consequences might result from an abortion, Dr. Trask said, especially one "produced by violent means on a woman five months advanced in pregnancy and previously subject to frequent attacks of menorrhagia." Such a procedure would likely leave "a very deleterious impression on the general constitution."

Under cross-examination, Trask acknowledged that Peter "was attentive to his wife during her confinement" with Edith; his manner was "affectionate and kind." Like her older sisters Mamie and Allie, Edith had been born at Waverly, and Trask assured the court that "the room in which Mrs. Strong gave birth to Edith was not an unhealthy one . . . in the cabinet of curiosities there was nothing calculated to injure the health of the people sleeping there."

"Do you think javelins, daggers and mummies are fit things to have in the view of a pregnant woman," Gerry demanded in his redirect, implying that Peter's memorabilia distressed Mary's womb. Several jurors laughed, but Trask considered the question carefully. "I would have considered it a suitable [room] for a lady," he answered.

Dr. Anthony E. Scheide, the Heckscher's family doctor, was called next. He testified that Lucretia Heckscher could not yet leave her house. Her health was still too delicate after her new son's birth a few weeks earlier. Her deposition had been taken and would be read in court.

Dr. Scheide then absent-mindedly walked off with Juror Long's coat instead of his own, to the amusement of everyone in the courtroom when he hurried back to return it.

CHAPTER 20

Sister, Nurse, Undertaker

WEEK 4

Trial Days 12 (cont.), 13

Tuesday, December 12 (cont.); Wednesday, December 13

Defendant's Witnesses: Lyman Bonnell, Lucretia Heckscher,

Madame Barbier, Nathaniel Wilson

SEVEN DEFENSE WITNESSES had already testified in two and a half days. Now, it was Lucretia's turn.

Three years older than Mary, Lucretia had been her sister's best friend in childhood, her companion on walks to school and visits to Aunt Em, her bridesmaid, and her adult confidante. Lucretia had taken Mary's family into her home at Whitlock Point for six months, becoming Mary's fiercest defender.

In October, at eight months pregnant, Lucretia had lumbered in person into the Court of General Sessions for Peter's manslaughter trial, against the wishes of her doctors, husband, and lawyers. "When the honor of my family was concerned," she said, "I chose to take the risks into my own hands." She waited in a back room to testify against Peter. Then—abruptly, shockingly— the judge, John T. Hoffman, had ordered the jury to acquit him. She had been angry and disappointed. Now, only her ill health after her fifth child's recent birth kept her from attending the Strong divorce trial.

In her place, the next witness, Lyman Bonnell, assured the jury that he had tried to subpoena Lucretia to appear in person but had failed to see her. Then Gerry introduced Lucretia's deposition and began to read it aloud. In it, she dutifully recited a few by now familiar dates and details, then arrived at more personal memories, including the events of March 1862 at Twenty-first Street.

"I called on Mary the day she was confined, but I could not see her. . . . [Matilda Mussehl] said Mrs. Strong was very ill, and [my] mother was with her." Concerned about the situation's stress on Abby, Lucretia advised her mother to go home. First, however, she suggested contacting a nurse she knew, Madame Barbier, to help Mary. Abby agreed and dispatched Peter, who had just returned to Manhattan from Waverly, to request the nurse's assistance. Soon afterward, Lucretia left, since there was nothing more that she could do for Mary.

Juror Long disrupted Gerry's reading with one of his frequent complaints: "We have too much draft here. This case will be stopped yet by my sickness." A court officer shut the window.

Gerry read on. Over the course of the next year, Lucretia stated, the Strongs' relationship noticeably soured. At Whitlock Point, in the summer of 1863, she witnessed a bitter argument. Entering the drawing room, she heard Peter lash out at Mary with the words, "'You lie!'" Lucretia instantly intervened. "I said 'I think such language comes with very little grace from you, as I wish you to know now that I, for one, know all.'"

"[Peter] said, 'All? What do you mean?'"

Lucretia recalled making a furious accusation: "'I know that you went for that woman, Mrs. Potter; that you procured instruments from her, and the directions how they were to be used . . . that she told you that in nine cases out of ten the mother's life was endangered as well as the child's, and I believe that what you have done would place you in the Tombs.'"

According to Lucretia, Peter turned pale, rose to his feet, and cried out that he "did it at her prayers." Lucretia testified that Mary bitterly denied his claim, contending that "it was done" because Peter threatened to take her children away, and that it was the price he demanded for burying her disgrace. Peter replied that he was ready to stand trial, since Mary seemed to want "to see the father of [their] children disgraced as well as their mother."

Lucretia had no doubt that Peter asked his wife to abort her pregnancy and supplied the necessary instruments and instructions. His actions ranked in her mind with the worst possible crime. "I considered him guilty of a double murder," she asserted in her deposition, "not only of the child but of the mother in his heart."

Cram took over from Gerry, reading the deposition's cross-examination. Lucretia testified that the argument at Whitlock Point wasn't the first time that she saw the Strongs quarreling. They had also exchanged angry words at her parents' dinner table in the spring of 1863. By then, the couple no longer shared a bedroom, but Lucretia hadn't thought to question what the change signified.

The judge called a thirty-minute recess. When court resumed, Gerry asked to postpone the rest of Lucretia's deposition. He wished to summon his next witness, Mrs. Barbier, who was feeling indisposed and wanted to testify so she could go home. Journalists and other observers were eager to hear her. It was well known that her failure to appear at Peter's manslaughter trial had helped him achieve a swift acquittal.

Mrs. Barbier—sometimes called Madame Barbier, presumably to enhance her image as a Frenchwoman of sophisticated skills—considered herself "a ladies' nurse" rather than a midwife. She cared for women during their confinement and after a newborn's delivery.

One evening about eight p.m. in March 1862, Barbier testi-fied, Abby Stevens sent Peter Strong for her. He explained that "he expected his wife had miscarried." Arriving at the Strong residence around ten p.m., Barbier found Mary upstairs, fully dressed, sitting in a chair in her bedroom, her worried mother in a chair beside her. Mary had been ill all day. The nurse helped put Mary to bed and sent Abby home. Abby gave instructions to call for her if needed.

Peter, who had previously left the house, briefly reappeared later in the evening at Mary's request. "I don't know what he did or said," Barbier stated. "He didn't stay long."

The family physician, Dr. Watson, visited, left, and returned about two a.m. "[Mrs. Strong] was delivered by the doctor, who handed the child to me." Barbier testified. She guessed that "it was five months old. . . . It was not alive when handed to me." She described a harrowing scene, explaining that "the doctor told me to put it away, and I put it in the bathroom, under the closet, until the next day. . . . At this time Mrs. Strong told me to bury it in the yard. The doctor said 'no such thing.' He would see to it, and I gave it to the undertaker about 11 o'clock." Barbier recalled that "it was a boy."

Barbier stayed with Mary for a week, caring for her. Peter returned several days after the delivery, again only briefly. Barbier recalled that "he sat on the sofa and shook his head, did not say anything to his wife, and went away." ·

Cram's cross-examination was succinct. He considered the topic of Mary's abortion essentially irrelevant to the task at hand and damaging to his client. To win Peter's divorce suit, he needed to prove Mary's adultery with Edward, and that relationship was his sole focus. He nevertheless reviewed Barbier's credentials: she had been a ladies' nurse for about eleven years, attended Lucretia three times, and was currently living in the household of John

Austin Stevens's brother Alexander in Astoria, Queens. Cram had no further questions.

Gerry proceeded to call Nathaniel Wilson, a Manhattan undertaker. Wilson testified that in the spring of 1862 he received a note from Dr. Watson asking for his services at the Strong household. On his arrival, he went upstairs, where a woman—presumably Barbier—gave him "something sewed up in a napkin or towel." He didn't know what it was, he remembered, nor did he wish to find out. He put the bundle in a paper box—it was not, he informed jurors, a coffin—and buried it. "It is not a usual occurrence with me to get such bundles," he said, either as a matter of factual information or as an excuse for his apparent callowness. He added that he was never paid.

Calling the nurse and undertaker seemed in some ways to have been an odd choice for the defense, for the decision to emphasize the abortion posed risks. If jurors accepted the abortion as fact, they might pity Mary for what she had suffered, but they might just as easily blame her, along with Peter, for the act.

The reading of Lucretia's deposition continued. After the heated argument at Whitlock Point, Lucretia did not see Peter again for several months. When she finally did, she no longer tried to be "polite and kind and make him welcome" as in the past but treated him with cold formality. Lucretia nevertheless admitted that "Mr. Strong was kind and affectionate to his children. They were very much attached to each other indeed."

She affirmed that Mary didn't want her current whereabouts known. Lucretia had last seen her sister in March 1864, and had corresponded with her since through Mary's counsel.

An altercation broke out between Graham and Cram, who wanted to omit selected sections of the deposition. How was it possible, Graham demanded, that Cram asked questions and then decided not to have the answers read?

"The deposition is considered a unit," Graham argued, "and should not be mutilated."

"It is so very dark here," Judge Garvin said, a hint of woe in his voice. "I will not go on further tonight. Adjourn the court till 11 tomorrow."

THE JOUSTING CONTINUED the next morning. Which passages of Lucretia's deposition to include? Which to omit? Cram wanted to exclude one section; Graham demanded exclusion of another. Cram changed his mind. Graham did not. The lawyers each won some bouts and lost others. Additional portions of the deposition were approved and read aloud.

One part provided further details about the Whitlock Point argument. Lucretia recalled hearing Peter exclaim that "he was going to hell as fast as he could and our family didn't care whether he went or not. . . . He threatened to claim a public divorce, saying he would have his rights. . . . I told him he and his family should suffer if he did anything against my sister," Lucretia rejoined.

Another section pertained to James Strong's wedding in June 1863. Mary was in delicate health at the time, Lucretia testified. But Mary's health was not the reason she stayed home. Peter refused to allow her to accompany him and took Mamie instead. He explained just enough to James "to account for Mary's absence and did not, to use [Peter's] own words, explain who was the other 'guilty party.'" Lucretia did not add that, by then, so many family members knew about Edward and Mary that James probably did as well.

More arguments ensued over the deposition's remaining sections. Garvin promised to review them later and decide what, if anything, to include. In the meanwhile, the defense should call its next witnesses.

Notably, nothing read aloud thus far in Lucretia's deposition had concerned Mary's relationship with Edward. Jurors most likely understood that this material constituted the disputed sections of the deposition and looked forward—if for no other reason than curiosity—to hearing them.

CHAPTER 21

A Mental Aberration

WEEK 4

Days 13 (cont.), 14

Wednesday, December 13 (cont.); Thursday, December 14

Defendant's Witnesses: James Barnes, Tappan Howell, Gunning
S. Bedford, John Sparks, W. W. Jacobus, A. F. Warburton,
Andrew Divine

DR. JOHN WATSON, who had attended Edith and Mary in their illnesses, died in July 1863. However, he had left behind a record of his professional visits, and the defense called upon his executor, James Barnes, to read it. Though factual and dry, it evoked a picture of sustained sickness and grief. It also affirmed that a male child's miscarriage had occurred the first week of March 1862, though it did not say whether nature or artificial means caused the event.

1861 Dec. 23, Mrs. Strong's infant, influenza; do 2 visits
24th, 25th, 26th, 27th, 28th, 29th, 30th, 31st; March 7, 1862,
Mrs. Peter Strong, miscarriage . . . male; March 7 two visits,
8th, 3; 9th, 2; 10th, 2; 11th, 1; 12th, 1; 14th, 1; 17th, 1; 23rd,
1; 24th, 1.

An appearance by Tappan Howell of the City Inspector's office followed. He recalled no certificates in the city records of March 1862 for a birth, death, or burial registered under the name of Peter or Mary Strong.

"Have you examined the books?" Gerry inquired.

"No, Sir."

"Well then, please do," Gerry said. Recordkeeping in New York was erratic until the late 1860s. Still, Gerry's request skewered Howell for incompetence.

In length and detail, the testimony of Dr. Gunning S. Bedford made up for the brevity of the previous two witnesses. The doctor began with a brief autobiography. He had practiced medicine for thirty years in New York, was a Professor of Obstetrics at New York University from 1841 to 1863, and had founded the first obstetrical and gynecological clinic in the United States. "By obstetrics," he noted, "I mean midwifery. I have written works on this subject; they have been translated in French, German, and Spanish."

Gerry's questions expanded on previous testimony by Dr. Trask, focusing initially on "the character of menorrhagia . . . and other matters related to abortion and childbirth." Cram instantly labeled the topics "disgusting," although Trask had testified about them before.

Asked if women tended to experience "mental aberrations" during pregnancy, Bedford answered that generally "women during pregnancy enjoy good health." However, he agreed with Trask that any serious blood loss, such as that associated with menorrhagia, would affect every "fiber of the body . . . none more so than the brain."

Sculpting a long and leading question, Gerry inquired whether a woman five months pregnant—a woman with an excitable and religious temperament and a history of menorrhagia, who had accused herself of incest without any motive and then consented at her husband's insistence to the violent destruction of her child—whether she might at the time have been suffering from "a mental aberration?"

Bedford acknowledged that "there were causes enough" for a mental disturbance, but whether one occurred in the particular situation under discussion, he couldn't say.

Cram surrendered to the temptation of sarcasm. "I should go further than the doctor," he interjected, "and say yes, it was clear proof that she was crazy."

Bedford explained the methods for producing an abortion by steel instruments. Reporters omitted Bedford's lengthy and detailed reply from the next day's news and instead referred readers to medical textbooks. After showing Bedford a book with an image of a five-month-old fetus, Gerry asked if the plate was correct. Assured it was, Gerry offered it to Cram to examine.

"No, sir," Cram waved it away. "I don't like to look at such things."

Then Gerry posed an age-old question, one that people still debate. "When does life actually begin in the child?"

"The father of our science, Hippocrates, contended, and for many years it was held, that the quickening was essentially the breathing of life into the child, which was at about four and a half months. . . . If you ask me my own opinion, I believe life commences simultaneously with fecundation."

Weren't the doctor's statements "sometimes falsified by facts," Cram inquired, again with sarcasm, highlighting the discrepancy between empirical fact and speculative opinion in order to undermine the doctor's credibility. Of course, he and the doctor both understood that facts—for example, the world's flatness—often turned out to be only speculation.

"My dear sir, if you will just specify some particular statement, I shall be glad to answer you."

The two sparred for a few minutes, ending with Cram's retreat. "I am frightened, doctor, with the learning in the case, and I would not attempt to go into these matters," he said. "In fact, doctor, I am afraid to go any further, and I will not ask you another question."

But, of course, Cram couldn't refrain. Questions, after all, were his business. Might not a woman suffering from remorse and repentance have a tendency to miscarry?

"I think remorse might affect her, but a woman who has fully repented . . ."

"Why do you say fully repented? I said nothing about full repentance."

"My dear sir, how can a woman *suffer* from repentance?"

"Do you think repentance is a glad emotion?"

"I do."

"Then there is where you and I differ. Would remorse have a tendency to produce a miscarriage?"

"Yes, sir."

Bedford was dismissed, and Gerry shifted temporarily from the topics of birth and death to child custody. Negotiations between Mary and Peter, Gerry explained, had broken down over arrangements for the children. He wanted jurors to understand that it was Peter—neither Mary nor the Stevens family—who definitively cut off negotiations.

Gerry's claim was valid. Negotiations had broken down over the children; however, the party responsible for that collapse remained open to interpretation. Mary's counsel during negotiations had suggested various possibilities for her role in the children's future. Perhaps Mary could help care for them if they were ill? Or the girls might attend boarding school, where Mary could visit them more regularly than if they lived at Waverly? Or the girls might spend some part of every summer with their mother?

Peter agreed to some flexibility but insisted on ultimate control, including the power to terminate Mary's access to their daughters. From his point of view, this was his patriarchal right, particularly given the nature of his wife's wrongdoing. From Mary's point of view, it was an intolerable punishment.

Gerry introduced and read aloud a letter from Peter's senior lawyer, Murray Hoffman, written in March 1864, that clearly set forth Peter's conditions for a separation. "What is insisted upon and indispensable," Hoffman had asserted, "is that the articles [of an agreement] shall explicitly provide that access to the children be left to the sole discretion and judgment of Mr. Strong." Mr. Strong had expressed "surprise and indignation that one who had so wronged him should seek to bargain on a footing even approaching equality." Any hope for an arrangement, Hoffman wrote, was at an end.

To emphasize Peter's unfitness to assume sole care of Mamie and Allie, Gerry turned to the plaintiff's previous manslaughter trial. The lawyer first summoned John Sparks, clerk of the Court of General Sessions, who confirmed the indictment against Peter and Mrs. Potter. Next, Gerry called W. W. Jacobus, a police officer, who testified about attempting to subpoena Madame Barbier, the nurse, only to be physically barred from her house. Some in the courtroom undoubtedly remembered the tale of the burly policeman chased from Madame Barbier's door. By describing the incident, Gerry aimed to undermine the import of Peter's acquittal. The verdict, he implied, was simply a matter of a witness's recalcitrance, rather than a result of solid, factual proof.

THE NEXT MORNING, Gerry called W. F. Warburton and Andrew Devine, stenographers for the Court of General Sessions, who read aloud selected parts of Peter's manslaughter trial.

The reading fully apprised jurors of the circumstances surrounding that trial's controversial verdict.

Tappan Howell of the City Inspector's Office returned to report that he had examined the relevant records from March 1862. There were no certificates for either the birth or death of a Strong infant, nor any record of a miscarriage. His testimony might have indicated a family's wish to hide a secret or simply the city's faulty recordkeeping.

Through the professional and clerical witnesses he had just questioned, Gerry had succeeded in extracting certain important points for the jury. Mary's state of body and mind from 1860 onward—whether as a result of breastfeeding Edith too long, adulterous relations, remorse, or repentance—were disordered by her diseased womb, leaving her vulnerable to Peter's insistence that she terminate her pregnancy. And Peter's acquittal in the abortion? A sham. His innocence was never proved.

And who was shamelessly responsible for bringing the Strongs' private marital troubles into a public arena? Not the Stevenses. It was instead the Honorable Murray Hoffman, sitting arrogantly in court, who had counseled Peter Strong to deny Mary Strong any guarantee of a relationship with her two surviving daughters.

CHAPTER 22

The Matter of
Mrs. Potter

WEEKS 4, 5

Trial Days 14 (cont.), 15, 16, 17

Thursday, December 14 (cont.); Friday, December 15; Tuesday,
* December 19; Wednesday, December 20*

Defendant's Witnesses: Louis Gazinsky W. B. Rankin, Rachel Walsh,
* J. E. Burke, Mary Smith, Arthur Jones, P. J. Davis, Sergeant*
* Dilkes, Captain Caffrey, G. S. Bedford, Jr., D. B. Hasbrouk*

THE TESTIMONY FOR the rest of the day no longer focused on
the impact of Peter's supposed abominable treatment of Mary—
his failure to provide adequately for her needs, his offer to forgive her if she had an abortion, his own commission of adultery.
Mary's lawyers no longer sought to establish exculpatory reasons
for her infidelity. Instead, they set out to prove Peter's unseemly
association with his tenant Electa Potter, his alleged lover and
collaborator in the crime of abortion. Rachel Walsh, the most
highly anticipated witness of the day, was one of two women (the
other, Mrs. Massey) who claimed that Mrs. Potter told them outright of her affair with Peter Strong.

John McKeon, however, did not immediately produce Rachel
Walsh. Instead, he called Louis Gazinsky, a clerk for the county

government. McKeon wanted Gazinsky, who had lived briefly at 124 Waverly Place and who radiated earnest respectability, to introduce the colorful topic of its other, less reputable boarders and their activities.

New York's boarding houses ranged from pleasant and comfortable lodgings for newly arrived bachelors and middle-class families of clerks and salesmen to dilapidated shanties for the unemployed poor. The Strongs' properties ranked among the better ones. After moving from 104 to 124 Waverly Place in 1862, leasing the whole residence, the Potters soon began to take in other tenants. Gazinsky testified that he moved there shortly after they did, agreeing to serve as surety for the lease and to contribute part of the monthly rent. Jurors might have noticed the coincidence in timing—if a coincidence it was—of Peter's leasing an entire house to the Potters, who could ill afford the full rent, in the spring of Mary's alleged abortion.

Initially, Gazinsky said, he was the Potters' only lodger, but a Mrs. Purdy came that summer and Rachel Walsh and other boarders followed. Mrs. Potter collected rent from the assorted tenants, paying the monthly total to Peter Strong or his agent. Or, as Gazinsky testified, not paying it. Despite his and other boarders' monthly contributions, rent was often in arrears. Moreover, life at Waverly Place was anything but congenial. "There was some quarrel between Mrs. Potter and Mrs. Purdy," Gazinsky said. "I don't know what it was. I had to go to a District Court to pay the rent. A charge of assault and battery was made against Mrs. Purdy by Mrs. Potter."

Furthermore, 124 Waverly Place not only served as a residence, Gazinsky explained, but also as the site of Mrs. Potter's medical practice. She posted a sign out front that said "female physician," listing her office hours. After a mere six months, he left to find other accommodations.

Gazinsky was dismissed, having evoked to McKeon's satisfaction the chaotic character of life at 124 Waverly Place.

Following Gazinsky, W. B. Rankin, a lawyer, testified to representing Mrs. Potter in her successful effort to evict the quarrelsome and aggressive Mrs. Purdy. Prompted by McKeon, Rankin also remembered reading three articles about the disreputable character of 124 Waverly Place, published in December 1863 in the *Police Gazette*. McKeon read one article aloud. Titled "Mysteries of Charity," it dealt with the fraudulent organization Mrs. Potter had founded, allegedly to help war widows. The article left little doubt that the money raised was never used for its stated purpose.

Next, McKeon called Rachel Walsh, the key to establishing Peter's guilt, either by association or, more seriously, for adultery, with the abortionist. Walsh testified that she had been a resident at 124 Waverly Place from 1862 until April 1864, when the Potters also moved out. She went on to describe the house's layout, explaining that its attractively furnished front parlor served as a drawing room and reception area, with the back parlor used as the Potters' bedroom and Mrs. Potter's office. Vernon Potter was away from the house from dawn till dusk, she confirmed. Peter Strong used to visit between noon and three p.m.

"I know Peter R. Strong by sight," Walsh said. "I saw him at Waverly Place more than once. . . . He used to go into the parlor and sometimes into Mrs. Potter's room . . . and used to stay a few moments or an hour. No one else would go in while he was there. The doors were closed." Although erratic, his visits were relatively frequent, often conducted in a most informal and familiar way. "He would come sometimes once, sometimes two or three times in a month. Mrs. Potter was dressed sometimes in a white wrapper, again in bed, again in a chair, sometimes in her usual day dress."

McKeon turned to the subject of Mrs. Potter's notorious profession. "I know Mrs. Potter to be a female physician," Walsh acknowledged.

"Do you know whether she ever sold instruments with which to produce abortions?" McKeon asked.

"I have seen such instruments. They were solid silver, with a curve at the end and a black handle, a long, hollow tube, about six inches long." Also, a closet in the back hall stocked herbal medications used in Potter's practice.

The court called a thirty-minute recess. Afterward, J. E. Burke, a reporter from the *Daily News*, read aloud an article he had written about Peter's manslaughter trial in October. The point, Gerry insisted over Cram's indignant objections, was to show that the jury answered "not guilty" only after the judge firmly directed them to do so.

Cram began his cross-examination of Walsh by asking about her personal history. Before focusing on Peter's relationship with Mrs. Potter, he first wished to discredit Walsh with pointed questions. Asked about her marital history, she testified that she had been separated from her husband for a number of years, moving from boarding house to boarding house before his death two years earlier. She staunchly denied being the mistress of another lodger at one of her temporary homes.

Shown a circular titled *The Metropolitan Society for the Relief of Widows and Families of Deceased Soldiers*, she admitted to helping Mrs. Potter produce and distribute it.

Cram read aloud:

. . . the assistance given in medical attendance, proper
food and nourishment, nursing, etc. to over 493 families
from October 2, 1862, to May 1, 1863, have [*sic*] severely
taxed the energies of the Society both in the outlay of

money and personal attention and labors. It being a purely
charitable undertaking, it is necessary to seek an offer for
aid [from] a kind and generous public to make a sufficient
fund. . . .

Designed for fund-raising, these assertions seemed at best
exaggerations and at worst total lies. Nevertheless, Walsh loyally
defended her partner. "I don't believe [Mrs. Potter] would write
anything untrue," she insisted. Her defense of Potter excused her
own participation in the scam.

Judge Garvin dismissed the jury early in order to hear arguments about which sections of Lucretia's deposition should be
read in court.

McKeon, usually controlled, urgently wanted the jury to hear
everything Lucretia had to say about Mary's relationship with
Edward—a very different story from the one Cram had told about
the affair. Highly agitated, McKeon burst out that Mary and her
lawyers had been "abused by the press for months, slanders and
lies have been told about us for months. . . . I want to read in this
deposition the facts of the case showing that—"

"The counsel must not go on this way," Cram interjected, coolly.

"I will not be interrupted," McKeon responded, heatedly.

"Oh, yes, you will. I protest against this discussion being held
unless in the presence of the jury, and if your Honor allows it,"
Cram said, "I shall take my papers and leave the court."

"The counsel can leave the case as soon as he pleases,"
McKeon agreed.

"I don't propose to leave the case, but the court," Cram corrected.

"I shall show, Sir, that this man, Edward Strong, ought today
to be on trial for rape," McKeon asserted. "I shall show that he
attained his purposes only at the mouth of the pistol, and—"

"I shall leave the court," Cram said. "I will not continue

here a moment longer." He put on his coat and walked out of the courtroom.

~~~

THERE WAS NO MENTION of rape or pistols when court resumed on Friday. Cram's cross-examination of Walsh rolled along with further questions about Peter's visits. She reaffirmed that he was always received in the back parlor—the Potters' bedroom. The doors between front and back parlors were closed during his visits.

Didn't Mrs. Potter customarily transact business in the back parlor, Cram asked, intending to make Peter's visits seem routine.

"Not always," Walsh stubbornly replied. Cram repeated the question six times before Walsh admitted that, yes, Mrs. Potter transacted business in the back parlor.

But Peter Strong actually had no business to transact there, Graham interrupted. Peter went to 124 Waverly Place solely to commit adultery, he argued. According to the building's lease, rent was always to be paid at Peter's office on William Street.

Whatever the reasons for Peter's visits, Walsh added a new twist, testifying that he visited even during an eight-week period in 1863 when Mrs. Potter suffered terribly with rheumatism. On one occasion, Walsh testified, "Mrs. Potter was in bed; this was in the middle of the day. Mrs. Potter said she was sick. . . . Her legs were swollen."

In his redirect, McKeon read aloud, over Cram's objections, Walsh's affidavit for the grand jury in Peter's manslaughter case. It included a graphic description of the abortion Mrs. Potter allegedly performed on Elizabeth Adams, said to have caused her client's death. While pointing a finger at Mrs. Potter, Walsh also managed to implicate herself in the sad and sordid situation, describing how she was summoned into the back parlor "and there on the bed was the corpse of . . . Elizabeth Adams . . . Electa Potter was sitting on the bed very much agitated and excited . . . [she] said to take the child with the instruments and leave them with Sarah Bixby. . . ."

Walsh did as she was told, she testified, taking the fetus and abortion instruments to Sarah Bixby—called Mrs. Massey after her marriage—who was then single and boarding at 104 Waverly Place. Both of Peter's rental properties, it seemed, had been rented to cohorts in illegitimate activities.

Changing the subject, McKeon asked Walsh to describe more precisely what went on between Peter and Mrs. Potter during their encounters in the back parlor. Walsh demurely replied that she saw nothing. The door was always locked.

Except, there *was* one time when she needed to ask Mrs. Potter a question and, after trying the door handle between parlors, she decided to enter through the hall door. Peter and Mrs. Potter stood in the middle of the room, she testified. His arm was around her waist, and he was kissing her cheek. Walsh backed out, offering her excuses for intruding. This was a scene that McKeon wanted jurors to remember from Walsh's testimony.

Dismissing Walsh, McKeon called his next witness, Mary Smith, another former tenant at 124 Waverly Place. *The New York Times* described her as a "voluble Irish woman," and she readily, without seeming embarrassed, told her personal story. Married five years, with her husband in the army for three of them, Mrs. Smith found herself hapless and pregnant in February 1863— she never said by whom—and turned to D. B. Hasbrouck, chief clerk of the police, for assistance. The police, as jurors knew, saw and heard everything that went on in their precincts—which houses were brothels, which ones provided abortions, which ones accepted only ordinary boarders. He directed her to go to see Mrs. Potter, and she did, hoping for help during her pregnancy and confinement.

It was a transactional arrangement. "They were without a girl," she explained. She received bed, board, and care in exchange for a maid's services.

She enthusiastically testified about what went on in the back parlor behind closed doors. "I saw a good deal in the back room," she said. On one occasion, "I pushed open the door because Mrs. Potter was sick, and Mr. Strong was in bed with Mrs. Potter, but what they were doing, I don't know. His clothes, hat and boots were on the chair. I shut the door and left."

Mary Smith stayed at 124 Waverly Place only about eight or nine weeks and was ill for two of them. "Medicine was given me that looked like tea; it made me sick at my stomach, and then I stopped [the medication]." It seems likely that she took a potion to induce an abortion but changed her mind.

Shortly afterward, the same week that Elizabeth Adams died, Smith left Mrs. Potter's establishment. This was in April, and she delivered her child in May. Her little boy, Smith said, was now more than two years old. She didn't mention that his life surely was saved by his mother's dislike of a foul-tasting abortifacient.

AFTER AN ILLNESS ON MONDAY, long-suffering Job Long returned to court on Tuesday, December 19, and proceedings resumed. It was the week before Christmas and the fifth week of the Strong divorce trial. *The New York Times* noted that "the usual cloud of witnesses, a host of detectives, a squad or two of policeman, and *oi polloi* innumerable" crowded the courtroom. Mrs. Potter's various homes remained the main topic, with detectives, lawyers, and policeman all testifying to the dubious character of her residences both on Waverly Place and on Sixth Avenue, where she moved in 1864.

A harness-maker by trade, Arthur Jones was the day's first

witness. Born in England, he had relocated to the United States from Canada four years before, moving from boarding house to boarding house with his wife and two children. In December 1864, his brother, Thomas, a New York City private detective, had offered him five dollars a week to watch the house at 386 Sixth Avenue, where the Potters were renting the second floor. Arthur Jones had accepted his brother's assignment to observe the house for several months and report on what he saw. Cram indignantly objected to the witness, demanding how the court could possibly accept the testimony of "a spy and a pimp," bought and paid for by the defense. The court ruled that testimony from a private detective—apparently, even a temporary and inexperienced one—was admissible.

While waiting to testify, Jones stated, he had been staying at Earle's Hotel. Others at the hotel associated with the suit included Sarah Bixby Massey and her husband. Jones acknowledged being paid sixty-two dollars for his court appearance, but did not know if the others also were paid.

He explained that he had dutifully written down the names or descriptions of persons he saw entering and leaving 386 Sixth Avenue. Then he read parts of his notes aloud. These reported that Peter Strong visited the building at least ten times over the course of two months, staying about an hour, always at midday when Vernon Potter was away at the market.

How did he recognize Peter, McKeon prompted. He was shown a photograph, Jones testified, without explaining who had furnished it. Asked to identify Peter in the courtroom, he pointed at the plaintiff.

The gaggle of witnesses following Jones was drawn from New York City's police force, an organization with a surprisingly turbulent past. It was relatively new, forged from a fierce rivalry between two separate organizations, the Municipal Police and the Metropolitan Police. Less than a decade earlier, the two had fought for control of the city, the battle between them escalating in 1857 into a riot worthy of the street gangs and criminals they were supposed to subdue. The Metropolitans emerged victorious and consolidated other local police departments into the New York City Metropolitan Police.

Several of its members were now summoned to testify to the curious goings-on at 124 Waverly Place. First among them, P. J. Davis, was a patrolman from the Sixteenth Precinct. He had noticed a sign "for sick children and wives of soldiers" affixed to the front of the house but had seen no one enter who matched that description. Instead, he "saw ladies of fashionable style go in. Also, gentlemen who were not soldiers." He added that "the general reputation of the house was not very good; the house was kept by women of bad character and was visited by women of that character."

Under cross-examination, Davis admitted that he "never saw a woman go in or out I knew to be a courtesan, but I saw those I thought to be such. . . . I can go on Broadway and pick them out as I can corn out of oats."

A sergeant of police, last name Dilkes, remembered receiving a report on the house from Davis but claimed to know nothing himself about the house's reputation.

"You may examine him, Mr. Cram," said Gerry, who had taken over the questioning from McKeon.

"I don't want to examine him," Cram replied.

Captain Caffrey of the Fifteenth Precinct, a six-year veteran of the force, reported five separate instances when "his attention" was called to the house, including a complaint of Mrs. Walsh against a man named Prentice for annoying her. Prentice was arrested and held on bail. Nevertheless, Caffrey "knew nothing definite about it. I did not direct my officers to watch the house; all disorderly houses are reported to me and I record them."

Gerry attempted to introduce into evidence a mortgage on Mrs. Potter's personal property to show that she was in debt, and that her debts were subsequently and mysteriously paid off, but the judge excluded the document.

G. S. Bedford, Jr., an assistant district attorney, son of the obstetrician of the same name, testified about efforts to bring Mrs. Potter to trial for homicide in the case of Elizabeth Adams, before Peter Strong's trial for manslaughter. The testimony seemed to accomplish little beyond once again linking Peter's name with Potter's in an unfortunate context.

"IN THE CONFUSION OF YESTERDAY," Gerry stated on Wednesday morning, "I forgot to call Mr. Hasbrouck, a name mentioned by more than one witness on the stand."

D. B. Hasbrouck, deputy clerk for the Police Commissioner, was responsible in 1862 for dispensing funds for the relief of soldiers' wives, a charitable pot of money raised by the Police Department. He had two thousand women listed on his books and paid them at his discretion. He recalled that Mrs. Potter once told him that he had referred Mary Smith to her, and that she thought Smith was collecting more money than she deserved. The sum had been based on Smith's having two children. "Mrs. Potter, when she called on me, stated that she knew nothing of Mrs. Smith having two children, and thought the officers had been imposed upon in this respect." Mrs. Potter doubtless wanted to remain on the best terms possible with the police, while taking revenge on that troublemaker, Mary Smith. However, in discrediting Mary Smith, Hasbrouck's testimony paradoxically seemed to help Peter, making it unclear why the defense had called him.

Nevertheless, in delving into the world of Waverly Place and its assorted inhabitants, McKeon and Gerry had done what they

set out to do: demonstrate that Peter clearly had an ongoing association with Electa Potter. What, exactly, was the nature of their
relationship? It was difficult, after all, to say with certainty. Many
of the witnesses seemed as unsavory as the accused might be, and
thus untrustworthy as truth-tellers, which was a conundrum for
the defense.

CHAPTER 23

Accusations and Rebuttals

WEEK 5

Trial Days 17 (cont.), 18, 19

Wednesday, December 20 (cont.); Thursday, December 21; Friday,
  December 22

Defendant's Witnesses: Lucretia Heckscher, Samuel Kramer,
  Bailey Doane, Hester Walker, John Haggerty, John Wylie,
  Frances Straithoff

Plaintiff's Witnesses: Mary Eliza Hillaker, Jason L. Burdock,
  Sarah Burdock, Vernon Potter, Joseph Daly, William
  H. Aspinwall, Horace Massey, Gouverneur Lancey

DEFENSE COUNSELS' STRATEGY had relied largely on mind-numbing repetition: policemen, detectives, and enigmatic women testifying to the seedy character of Waverly Place. Was it surprising if jurors' minds started to wander?

Five days until Christmas. Visions of sugar plums. Newspaper advertisements overflowed with gift suggestions. Perhaps, for the wife, an ermine muff to warm her hands while skating, or a blanket of fox skins to cosset her when sleighing? For the husband, a handsome new overcoat or a black velvet opera cloak? Anchored at Ninth Street by the A. T. Stewart department store, a magnificent iron palace, shops up and down Broadway stocked music boxes, Parisian perfumes, parasols and umbrellas, bonbons and confections, the latest in fashions, and extravagant items for the home—Aubusson carpets, pianos, rosewood bedroom suites. Displays of board games, wood trains, spinning tops, and dolls of every kind tempted parents and delighted children. Penniless, hungry boys roaming the streets in the wake of the war looked longingly in shop windows and begged for money and food.

Both Peter and Mary may have dreamed of daughters, living, lost, and dead. Eleven-year-old Mamie, while surrounded by loving relatives at Waverly, likely still grieved her multiple losses, remembering her mother, thinking of little Edith, and missing Allie, too, who was with Mary somewhere, but where?

And six-year-old Allie, who had vanished from New York a year and a half ago? Of whom did she dream that holiday season? Was it an exciting adventure for a little girl, or a terrifying nightmare, when she had been suddenly carried off? What did she see now when she looked out her window? Who, in addition to Mary, was there to pamper, play games, read books with her, and give her gifts?

Troubling questions like these haunted the courtroom, but no one introduced them.

In the meantime, the judge had ruled in favor of reading the rest of Lucretia Heckscher's deposition. At first, there was little that jurors hadn't heard before, including Lucretia's angry accusation that Peter "procured instruments [for an abortion] and the directions how they were to be used," and provided them to Mary. Guilty in his heart of a potential double murder, Lucretia testified, he knew that "in nine cases out of ten the mother's life was endangered as well as that of the child."

The repetition ended with an explosive newly read section of the deposition, focused on an intimate conversation between

Lucretia and Mary. According to Lucretia, while the Heckschers were living in Manhattan at the St. Denis Hotel in the spring of 1863, Mary visited and shared a version of her story that she had told no one else. She confided that, after returning from Europe, she and Peter grew apart, and that Edward had gradually grown more attentive to her. Mary didn't deny "that she was gratified by all these kindnesses and the interest [Edward] showed in her," Lucretia recalled, "but she never had a thought of wronging her husband in any way or shape."

However, Mary told her sister, the situation took a drastic turn one morning at Waverly. "After breakfast," Lucretia testified in her deposition, "Mr. Edward Strong said, 'Mary, I want to speak to you in my room; they were in the habit of going to each other's rooms very freely. . . . They all lived together in the family. When she got into the room, he locked the door and pointed a loaded pistol at her and said, 'Mary, if you scream, you are a dead woman.' She replied, 'You would not shoot me, Edward?' Said he, 'As that fly on the wall.'"

Edward's assaults didn't end with that single episode, Mary claimed. Instead, Edward repeatedly threatened her with violence, and she knew that he usually carried a pistol. Sometimes, when he pressured her to accompany him on a walk or drive, she would try to refuse his demand. Then Peter, unaware of the real situation, would take his brother's side, urging her to accept Edward's seemingly benign invitation, lest she appear disagreeable or capricious.

While visiting Newport on one occasion, according to Lucretia, Mary went for a drive with Edward at Peter's insistence. As he talked with her in the carriage, Edward "became very much excited and threatened to throw her from the cliff; that he very nearly did so." Lucretia added that Mary "said she thought herself lost."

Asked if Mary pretended to be "innocent in her relations with Edward Strong," Lucretia responded carefully. "Not totally so," Lucretia began. "She said that Edward Strong had violated her, and that after that he had taken advantage of his position, threatening her with discovery, whenever he possibly could, to gratify his own passions." Lucretia's deposition continued the sordid story: "She told me, also, that she had begged and implored him to leave Waverly. That he could do so and she could not."

Why had Mary Strong never told anyone of her misfortunes, Lucretia had been asked.

"She said she was afraid of bloodshed."

Lucretia's deposition ended the case for the defendant on a note of high drama. Loyal and staunch, Lucretia had stood by her sister, and her account transformed Mary from a wanton seductress into a tragic victim. Nevertheless, some doubters in the courtroom surely added "dupe" to Lucretia's name and "liar" to Mary's as they thought about what they heard.

Rebuttal witnesses on behalf of the plaintiff came next, their testimony intended to counter any persuasive points or impressions made by the defense's witnesses.

Mrs. Potter's niece, twenty-four-year-old Mary Eliza Hillaker, was the first among this group, summoned to counteract any impression that Peter was her aunt's lover. Married in 1860, Hillaker had moved into her aunt's home at 124 Waverly Place when her husband went to fight in the war in 1862. What she recalled most vividly was her aunt's illness during the winter of 1863, the sufferer's rheumatism so terrible that each one of her legs swelled to the size of two and her feet were round as apples. A miscarriage that produced a great flow of blood added to her aunt's misery that March. "She could not move in bed or be touched even without screaming. . . . If she got out of her bed she had to be lifted out into a chair by the side of the bed."

Hillaker remembered seeing Peter Strong visit one day that same winter. Whatever intimacies Mary Smith claimed to see that day absolutely could not have happened, Hillaker testified. Not only was her aunt too ill for embraces, but Mary Smith was too nearsighted to be a reliable witness about what she saw. In addition, Smith was wholly untrustworthy, with a reputation for stealing.

Collecting rent was the only reason Peter Strong had visited, Hillaker assured the courtroom, and it wasn't surprising that he came in person to demand it. Mrs. Potter was so far behind in payments that she loaned her aunt the rent money, pawning a white crepe shawl, a silk dress, and silver spoons in order to raise it.

She left Waverly Place in the spring of 1863 but lived with the Potters again when they moved to Sixth Avenue in 1864. Hillaker swore that Peter Strong to her knowledge never visited there once.

Gerry swiftly attacked Hillaker, aiming to erode her respectability. Was she admitted to Bellevue Hospital in November 1864? Hillaker acknowledged that she had been.

"Were you not taken into the venereal ward of the hospital?"

"I was not."

"Will you swear distinctly that you were never under treatment for venereal disease."

"No, sir. I was not."

Questions about Mrs. Potter's pregnancy and miscarriage ensued.

"Did Mrs. Potter ever tell you she produced a miscarriage on herself?"

"No, sir."

After a series of questions about how frequently Hillaker pawned items in order to pay bills—queries intended to show that

Mrs. Potter and her family, although virtually poverty-stricken, were nevertheless renting a house far beyond their means—court adjourned until the following morning.

～✑～

On Thursday, Gerry continued to barrage Hillaker with questions about her personal finances, queries that Cram deemed irrelevant. Graham defended his colleague's approach, noting that Hillaker seemed to have no history of legitimate employment and thus must have supported herself in immoral ways.

Hillaker responded in detail, noting how she had sewn vests at six shillings a piece, two a day; sewn buttonholes in soldier's coats at seven cents a day; collected two dollars and fifty cents a week from the city and the same from a police relief fund, and received twelve dollars and fifty cents a month from her husband, although on an irregular basis.

Asked to elaborate on Mrs. Potter's miscarriage in the spring of 1863, she replied that she did not know what had caused it.

"What became of the child?"

"It was put in a bottle by Mrs. Potter's directions."

"What was done with it then?"

"This is improper, irrelevant, and indecent," Cram barked.

The judge excluded the testimony.

"From the time you entered Bellevue Hospital until you left there, was there any child born?"

"I expect there was a great many."

"To you?"

"I decline to answer."

Hillaker stepped down and was replaced by an elderly man, Jason L. Burdock, whose kindly demeanor momentarily diffused courtroom tensions. More effective at bolstering the plaintiff's case than Hillaker, Burdock essentially served as a character witness for Mrs. Potter. He had long been a missionary in the Sixth Ward, site of the infamous Five Points, where he was employed by the philanthropic Tract Society, and he testified that he and his wife had lived with the Potters at the same boarding house in the late 1850s.

"Mrs. Potter used to sew then," he said. "She had no sign as a doctress up then; she said she used to attend lectures."

The Potters remained friends with the Burdocks, who visited them frequently over the years, including at 124 Waverly Place and on Sixth Avenue. There was a time when Mrs. Potter was quite ill, Burdock recalled, and he often saw her in her bed.

His wife, Sarah Burdock, recalled hearing that Mrs. Potter had once kept a millinery shop while living in Utica, her home-town. She might have felt the detail was important, millinery seeming a most reputable and ladylike pursuit.

Vernon Potter, Electa's husband, was now the main attraction. Reporters found him unimpressive, one journalist characteriz-ing him as "to all appearance . . . not quite so smart as his wife is reputed to be."

Much of Vernon's testimony duplicated that of other wit-nesses, affirming the chronology of the Potters' living arrange-ments and their problems paying rent at their various residences. He remembered seeing Peter at 124 Waverly Place several times on business matters pertaining to rent or repairs. He also testified, as had Mary Hillaker, that Electa Potter suffered terribly from rheumatism in the winter of 1863. Perhaps oddly, he claimed not to have known that his wife had a miscarriage.

ON FRIDAY, Vernon was cross-examined about his wife's con-finement in the Tombs for her alleged role in Mary's abortion. He didn't have the money to post the bail for her release, Vernon testified, nor did he know who did pay it. The people he approached weren't able to raise sufficient funds.

His wife was innocent of the homicide charge in the case of Elizabeth Adams, he asserted. It was Mrs. Walsh, not his wife, who performed Mrs. Adams's abortion. At the time, Mrs. Potter was so ill that she could hardly move, he claimed.

"Did you know that this evidence of Mrs. Hillaker was intended to defend your wife on an indictment for the death of Mrs. Adams?"

"No, sir."

"Did you not hear it said that the only way in which your wife could be proved innocent was to prove that she was in such a state of sickness during that time that she could not perpetuate an abortion?"

"No, sir."

As Vernon's testimony suggested, Electa Potter had managed to elude a prison sentence on both the manslaughter charge in the case of Mary Strong's abortion and the homicide charge in the case of Elizabeth Adams. Following Peter's acquittal, the parallel charge against Mrs. Potter for manslaughter had evaporated. Both her niece, Mary Hillaker, and her husband, Vernon Potter, had placed the blame for Adams's death on Mrs. Walsh. Electa Potter had cleverly salvaged her freedom, barely, from the criminal abyss.

The next witness, Joseph Daly, who had worked as a clerk for Peter in the early 1860s, testified that he had collected rent from Mrs. Potter about a dozen times, the money usually received in the back parlor, and once when she was ill in bed. On several occasions, she gave him counterfeit money, and she sometimes tried to borrow money from him to make up any shortfall. His testimony cut two ways. It confirmed that Mrs. Potter indeed used the back parlor for business, but also reaffirmed that she was no stranger to attempted fraud.

While the previous five rebuttal witnesses had been part of Peter's shadow life with Mrs. Potter and her associates, the next witness, William H. Aspinwall, told tales of a sunnier time in the Strongs' marriage. A railroad magnate, he recalled the days when the couple's travels in France and Italy reflected their status in society, and their friends came from an elite circle of old New York families. Aspinwall's role was to validate Peter's identity as a respectable upper-class gentleman who would never have descended to the unseemly acts that had been charged.

Following Aspinwall, the next witness, Horace Massey, returned the courtroom from the glamorous past to the dingy present. Massey's wife, also known as Sarah Bixby, had joined Rachel Walsh in claiming that Peter Strong committed adultery with Electa Potter, and that Electa herself had told them so. The Masseys had been boarding at Earle's Hotel in Manhattan, ostensibly waiting their turn as witnesses, at the defense's expense.

Cram had summoned Massey to demonstrate his unreliability as a witness. What amount of money, the lawyer demanded, did Massey have when he moved into the hotel? Eliciting spectators' laughter, Massey replied, "I had a bad fifty cent stamp." Cram didn't find the answer amusing. The sums involved in housing the Masseys, Cram asserted, were far higher than they should have been. "We offer to prove that there has been paid to [the Masseys] between three thousand and four thousand dollars. . . . There is no room for pretense that this sum was necessary for their maintenance, for they have indulged in luxuries, carriages, liquors, theaters." The money, Cram claimed, was a bribe paid to Massey by the defendant's brother, John Austin Stevens, Jr.

For technical reasons, the court excluded Horace Massey's testimony. Nevertheless, the cashier of Earle's Hotel in Manhattan, Gouverneur Lancey, was allowed to testify that Mr. and Mrs.

Massey indeed had lived there for a time. Lancey was the last of Peter's rebuttal witnesses.

The defense now had a chance to rebut the rebuttal of the plaintiff. A hodgepodge of witnesses testified, their testimony aimed at further discrediting Mrs. Potter's niece, Mrs. Hillaker, who had denied her aunt's affair with Peter.

Samuel Kramer, a pawnbroker: Mrs. Hillaker often gave him false addresses.

Bailey Doane, a physician: Mrs. Hillaker was admitted to the maternity ward at Bellevue Hospital in late 1864.

Hester Walker, a landlady: Mrs. Hillaker boarded her two children with her in March 1864 for a number of months, paying five dollars every two weeks. Mrs. Hillaker was seen at the time frequenting various bawdy houses.

John Haggerty, a carpenter: Mrs. Hillaker's room in the Potters' Sixth Avenue apartment had a window painted black and nailed shut, preventing anyone inside from opening it or outside from looking in.

John Wylie, a painter: the window had been painted black more than a year ago. The timing corresponded to Mrs. Hillaker's living there.

Frances Straithoff: the nail had been in the window since she had moved into the building.

And on that anticlimactic note, the last of the witnesses—plaintiff's, defendant's, and both rebuttals—finished testifying. The judge reminded the jurors leaving that Friday afternoon to remain unbiased and sent them home until Tuesday, since Christmas was on Monday. The jurors emerged into the New York twilight, their minds filled with a parade of witnesses, and perhaps encountered on the streets home the lyrics and melodies of the season's carols.

CHAPTER 24

Closing Time

WEEK 6

Trial Day 20, 21, 22

Tuesday, December 26; Wednesday, December 27; Thursday,
December 28

Defendant's Attorney: John Graham

Plaintiff's Attorney: Henry Cram

GERRY, THE JUNIOR MEMBER of Mary's legal team, stood at a small table at the front of the courtroom, meticulously arranging legal tomes and more than 3,000 pages of courtroom testimony on its surface. Then he stepped aside and sat next to McKeon at the lawyers' longer table. John Graham rose, taking up a position behind the small table with its imposing stacks.

In their closing arguments, the two lawyers chosen for the task—Graham for the defense and Cram for the plaintiff—planned to offer differing interpretations of the law, facts, and witness testimony, carefully crafted to present their side's version of the Strong marriage. Each lawyer intended to convince jurors that his client was innocent of adultery, and that the other party to the divorce suit was guilty of it. The judge had allotted three days to this process.

Graham began with a conventional greeting to jurors, thanking them for their courtesy, attention, and patience. Then he moved immediately to legal issues. Adultery was deemed an "offense" in New York State's statutes, he stated, and the defendant was therefore entitled to two principles of law: "First, that she is innocent until proved to be guilty; second, that every reasonable doubt is her property, and that the plaintiff must prove her guilty beyond every reasonable doubt before a jury can find her so."

Graham reminded jurors that the defendant, while accused of adultery with Edward Strong, had claimed that she was raped. She had not made this claim under oath, Graham acknowledged, but it was nevertheless admissible.

On the other hand, he argued, Mary's confessions should not be considered even though admitted. "In reference to confessions, we say [the defendant] cannot be convicted by her own admissions." The ones Mary wrote evidently were "wrung from her by her husband." Oral confessions were equally suspect, Graham warned, dismissing the testimony of Peter's sister Julia Bedell and sister-in-law Fanny Hoffman as misguided and misleading. Graham described the two women as the plaintiff's accomplices. Not only had they lured the defendant into confidences against her own interests, but Julia had also destroyed the supposed crucial evidence of Mary's confessional letters.

Nevertheless, Graham asserted in an about-face, anything incriminating that Mary might have said had to be discounted. She was a sick woman at the time of her so-called confessions to her sisters-in-law, half out of her mind from Edith's death, an abortion, and a debilitating woman's disease. She was to be pitied, not persecuted.

He reminded jurors that circumstances existed under which divorce could be denied. If Mary had committed some transgression—unlikely though that was—all had clearly been forgiven, Graham stated. If jurors believed that "the plaintiff openly admitted her as his wife before the world" while at Islip, then that fact demonstrated the couple's voluntary cohabitation. Moreover, if jurors believed that "she was forgiven conditionally, and she kept her conditions," then she was entitled to "the benefit of forgiveness."

Connivance was another reason for denying a divorce. Peter's negligence and carelessness had serious consequences, allowing Edward's grave and inexcusable actions against Mary. Indeed, Graham argued, "the law imposes upon the husband the duty of protecting his wife and shielding her from the [wiles] of the seducer. And if this duty is not done and she falls, then the husband connives at her guilt."

Turning to the topic of character, Graham extolled Mary's virtues. She was pure when she married and became an ideal wife and mother, "religious from her young days. She eschewed gaiety, and acts of charity and religion occupied her leisure time. . . . She was . . . beautiful . . . virtuous against the world."

Peter, on the other hand, was untrustworthy at best. "When a man has the shrewdness of a lawyer, but without his industry, he is an uncomfortable member of any family." Among Peter's vices, he was avaricious and selfish, qualities that prevented him from adequately performing a husband's duties. "If he had a small income, why didn't he take off his coat and go to work and provide for his family?" Graham demanded, reminding jurors that Mary had longed for a home of her own, however humble, and that Peter had consistently ignored her wish. "There is scarcely an oasis in the great desert of his non-attention."

And what about "the irresistible deacon" Edward Strong? Graham lavished scorn not only on Edward but also on the rest of the Strong family for their repugnant acquiescence in his behavior. "If [Edward] should swear on a pile of Bibles as high as this building, no one would believe him. Where is he? Why, he is within fifty miles of the city and visited by his family. He is enjoying himself boating and sporting, and when you declare Mary Strong guilty, he will be taken home again."

The Strongs, riddled with their own flaws, dared to stigmatize the Stevenses by calling Mary's father "a purse-proud, aristocratic man?" Such claims, Graham advised the jury, were shocking and unjust. Did John Austin Stevens "look like a king? Was it a sin that he stood by his daughter?"

The plaintiff's counsel, Graham asserted, had wrongfully accused Mary's father and brother of dragging Mary into court and parading the scandal instead of settling it. But, in fact, it was Peter's own senior counsel, Murray Hoffman, the former Superior Court justice and a Strong family member, who drove the matter into public view by refusing reasonable custody terms. In the course of negotiations, Graham explained, Judge Hoffman had written that Peter alone should be the arbiter of Mary's relationship with her children. "What mother," Graham demanded, "would not *get her back up at that*?"

Moving on from the issues of personal character and familial relationships, Graham asked jurors to contemplate the concrete evidence presented to them. They could not render a verdict against the defendant without enough evidence against her. But neither the plaintiff's witnesses nor his lawyers had offered substantive proof of the defendant's adultery. Matilda Mussehl, the children's governess, described suspicious scenes—for example, seeing Mary flee Edward's bedroom one evening—only to rescind her testimony under cross-examination. Graham ended the afternoon by accusing Mussehl of perjury.

❧

"I NOW COME TO a very important point," Graham announced on Wednesday morning. "It is the question as to whether there was an abortion" and who arranged it. It could not have been Mary, he insisted. She had no motive, as she knew Peter to be the unborn child's father, and she feared the danger of infection or even of her own death from an abortion. In addition, according to Lucretia Heckscher, Peter had confessed to obtaining instruments and instructions from Mrs. Potter for the deed.

"And now, in regard to Peter and Mrs. Potter," Graham said, introducing Peter's alleged adultery at last. Jurors had heard three witnesses—Rachel Walsh, Mrs. Potter's business partner; Mary Smith, one of Mrs. Potter's boarders; and Arthur Jones, a detective—provide detailed descriptions of the intimacy between Peter and Mrs. Potter, including scenes of the two in bed and also of them kissing. Other suspicious clues existed as well, Graham said. Why had Peter indulged his tenant in her nonpayment of rent? Why had he allowed her to lease an entire house, 124 Waverly Place, when she and Vernon clearly could not afford it? Why had he continued to visit her on Sixth Avenue, when she was no longer his tenant, if not to engage in adultery? "The darkest day Strong ever knew was when he made the acquaintance of Mrs. Potter. She has her hand on him, and he dare not desert her," he went on.

Having accused Peter of abortion and adultery, Graham returned to the topic of personal character. "This is the man, you are called to hug to your breasts, to give the benefit of a divorce, and send his wife out upon the rough highway of an unfriendly and unsympathizing world." He concluded with the now familiar plea, used by lawyers for both sides to suit their own purposes. The children! What would be best for the children? "Do not stand at the side of this father but remember these little ones, help them, do them justice, give them the protecting love of their mother."

In his closing argument, Graham had covered a wide swath

of subject matter, with some elements more relevant than others. He had praised Mary and her family, disparaged Peter and his, summarized witness testimony about Peter's suspicious interactions with Mrs. Potter, and demeaned Peter as a husband and father. When Graham concluded his eight-hour summation, a presentation that had consumed a full day and a half, his admirers surrounded him, clapping him on the back, complimenting him, and shaking his hand. Robinson, one of Peter's lawyers, elbowed his way around the group and cleared Graham's books and papers from the table, readying it for the next round of argument.

It was already late in the day. The judge inquired whether Cram wished to begin the closing argument for the plaintiff or wait until morning. Cram preferred to start. At that point, having received many compliments, Graham left the courtroom, although he would return the next day to hear the second part of Cram's argument.

Cram began in a matter-of-fact manner, point by point countering Graham's arguments. He started with the admissibility of confessions: "Confessions of adultery by the party accused are the highest species of evidence when real and bona fide and free from all suspicion of either duress or collusion." By implication, Mary's confessions, unless convincingly proved otherwise, were solid evidence of her guilt.

If jurors, as Cram expected, found Mary guilty of adultery, they were obligated to vote in Peter's favor. They had no reason not to do so. The defendant's infidelity had been committed without "the consent, connivance, privity or procurement of the plaintiff." Neither had Peter forgiven Mary for her adultery, demonstrated by clear evidence that "the plaintiff and defendant commenced and continued to occupy separate rooms and separate beds."

There had been no abortion, no matter who stood accused of

the deed. "It was not an abortion at all. It was a miscarriage, and no human being has proved it was anything else."

However, even if there had been an abortion, it would have no bearing on the issue of forgiveness. "If the alleged agreement for future forgiveness is conditioned upon the commission of a crime by the party guilty of adultery . . . the fact that such crime is afterward committed does not make such . . . agreement amount to the forgiveness which is a bar to the suit for divorce."

As for Peter's supposed adultery with Electa Potter, it was a fiction entirely without proof. "The plaintiff is entitled to the benefit of the same rules of law which are claimed by the defendant. . . . The circumstances to prove guilt must be such as would lead the guarded judgment of a reasonable and just man to the conclusion, free from any reasonable doubt. Circumstances merely suspicious are entirely insufficient."

He elaborated. "The adultery will not be taken as proved merely because a pretended eyewitness testifies to it, for the jury must be satisfied that the story of such witness is probable, that the witness himself is honest, not mistaken, and his testimony true."

Having dismissed any possible reason for denying Peter a divorce, Cram went on to label the opposition's argument an entirely inadequate and incoherent assemblage of untruths and inconsistencies, "a bundle of speculations, disjointed and incohesive." While Mary's lawyers had "heaped charges on the plaintiff of avarice and neglect and cruelty," their insults had added up to nothing but a lot of contradictions. "They charge him to be a man accustomed to all the vices of the Old World, and yet they make it a crime that he prefers the pure and simple pleasures of a country life to the life of a city. . . . They say he wants to get a divorce and marry again, and, in the same breath, that he wants to pursue an unlicensed course of adultery. Think of the inconsistency!"

Given that the opposition had no substantive case to present, Cram asked jurors to consider why Mary and Peter had been unable to settle their differences out of court. There was only one reason: the guardianship of the children. The Stevenses "insisted that [the children] be sent to school, and the mother have certain rights, and when they were away from school the mother should have absolute rights of keeping the children one-half of the time."

Such an arrangement, Cram argued, would have violated the natural order of things. Decisions about the children and their care, and about the mother's privileges, should have resided entirely with the father, not only by right and custom but also as a matter of common sense. Who had been the innocent party, the injured spouse? Who had been the party at fault? The mother's "conduct, not her affection for them, should determine whether she is the proper person to have custody of the children." Clearly, Peter's custody would serve the children's best interests. "There is no affection so pure, so gentle, so delicate, so refined, so intense, so self-sacrificing as the love of a father for his daughters," Cram said, discounting a mother's love.

Instead, the Stevenses resisted this arrangement, the mother fled with the child, and the result was scandal and horror. What gave the Stevenses the right to "openly defy the law"? They had, Cram asserted, "a cosmogony of their own. They truly believe that when God made the world, He first made the Stevens family, then angels, then men."

Judge Garvin adjourned the court shortly after Cram had so vividly evoked the self-regard of the Stevens family, ranking themselves higher than the angels.

THE NEXT MORNING, THURSDAY, Cram allowed an uncharacteristic degree of visceral anger to show. It was aimed at Mary's father and brother, as well as at her lawyers, for their tactics.

In fact, Cram asserted, the tactics of the other side had not only been unprincipled but had done Mary far more harm than good. Mary's "pretended friends" and counsel had "made her name a byword, paraded her diseases before the public, instead of assenting to some reasonable settlement. . . . We condemn them for this, as well as for the infamous allegations against the plaintiff . . . and bribery which they have employed in the case."

He became shockingly direct in his accusations. "We blame John Austin Stevens, Jr. Not for defending [his sister] but for the mode of his defense." Cram did not cite Austin's alleged misdeeds, but listeners both in and out of the courtroom knew the rumors. Who had helped Mary disappear? Who had planted the false newspaper report of Allie's death? Who had manipulated the legal system into arresting Peter and Mrs. Potter on criminal charges? Who had arranged inappropriate payments to trial witnesses? Were Austin to step out into the community at that moment, Cram vowed, "every man will turn from him with loathing and abhorrence for what he has done."

Courtroom spectators were stunned by this ad hominem attack, so unlike Cram. This moment would have repercussions for both Austin and Cram beyond the trial's outcome.

Cram finally returned to the calmer, more analytical approach he usually employed. In contrast to the opposition, Cram now presented himself as someone who had tried to tell one coherent story and—he hoped—succeeded in communicating it. He wished only to prove which one of the two parties to the Strong divorce suit was responsible for committing adultery, an irredeemable offense in his view.

And who was the guilty party? Cram assured jurors that it was Mary, and Mary alone. "Her refusal to appear in answer to the habeas corpus, her abduction of this child, and her flight, are utterly inconsistent with innocence."

Moreover, he asserted, Mary's tale of Edward's brutal ravishment only reinforced her guilt. In accord with then-current views on sexual assault, Cram insisted that a woman in the midst of a sexual assault would have raised a "hue and cry" and resisted; she would have had physical wounds to show from the violence inflicted on her. Instead, he pointed out, Mary and the perpetrator of the so-called crime continued their relationship. They could often be seen strolling and riding together and attended church together. "The fact that she told that palpably false story is to me one of the strongest evidences of her guilt."

Cram acknowledged that some people might ask: what about the other participant in the affair, Edward, who was said still to be embraced by the Strong family? Admittedly, Edward was a "scamp," Cram said, but every family had one. "The worse he is, the more the mother and sisters love him."

Like Graham, Cram reviewed witnesses' testimony in detail, presenting a reverse image of the opposition's argument. Rather than questioning the motives of Matilda Mussehl, Julia Bedell, and Fanny Hoffman Strong, he stressed their righteousness, propriety, and integrity. Who could disbelieve such paragons of womanhood?

Then he asked jurors to consider the characters presented by the defense: Rachel Walsh, who helped perform abortions; Mary Smith, a suspected prostitute and proven liar; Arthur Jones, a so-called detective, paid to present whatever testimony his client wished. Cram hoped that the contrast resonated.

Wrapping up his argument, Cram asked the jury to arrive at what he called a morally just verdict. The Strong marriage had no hope of survival, for "you never could reunite these parties together again." The fate of the children, however, could be salvaged. "I present their little hands, raised in supplication to you, to unite them and bring them together again, and restore them to their father. . . . Their mother has brought horror and desolation upon them; they ask you, though they cannot escape the past, to rescue them for the future, and shall they plead in vain?"

It was late afternoon, Thursday, December 28, when Cram concluded. Usually chilly and steamy by turns, the courtroom had been consistently freezing all day, and most of those there sat bundled in their overcoats. One juror had unceremoniously draped his capacious pocket handkerchief over his head to ward off the draft on his ears.

Together, the arguments for the defendant and plaintiff had consumed three days. The lawyers told different stories but used similar tactics. They commended their own witnesses for their fine performances and attempted to discredit the other side's witnesses and evidence. They attacked the moral character of selected parties on the opposing side. They made sentimental pleas on behalf of the children, each lawyer claiming to represent the girls' best interests. They reminded jurors that the Strongs' marriage was already dead. They thanked jurors for their kindness and patience but warned that the future would remember them harshly should they fail to reach a just verdict.

Judge Garvin was brief in his remarks, announcing that he would deliver his charge to the jury the next day, Friday, at eleven a.m.

CHAPTER 25

A Long and Painful Investigation

WEEK 5
Trial Days 23, 24, 25
Friday, December 29; Saturday, December 30; Sunday,
  December 31
Twelve Jurors

CHARLES BERRY WAS LATE the next morning. Eleven o'clock
came and went. The butter-and-cheese dealer had been worried
about the toll his absence was taking on his business. Was he
delayed by work? Or, like Job Long, seized by illness?

John and Austin Stevens, their faces wan with exhaustion, sat
quietly with in-laws Richard Heckscher and Joseph Norris.

Peter, seeming surprisingly at ease, chatted softly with brothers Benjamin and James.

At 11:20, Charles Berry appeared, no excuses given—at least
not publicly. Jurors were now all present and accounted for:

Edward Draper, the jury's good-natured foreman, owner
  of a dry goods store;

Charles Berry, this morning's latecomer;

Nathaniel Betts, shoe salesman;

Francis Burke, merchant, always woeful in demeanor;

Wilkes Gay, clerk;

Job Long, the ever-ailing butcher and distiller;

Robert Mackie, another merchant, at ease with himself,
content to quarrel or tell jokes;

James Rufus Smith, a third merchant, intelligent, bone-
thin, and sharp-eyed;

I. N. Sickels, pattern maker;

John J. Sigler, maker and installer of moldings;

John Willets, a fourth merchant, scrappy
and argumentative;

John Worstell, agent, a middleman between wholesalers
and retailers, confident he knows all about everything,
and boastful of his prior jury experience.

Twelve men waited for the judge's charge. While the jurors
would make their own decisions, they would depend on the
judge's guidance for interpreting certain factual and legal matters.
Garvin, tall to begin with, seemed to loom even higher with the
responsibility. He was, as always (except when the lawyers' fighting provoked him), composed.

In contrast to the lawyers' closings, Judge Garvin intended his
instructions to the jury to be brief, taking not more than an hour.
But he began with a statement as sweeping and extravagant as any
of the lawyers dared to make. "This has been a long and painful
investigation," he said, "such a one as perhaps has never been seen
in this or any other court."

Garvin acknowledged that jurors had seen a great many witnesses and heard a great deal of evidence. While he might have limited some of the testimony, he had decided that jurors needed to hear it in full, as it bore on Mary Strong's health and state of mind, as well as on the nature of events at 104 and 124 Waverly Place. He explained that he did not plan to dwell at length on the statements of witnesses, but that he would refer to the testimony as necessary in relationship to the application of the law.

Despite the amount of time the case had taken, the issues, according to Garvin, were "few and very simple." He summarized them efficiently. "The charge against the defendant is adultery," he stated. "The defendant denies that charge. Is a positive denial made out, and if not, has there been forgiveness on the part of the plaintiff? The next issue is, has the plaintiff himself been guilty of the same offence with the individual about whom you have heard so much?" He instructed the jury that "on all questions of fact, you are the sole and only judges," but that "with questions of law you have nothing to do. You take those from the court."

He asked jurors to consider the trial's impact. Who would be most affected by the outcome? He wanted jurors to understand that, in addition to the spouses, two other concerned parties had a deep investment in the jury's verdict. One was the People, whose interest had been demonstrated by the courtroom crowds. He did not elaborate further on what everyone knew: the well-being of the state and the nation relied on the stability of the institution of marriage.

The children, Mamie and Allie, were also a critically important party in the suit, Judge Garvin said. As permitted by evidence and the law, their interests had to be served. His emphasis was surprising and, to some degree, bold. While the Strongs had made custody a centerpiece of their battles, and the lawyers had issued sentimental appeals on the children's behalf, Mamie and Allie had remained shadowy figures in their parents' drama, secondary characters in the stories told. In raising the children's best interests as a factor to be considered along with their father's traditional patriarchal rights or their mother's purported wrongdoings, Judge Garvin highlighted the significance of an evolving legal precept.

He introduced another surprising directive. He instructed jurors to deal justly with the plaintiff and defendant without regard to their sex. "You are to extend no favor to her because she is a woman. You are to give him no right because he is a man." In asking jurors, in effect, to dismiss their preconceptions about men and women, he surely took some of them aback. Garvin was asking jurors to base their decisions on the evidence, not on the rights or roles of men and women.

What, then, were jurors to look for in the body of evidence they had seen and heard? Garvin explained that not all evidence was equal. On confessions, he weighed in on the side of Mary's lawyer John Graham. Confessions, Garvin explained, were corroborative evidence only. Witness testimony, on the other hand, was key. Garvin instructed jurors to take into account a witness's "conscientiousness, knowledge of facts, ability to remember, whether what [was] stated was true." He stressed also that a jury was obliged to consider the contradictions between what emerged in direct examination versus cross-examination.

As he drew to a conclusion, Garvin highlighted the importance of the task at hand. "I feel I have tried to do my duty," Garvin said. "It remains for you now to do yours. . . . You must agree on a verdict and give us the result of your deliberations."

In his diary, George Templeton Strong complimented the judge on his even-handed charge to the jury. Somewhat reluctantly he admitted to having formed a high opinion of him.

The jurors retired to the jury room shortly after noon. Courtroom observers whispered among themselves, taking bets on the verdict. Most thought that it would favor Peter, and that jurors would deliberate no more than an hour.

They were wrong. Two hours passed. Spectators wandered out into the daylight, shielding their eyes from the bright sunshine after the dim courtroom. Some sat on benches in City Hall Park, savoring the unseasonably warm weather. Several undoubtedly dashed across the street to the oyster bars on Broadway, slurping down the slippery morsels to appease their hunger and pass the time. Others, standing on the grimy Tax Building's steps to catch a breath of fresh air, exchanged gossip or chatted about matters unrelated to the trial. As members of the courtroom crowd came and went, the same questions were repeated. What's happening? What have you heard? Will it be long now?

At 3:30, the jury asked for further instruction. The jurors reentered the courtroom, seeking guidance on the issues of forgiveness and cohabitation. The judge had given previous direction—cohabitation had to be voluntary, with a married couple choosing to live together as a husband and wife, not as a brother and sister. Now Garvin elaborated: cohabitation required express proof of sexual intercourse in order to deny divorce on the basis of forgiveness. He did not mention the topic of separate beds, described by witness after witness, but the image had seared itself in jurors' brains. They seemed satisfied by his answers and returned to their deliberations.

George Templeton Strong left the courtroom—still packed with people—at five p.m., dined uptown, and took the omnibus back downtown at nine p.m. to see whether there'd been a verdict. He passed by Union Square at Fourteenth Street, the northern outskirts of the city when he and Peter were young, currently surrounded by elegant homes. The previous April, its greenery had been draped solemnly in black for Lincoln's funeral. The city now extended well beyond Union Square, even beyond Fifty-ninth Street, site of the newly created, still unfinished paradise of Central Park.

A line of streetlights, like tall sentinels, brightened Broadway's long expanse. George passed by Bleecker Street, packed with boarding houses, where the Stevens family once lived in the handsome townhouse where he had met his wife, both of them guests at a long-ago Christmas Party. George passed by shops, restaurants, hotels, churches, taverns, the neighborhoods getting shabbier as he traveled south. Broadway was lively and crowded in many places, but largely hushed in the business district, where shops were closed. *The New York Times* building and other newspaper and printing businesses still bustled with activity. The cupola of City Hall towered over the silent park below, its paths and benches empty in the night. George disembarked, walked to the courthouse, and found its doors locked but the lights shining in the jury room windows, the jurors still deliberating.

The jurors remained there all night. "They argued and slept, and discussed, and rested," one reporter wrote; another newsman added that they were snug alongside a good fire. Genial Edward Draper, the foreman, helped keep tempers in check. Robert Mackie catnapped on the floor, snoring as if he were at home in bed.

That morning, Saturday, December 30, a brutal snowstorm buried the city as "hard & cold & spiteful & bitter & malevolent as either of the two J. A. Stevenses," George wrote.

The jurors peered out at the howling gusts, their minds on the travails of getting home in the storm and the festivities of the coming New Year celebrations. Restless and weary, frustrated and angry, they asked to see the judge, who had been waiting in the office of A. Oakey Hall, the district attorney, who—so the Strong family insisted—was in the pocket of the Stevenses.

The jurors informed Judge Garvin that they wanted to be

discharged. There was no chance of their reaching agreement. Garvin refused to let them go.

The jurors remained sequestered in the jury room all day. By five p.m., after almost thirty hours of debate and courthouse rations, they were ravenously hungry and thirsty. The storm had abated. Did they have to remain in the courthouse? Might they go to a nearby restaurant? Judge Garvin gave his permission. Only Job Long and John Willets stayed behind, neither one feeling up to going out.

Draper ordered liberally and made sure that his hungry crew did the same. Eight of the men sat together at a long table, in the company of two court officers; they were a cheerful group in the crowded and noisy restaurant. Smith and Burke sat at a separate table, Smith looking sour, Burke despondent as ever.

When they returned to the jury room, the men occupied themselves as best they could. They whittled, napped in ragged blankets supplied by the court, joked and argued, and, of course, deliberated at intervals. Cigar smoke curled toward the ceiling. John Worstell, confident in his own opinions and sure he could convince others to agree, firmly believed that his compatriots could, in the end, arrive at unanimity. Only two men dissented to the majority opinion. The other ten men hoped to persuade them to change their minds.

At nine p.m., eleven p.m., and again at midnight, the jurors sent for Judge Garvin, asking for instructions on various points. Garvin wearily advised them that "so long as any of the jury think there is a possibility of an agreement, I shall deem it best to keep you. I will now go home for the night, and will respond to any summons you may send."

Sunday, December 31, the morning of New Year's Eve, brought gloomy weather, snow melting into slush beneath gray skies. Cram and Gerry entered the jury room at almost the same time. The courtroom was otherwise empty except for a few court officers. Shortly after nine a.m., the jury again sent for Judge Garvin. As soon as he arrived and was ready, the jurors emerged, bleary-eyed from their long night.

Had jurors come to a verdict or were they likely to do so, Garvin asked, as he had twice previously.

"No," Draper answered.

After almost forty-five hours of deliberations, the jury was deadlocked. There would be no divorce.

Jurors were unanimous in finding Mary guilty of adultery, but only ten men agreed that Peter, who had been countersued by Mary on the same charge, was innocent. Two men, John J. Sigler and James Rufus Smith, pronounced him as guilty as his wife. They insisted that Mary Smith and Rachel Walsh had been truthful and reliable witnesses in testifying to Peter's adulterous relationship with Mrs. Potter. Since jurors could not agree that one spouse alone had been at fault for the marriage's failure, divorce could not be granted under New York State law.

The absence of a verdict favoring either the plaintiff or defendant was a sad and serious matter, and Judge Garvin expressed his profound disappointment. Nevertheless, he affirmed that he would not detain the jury any longer. He wished jurors the compliments of the season and discharged them.

John Worstell, however, wasn't ready to be discharged without a fight. He loudly called out that he wanted to make a statement. By this time, the press had arrived, and journalists were eagerly scribbling away. Gerry objected to Worstell's request, and Cram predictably objected to Gerry.

"Will not your Honor permit the juror to make his statement," Cram asked.

"The jury is discharged," Garvin replied, "and can make what statement they like."

"Sometime before the close of this trial I saw Mr. Sigler going away from the court in company with the [defendant's] detective Arthur Jones," Worstell said. "Immediately after that I had a conversation with Mr. Sigler, and he said he had made up his mind on the subject of Mr. Strong's guilt and nothing would ever induce him to change it."

The implication, of course, was that Detective Jones, a witness for the defense, had engaged in jury tampering. Worstell proceeded to launch into an attack on the arguments presented throughout the night, but the judge interrupted him.

For Garvin, the trial was over.

Cram was not to be silenced. He denounced the defense for sending its own witness, a paid detective, after a juror with the obvious intention of corrupting him. Referring to previous accusations against Austin Stevens for bribing Mary Smith and Rachel Walsh, Cram added that anyone who would pay a detective to corrupt witnesses wouldn't hesitate to use them to corrupt jurors. "The money of the other side and its influence has been too powerful," Cram stated grimly.

"That's so," shouted some of the jurors. They gathered around Cram, shaking his hand.

Four of the jurors—Long, Worstell, Willets, and Mackie— handed Cram a signed statement that they intended to share with the press:

... we had all agreed that the defendant had been guilty of adultery, and that the plaintiff had not forgiven her.

On the remaining question, the charge of adultery against Mr. Strong, ten of us were for a verdict in his favor, and the remaining two jurors, James Rufus Smith and John J. Sigler, refused their assent to this, and it was upon the disagreement on this point that the jury were discharged this morning.

As the group exited, Cram turned to the men around him. "Gentlemen, ten of you are noble men—I thank you deeply. . . . I shall never forget you." Then he added, "And I shall never forget the other two, either."

Four years after Edith's death and Mary's confession, on the eve of the new year, 1866, Mary Strong in absentia remained Peter Strong's lawfully wedded wife.

PART 5

Endings, Beginnings

CHAPTER 26

Post-Trial Battles

THE TRIAL ENDED but its effects did not, both short-term and lifelong. Austin, outraged at Cram's accusations in the trial's last days, sent him a letter threatening reprisal.

What exactly did Austin intend, George Templeton Strong wondered. To hire bullies with cudgels to follow and attack the distinguished lawyer? Some milder legal remedy?

John Austin Stevens gave his son no encouragement on the matter of bludgeoning the opposing counsel, too preoccupied with plans to retire from the Bank of Commerce. He was ill and exhausted. The Bank's board of governors, an elite group of old New Yorkers, expressed regret at John's retirement, offered sympathy for his ordeals, and reminded him that the bank's impressive record was also his own, and "as such will form an important chapter in the financial history of the Country." His reputation was secure.

Unsettled by the continuing rancor against him, Cram had Austin arrested for making threats and a belligerent in-person visit. Released after pledging to pursue revenge no further, Austin traveled to Paris in March on business and stayed abroad several months.

From the Stevens family's perspective, what was the point in continuing any post-trial battles? Mary, while unanimously voted guilty of adultery by the jurors, had nevertheless won a victory of sorts. Peter not only lost his divorce suit but emerged with a reputation almost as tarnished as hers. She and Allie remained in hiding, lest Peter seek a new trial.

There was talk on the Strong side of doing so, but Peter failed to move ahead, worried that he lacked enough money, according to George, who called his cousin's indecision "a condition of moral flabbiness." Although Peter claimed to have already spent the enormous sum, at the time, of $20,000 to divorce his wife, George thought the case should be pursued as a matter of conscience and pride. On the other hand, he recognized that "the public is sick of this horrible case." Indeed, he wrote, many reporters felt that there was "little to choose" between Peter and Mary, neither of whom seemed particularly admirable. Some had commented that Peter and Mary seemed "so well matched" it would be "a pity to divorce them."

That June, to make the situation more infuriating for Peter, the matter was dragged back to court. Mary's lawyers sued on her behalf for counsel fees, a move that cousin George viewed with professional approval as brash and clever, even though the motion targeted his cousin.

The judge considered the motion carefully. A defendant who either denied her guilt or set up defenses such as forgiveness or recrimination (a counteraccusation like the one in Mary's Supplemental Answer) was entitled to alimony and counsel fees, unless the court found that she was altogether in the wrong.

Although the judge alone was to rule on the current motion, he took into account the jury's findings in the Strong trial. Since two of those twelve jurors believed that Peter, as well as Mary, was an adulterer, "I have come to the conclusion," the judge wrote, "that counsel fees and alimony should be allowed. As, however, defendant's counsel . . . expressly waived and abandoned that portion of the motion which called for alimony . . . I shall not order it." The judge did skimp on the amount of counsel fees allotted, allowing a mere one thousand dollars, despite the Stevenses' claiming to have spent five thousand.

Mary's small triumph received little press coverage—brusque and factual rather than melodramatic and editorial. Newspapers now were focused on the larger news of the nation: the struggle over Reconstruction and the readmission of the eleven former Confederate states into the Union. President Johnson, deeply sympathetic to the South, had tried to enact policies for their governance considered far too lenient by many in the North, and he had vetoed legislation designed to protect the rights and safety of the South's formerly enslaved population.

That June 1866, both houses of Congress passed the Fourteenth Amendment with enough votes to send the amendment to the states for ratification. The amendment provided that anyone born or naturalized in the United States was a citizen, and that no law could abridge the privileges or immunities of citizens or "deprive any person of life, liberty or property, without due process of law."

The amendment's provisions were sweeping, as, indeed, would be its long-term ramifications, but it ducked the subject of suffrage. Rather than granting the vote to all adult citizens, the amendment proportionately reduced a state's congressional representation if that state denied the right to vote to "any of the male inhabitants of that state, being twenty-one years of age." Although the amendment essentially punished states if they did not allow African American men as well as white men to vote, its stance on suffrage was ambiguous enough that new amendments on voting rights would be required over the next 150 years. However, one thing was absolutely clear: the Fourteenth Amendment had inserted the word "male" for the first time into the Constitution. Voting rights were denied to women, whatever their race.

Many women's rights activists who supported African American male suffrage were outraged. If the federal government failed to ensure women's right to vote, how could women elect representatives who would fight on their behalf? Denied the right to vote, how could women influence the laws, policies, customs, and attitudes that shaped their lives? Who in government would speak out against the laws and traditions that discriminated against women in government, education, and the workplace; that limited their wages and opportunities; that regulated every aspect of home and family life—including marriage, adultery, divorce, child custody, and abortion, all the issues raised by the Strong divorce trial?

After all, who stood in the courtroom that same June to argue and decide the fate of Mary Stevens Strong's petition for payment of her counsel fees? There were several lawyers and one judge. Of course, all of them were men.

Men.

Not only because Mary was physically absent. But because it was men who elected the men who wrote the laws, and it was men who served as judges, lawyers, and jurors.

"I want women to have their rights," insisted Sojourner Truth, a warrior for both abolition and women's rights, in one of her speeches.

In the Courts women have no right, no voice; nobody speaks for them. I wish woman to have her voice there among the pettifoggers. If it is not a fit place for women,

it is unfit for men to be there. I am above eighty years old;
it is about time for me to be going. I have been forty years
a slave and forty years free and would be here forty years
more to have equal rights for all.

In the United States, women would not win the vote until
1920. In New York State, women would not be accorded the right
to sit on a jury until 1937.

HAVING LOST HIS LATEST COURT FIGHT, Peter continued to
live at Waverly, where Mamie had the company of her paternal
grandmother, aunts and uncles, and young cousins. One October
morning in 1866, cousin George took the ferry across the East
River to visit his extended family. He was picked up by Peter and
greeted hospitably at Waverly, especially by seventy-eight-year-
old Aletta, who was cheerful and good-natured as ever, George
wrote. The day sparkled with fall light, and Peter took him fishing
and for a walk around the village of Flushing, which was rapidly
being transformed into a busy hub of homes and businesses. Then
they returned to Waverly, where Mamie joined them.

"Little Miss Mary is a sweet child," George wrote, "rather pre-
cocious for her twelve years, full of life and spirit."

Some family gossip intrigued him. Edward Strong, still living in Connecticut, was engaged to be married. His bride-to-be,
Evelina Kearney, was a friend of the Strong family, her relationship with Edward vaguely described by George as "growing out
of that domestic tragedy of 1862, & all the doings of both parties
thereto ever since . . . & almost passing belief." While George's
diary entry was oblique, it's possible to speculate that a romance
ensued after Evelina offered Edward sympathetic companionship
during the ordeal of his brother's divorce scandal—just as Mary

had once offered Edward sympathetic companionship in the wake of his first wife's death.

A week after George's visit to Waverly, thirty-nine-year-old Edward and twenty-nine-year-old Evelina were married. Not even a full year had passed since the Strong divorce trial.

ON MAY 26, 1868, following another trial that drew immense public interest, the United States Senate acquitted President Andrew Johnson, the first president in the nation's history to be impeached, of high crimes and misdemeanors. The Senate failed to convict him by one vote. It was paradoxically both a dramatic and an anticlimactic conclusion to a multiyear battle—in that sense, not dissimilar to the Strong divorce trial's unsettled end.

But the end of the Strongs' battles approached. On June 6, 1868, less than two weeks after Johnson's acquittal, with no publicity or fanfare, Peter Strong submitted a document to Judge Samuel Garvin of the Superior Court of New York requesting that his divorce action be reopened under very specific circumstances. Signed by Peter, the document stated that he, "being desirous of bringing to a close the above action and avoiding the scandal of a second public trial does consent that the above-named defendant [Mary E. Strong] shall have the tuition, care, and maintenance of his daughter Alice Strong until she has arrived at age 18, provided said defendant, her mother, shall so long live."

In a second document, submitted to the Court on June 9, Mary and Peter waived their right to a jury trial and stipulated and agreed that all issues addressed in their original trial should be referred to a referee for his investigation and opinion.

In effect, Mary had agreed not to fight a divorce action, but to abide by the decision of a referee, so long as she was awarded custody of Alice. Depending on the referee's decision, Peter would gain his freedom, official custody of Mamie, and some measure of satisfaction in Mary's being found legally at fault, at last, for adultery. This set of agreements had required careful and prolonged negotiations, as well as a high degree of coordination in the preparation of documents to ensure that the referee would make the right recommendations to the judge.

Henry Nicoll, the referee Garvin appointed, was a fifty-six-year-old lawyer, a Democrat, a former representative in the United States Congress, and a social acquaintance of George Templeton Strong and Murray Hoffman. Henry Cram oversaw the submission of the plaintiff's evidence to Nicoll; John McKeon did the same for the defendant.

Selected transcripts from the 1865 original trial were presented for Nicoll's review. These included the sworn trial testimony of Matilda Mussehl, the Strong family governess, and Fanny Hoffman Strong, wife of Benjamin Strong and daughter of Murray Hoffman. With their vivid scenes of intimacy and confessions of adultery, these served as examples of the evidence proving Mary's adultery.

None of the testimony pointing to Peter's alleged adultery or to his participation in an abortion scheme was included among Nicoll's official documents. Instead, a variety of new affidavits were presented to him, focused almost entirely on who was fit to assume custody of the children. The affidavits represented an impressively united front among former foes.

Murray Hoffman, Fanny's father, testified that he visited Waverly monthly, and that Mamie was now between fourteen and fifteen years old. Peter, he said, was a "tender and devoted father" and Mamie received every advantage of a good home.

In turn, John Cotton Smith, minister of the Church of the Ascension, testified to his frequent conversations with Mary in 1863–64 about her difficulties. She was sincerely repentant, he testified, had great maternal affection for her children, and was an accomplished woman who benefited from a careful religious education. "There is, of course, a serious disqualification," he admitted delicately, "but in consequence of her sincere penitence and fitness in other respects and her earnest interest in the welfare of the child, Alice Strong, at the child's present tender age I think it is in the interest of the latter to be in the mother's care."

Peter's sister-in-law Julia Bedell, the bishop's wife, swore earnestly that she had received letters several years before that evidenced Mary's "repentance and sorrow for her sin." She had not, she primly added, been in contact with the defendant since Mary left New York.

Mary's brother, Austin, had recovered from the insults he had suffered. A well-respected businessman, diplomat, and frequent traveler to Europe, he testified that he had been in continuous contact with his sister over the last several years. "Her conduct and behavior," he said, "are irreproachable; she is devoted to the care of her child and never absent from her."

Nicoll reported to Garvin that he found in favor of the plaintiff on the facts of the case: that Mary E. Strong had committed adultery and experienced frequent carnal connection with Edward Strong at "diverse times and places," and that these acts had not been forgiven, connived, nor procured by the plaintiff. As a conclusion of law, Nicoll wrote, Peter R. Strong was entitled to a divorce.

Acting on Nicoll's report, in July Judge Garvin "ordered, adjudged and decreed" that the Strongs' marriage was dissolved. Moreover, it was lawful for the plaintiff to "marry again in the same manner as though [the defendant] were actually dead." It was not lawful for Mary—the party judged at fault—to remarry "until he [Peter] be actually dead," a usual ban against the guilty party's remarriage.

Accepting the recommendation that Henry Nicoll, as referee, expressed in his official report, Garvin decreed that Peter be entrusted with "the care, custody, education and support" of Mamie, and that Mary be entrusted with that of Allie until "said child shall arrive at the age of 18."

It was over. Peter and Mary Strong were divorced. The newspapers took no notice.

Peter was a free man, permitted to remarry at any time. He had won custody of Mamie, and the two of them continued to live, as he had for most of his life, at his mother's home of Waverly.

A woman divorced for adultery, deemed legally at fault for her marriage's failure, Mary was forbidden to remarry until her former husband died. Nevertheless, Mary had, against enormous odds, won custody of Allie. No longer fugitives from justice, the two of them were living . . . where?

CHAPTER 27

The Changing World

"I HAD A FEW LINES FROM MARY," Lucretia wrote to her mother, Abby, in 1869. "She and Alice seemed happy and well. . . . I have promised to send Mary a photograph of myself and the children by May. Where is she, and how is she to be reached?"

The likelihood is that Mary and Allie had been living in or near Paris for several years, among a large American community that consisted of expatriates, temporary residents such as diplomats, artists, and students, and tourists passing through. Austin and his family had moved to Paris in 1868 for an extended stay. Mary also had other relatives there, including the Jones family, whose daughter, Edith—one day to be known by her married name, Wharton—was a little younger than Allie. Whether the Joneses welcomed their disgraced family member, or whether Mary socialized at all during this period, is doubtful. Though officially divorced, she seems to have remained for a time as anonymous as possible among her fellow countrymen, discreet about her exact whereabouts.

France was about to enter a tumultuous and violent period, declaring war on Prussia in 1870. After several humiliating defeats, Louis Napoleon's glittering Second Empire collapsed. With Paris besieged and bombarded by the Germans, the French quickly established a new government, the Third Republic, which in turn was attacked by a revolutionary faction that set up a rival government—the Commune. While a treaty was in negotiation between representatives of the Third Republic and the Germans, the Communards—composed largely of radicalized poor and working-class Parisians—fought the regular French Army in a bloody insurrection that was violently suppressed within a few months.

Mary, like most Americans, left the city during this two-year period of extended violence and chaos. The number of Americans in Paris dropped from several thousand to a few hundred, the memory of brilliantly lit boulevards, fashionable shops, famous museums, and the finest restaurants seeming a dream.

Mary's sorrowing heart was with the Communards, who were known as the Reds because of their red flag. She sympathized with their suffering and proletarian ideals. Nevertheless, her political views apparently were chastened by the terror of the times, at least according to Lucretia: "Even Mary Strong seems to have deserted . . . the Reds and says she hopes to see 'a limited monarch' established in France."

After the Third Republic defeated the Communards, and Prussia defeated France—forcing a harsh treaty on the French—order was restored. Mary and Allie returned to Paris.

During these years of turmoil abroad, Peter and Mamie remained under his mother's benevolent wing at Waverly, as did his siblings Benjamin, James, and Elizabeth Jane, together with their families. Julia and her husband remained in Ohio. Edward moved from Darien, Connecticut, to the small Westchester village of Sing Sing, now known as Ossining, in New York. His wife, Evelina, had given birth to a daughter in 1867, nine months after the couple's marriage.

Remarkably for one of old New York stock, Peter refused to keep a low profile after his very public scandal. He retained an office in downtown Manhattan, frequented his favorite club, the Century Association, with his cousin George, and penned satirical lyrics, primarily about the foibles of New York society high life, for the *New York Evening Post*. A book of his poems was published under the title *Awful! And Other Jingles.* "Awful" was the title of the first poem in the collection.

I.

I was dining at Delmonico's, a week or two
    ago,
With a charming little maiden and her dapper
    little beau;
And I tried by close attention, as I trifled with
    my fork,
To arrive at a solution to the meaning of their
    talk.

II.

It was all about a party, which, they said, was
    "awful jolly,"
Where their "awful pretty" hostess had an
    "awful handsome Dolly;"
And an "awful cunning necklace," which her
    "awful good papa"
Had procured for her at Tiffany's while shopping
    with mama.

Through several more verses, the poet finds himself baffled by the couple's repeated use of the word "awful" such as "awful stylish," "awful swell," and "awful little minx."

In 1873 Austin Stevens returned to the United States after five
years abroad. There, like Peter, he started contributing pieces to
the newspaper—but in a style more befitting the decorous ways
of old New York. He wrote for *The New York Times* under the
pen name "Knickerbocker," an ironic yet affectionate moniker for
descendants of New York's early Dutch settlers. Expounding on
serious topics such as the important financial questions then fac-
ing the nation, Austin was lauded by his employer as a columnist
of wisdom and experience.

Austin's departure was a sad blow to his sister and niece, who
followed him to the United States for a visit—it may have been
their first since they left the country. Whether they saw Peter
or Mamie or both in New York is unclear. Upon their return to
France after several months, Mary missed her brother, Austin,
terribly and longed for her beloved parents in New York as well as
Aunt Em in Maine.

"Poor Mary seems to have at last felt her burdens more than
she could bear," Lucretia wrote. Mary wanted to move back to the
United States, dreamed of living with Aunt Em in Brunswick, far
from New York society's prying eyes and disapproving looks, but
Lucretia warned that such a move was premature. While Mary's
legal matters had been resolved, her disgrace endured. "I have
begged her over and over again to give up this passionate longing
for the unattainable in respect to Maine, assuring her that a kind
Providence, and Time, could do more for her and in a better manner than anything she could herself bring about." Mary and Allie
remained in France.

The next year, 1874, Peter and Mamie visited Paris, by then a
routine cultural excursion for the well-to-do but also, perhaps, an
opportunity for Mamie to see her mother and sister, and for Peter
to see Allie. In October, news arrived from New York that Mary's
father, seventy-nine-year-old John Austin Stevens, had died. He

was a man "so affectionate, so generous, just and true," Lucretia wrote sadly. Mary must have felt his loss keenly. He had done what few other men of his day would have done for a daughter so transgressive, who so risked the honor of the family's name: he protected and supported her and fought for her to keep custody of her younger daughter.

George Templeton Strong, of course, felt differently. "I always got on with [Stevens] well enough," he wrote, "but when crossed he was the most vindictive, unscrupulous, and hateful of men."

Two weeks after John Austin Stevens's death, Peter, while still in Paris, drew up his first and only will. Its contents suggest that Peter through the years had taken his paternal responsibility for Allie seriously and felt lasting affection for his absent child. He bequeathed his estate in equal shares to his two daughters. On his death, Mamie and Allie were each to receive income until the age of twenty-five, and then inherit her designated share of his estate.

There was one exception to the equal division of assets. Mamie, whom Peter alone had raised, would alone inherit his personal property, including his furniture, books, paintings, and other such items with which she was familiar—perhaps even the items held in his "cabinet of curiosities," so much discussed at his trial—a dagger, Armenian dresses, a mummified human foot.

In November, a month after John Austin Stevens's death, Peter's mother, Aletta Strong, died. "A most excellent old lady," cousin George commented.

Fifty-five-year-old George Templeton Strong died the following year. While his views and opinions on many topics were not always admirable, he nevertheless tried to act in accordance with an ideal of civic virtue and responsibility. He had dedicated himself not only to the well-being of his wife, son, and community of friends and family, but also to the welfare and improve-

ment of his city and to the Union's wartime efforts. An acute
observer of society, he left behind one of the great and enduring
records of nineteenth-century life: the more-than-two-thousand-
page, four-volume diary that he started in 1835.

Tucked in its pages he had kept a small sketch of Mamie and
Allie Strong, undated, artist unknown, drawn when they were
little girls, perhaps eight and three respectively, before they were
separated. Allie is face forward, while Mamie's face is slightly
tilted as she peeps out from behind her younger sister. Both
girls are achingly beautiful, with large, bright eyes and rosebud
mouths, their oval faces framed by light-colored curls. Mamie's
frank and open expression, with its hint of a smile, contrasts with
Allie's more serious—one might even say sad or anxious—look.
It's easy to imagine that Mamie, born in 1854, having spent her
early years in a household that seemed relatively stable, was a more
secure, steadier child. Allie, born in 1859, had known sorrow and
upheaval from her earliest days.

Neither girl seems to have left any evidence—childhood
drawings or scribbles or, later, a note to a friend or in a diary—to
indicate what they felt as they watched their parents' relationship
deteriorate and were then so dramatically separated, to grow up
far away from one another. To my knowledge, personal records
of the girls' inner lives in childhood and youth, if any documents
existed, have not been preserved, although public records reveal
the shape of their outer lives through the years.

In 1879, twenty-four-year-old Mamie was engaged and planning a spring wedding, and nineteen-year-old Allie, though raised
in France, had an American beau. Both men were similar in some
ways to Peter—affable clubmen, sons of well-to-do families.
Mamie's fiancé, twenty-three-year-old George Bech, hailed from
Poughkeepsie, New York, and was heir to an iron-works factory
and fortune. He especially enjoyed yachting. Allie's beau, Charles

Macalester, age twenty-four, was from a prominent Philadelphia family and noted for his skill in competitive pigeon shooting.

Peter didn't live to see Mamie's April wedding. He died at age fifty-five, in February 1879. His obituary in Newtown's local newspaper, after lauding his "ready pen in prose and poetry," described Peter much as his cousin George might have done in their youth: "Genial, full of anecdote, and having a happy disposition."

Although still mourning her father' death, Mamie went forward with her spring wedding to George Bech. Soon afterward, newly married, she visited Philadelphia, where her Aunt Lucretia, Mary's sister, resided, as did Charles Macalester, now Allie's fiancé. Lucretia wrote glowingly that Mamie was "a sweet, gentle affectionate girl, easily made happy, and very susceptible to kindness."

Mamie's life was not a long one. She died in childbirth, along with her baby, in January 1880, nine months after her marriage. She and her child were buried in the Bech family mausoleum in Poughkeepsie, New York.

That March, two months after Mamie's death, Allie married Charles Macalester. The couple planned to settle in Philadelphia but to live some of the time in Seaville, New Jersey, an ocean resort town a few hours from the city, and some of the time in France.

Lucretia received news of Allie when her niece visited New York. "Mrs. Neill, Sr. told me the other day that Alice McCalester [*sic*] had been to their house; that she looked very handsome and happy," Lucretia wrote, "and that they thought she was fascinating. . . . She is a funny girl, with cheek eno' for two."

The woeful little girl in the picture George Templeton Strong kept in his diary apparently had matured into a beautiful, intriguing, and tough young woman. With her combination of charm and cheek, Allie was her mother's daughter.

Mary was in the United States for some part of 1879 and 1880.

It's doubtful, given the scandal of her past and the strict scruples of those in her one-time social circle, that she was invited to either of her daughters' weddings, not even to Allie's. Still, her presence in her former homeland surely allowed her to experience the hopes and sorrows of these years—two marriages, a birth, and three deaths—more intimately than if she had been far away.

Then she returned to France. Her divorce decree had banned her from remarrying during Peter's lifetime. Now, thirteen years after her official divorce and two years after Peter's death, forty-eight-year-old Mary was about to enter into a new life. She was to be married to Philippe Michel Maurice Bonjour Picot de Limoëlan, a wealthy member of a distinguished French family.

Mary, who had allowed herself in recent years to live more openly, may have been introduced to Philippe by a mutual acquaintance, or perhaps met him at one of the elite social events held at the American Legation in Paris for the international community. It was here that many a rich man's unmarried daughter met the eligible French nobleman of her dreams. Mary's situation as a divorced woman of course had marginalized her. As a widow, however, she was both accepted by society and deemed free to remarry by the Catholic Church, to which Philippe belonged. The passage of time and French sophistication also would have made her past less an issue than it remained in the minds of old New York.

While not a titled aristocrat, forty-seven-year-old Philippe had been made a Knight of the Legion of Honor—France's highest decoration for civil and military merit—and held a high-ranking position at the prestigious Maritime Ministry. He lived in a fine building in one of the most attractive districts of Paris, was lifetime heir to his family's magnificent eighteenth-century chateau in the town of Sévignac in northwest France, and moved in the highest circles of French society. More important than his wealth or position, after many years of hardship, Mary bloomed in the light of his affection.

"She seems like a young girl," Lucretia wrote to her mother, after reading a letter from Mary. "As tho' her life were just at its dawn. I am sure I trust she <u>may</u> find <u>happiness and rest</u>. She will at last have a respectable name, a home, and a protector, being as she is, it is a fortunate thing, I think."

What did Lucretia mean by the phrase "being as she is"? Her husband, Richard, thought that in cases such as Mary's a flaw could be a virtue. "Richard thinks after all 'self-seeking people' get along best in this world," Lucretia continued. "Mary has certainly worked with a will few could withstand to accomplish what she has considered best for Alice's and her own happiness."

Lucretia believed that Mary and Allie, contented at last, might become more feminine and nurturing. "If they both find [happiness], perhaps the more womanly and loveable points of their natures may develop." She hoped that they would conform more successfully with society's expectations of a woman.

Mary and Philippe were married on June 2, 1881, at the Paris City Hall. The company gathered to witness the ceremony included—along with Allie and her husband, Charles—a marquis who was also a senator; two Knights of the Legion of Honor; and Edward Noyes, Minister of the United States to France. Mary, the marriageable girl of old New York who, in her first marriage, had shockingly violated a host of norms, laws, and social conventions, now found herself in later life, as she had been at the start, respectable.

MARY'S YEARS WITH PHILIPPE WERE FEW. In 1886, near the chateau in Sévignac, a horse harnessed to his carriage suddenly reared up, and Philippe was killed. The accident eerily evoked the tale, told often at the Strongs' divorce trial, of the fractious horse that tried to throw Mary and, once, to overturn the cart that she was driving.

Despite her terrible loss, Mary seems to have led a comfortable life after her husband's death, dividing her time between the chateau and an apartment in Paris. A convert to Catholicism, Philippe's religion, she found solace in Sévignac's historic church and generously contributed to it. She died in 1895 at age sixty-two, nine years after Philippe's death, praised for her gifts to the church and charity to the poor.

Mary was not alone in finding respectability later in life. Her former lover and brother-in-law, Edward Newton Strong, also died in 1895, a long-time resident of Ossining, New York, survived by his wife of almost thirty years, Evelina, and their daughter. The past had receded for him, as it had for Mary.

For the memorable Mrs. Potter, too, the late-nineteenth-century world proved forgiving. Beyond the lingering influence of old New York, reputations could be redeemed. To all appearances, she led a quiet and uneventful later life. In 1880, she and her husband, Vernon, who was listed on the census of that year as a retired merchant, were living in Hoboken, New Jersey. Rather than using her first name, Electa, she had chosen to call herself by her middle and less notorious name, Minerva, the name of the Roman goddess of medicine as well as wisdom. Widowed in 1898, she died in 1906 at age seventy-nine.

The Strongs' trial, of course, had involved many people other than Peter, Mary, Edward, and Mrs. Potter—judges, lawyers, servants, relatives, medical men and women, policemen, friends, and jurors. While their lives overlapped with that of the Strongs, these individuals largely went their own way post-trial, returning to their private worlds. A few, however, were public men whose careers were covered by the press. John T. Hoffman, Recorder at the time of Peter's manslaughter trial, served as mayor of New York City from 1866 to 1868, then as state governor for a four-year term. A. Oakey Hall, New York's district attorney at the time of the divorce trial, followed Hoffman as mayor. Almost three decades after the Strongs' marriage collapsed, John Graham, Mary's lawyer, and Henry Cram, Peter's lawyer, died on the same day: April 9, 1894. Graham's obituaries were as long-winded and flamboyant as he was in life. Cram's passing received small notices, dignified and modest.

Allie, a little girl when her parents divorced, not surprisingly outlived all the other major players in the Strong saga. It seemed possible that Allie, after her marriage, might lead a somewhat conventional upper-class life, visible only insofar as she was covered in the pages of society newspapers, perhaps glimpsed at a fashionable party or a resort town like Bar Harbor. But her later life turned out to be as dramatic as her childhood. A scandal that rivaled her parents' infamous one brought her vividly back into the public eye.

In 1893, Charles Macalester, Allie's husband of thirteen years, fell in love with Olive Wilkinson, the sister of his dear friend Walter Wilkinson of Baltimore, a man his equal in social prominence. Ollie, as she was called, was ten years younger than thirty-four-year-old Allie and said to be a skilled linguist and a beautiful blonde. Distraught over her husband's betrayal, Allie turned for comfort to Ollie's brother, Walter. Before long, their relationship also blossomed into a love affair and led to Allie's divorcing Charles. Almost immediately after the Macalesters divorced, Allie married Walter, and Charles married Ollie, making Allie's new husband her ex-husband's brother-in-law.

Journalists gleefully reported on these events as though on a French farce, writing that the two weddings took place within days of each other an ocean apart, Allie's to Walter in Paris, where her mother lived, and Charles's to Ollie in Baltimore, her family's home. In an ever-changing world, the two couple's reshuffling of family relations at first seemed to receive an amused and tolerant reception from friends, relatives, and society. It's notable, however, that Allie and Walter spent much of their married life in France, and that Ollie and Charles moved to Virginia, far from Baltimore's wagging tongues.

Allie gave birth to two sons, Walter Scott in 1895, and Stevens Austin in 1899. When her husband died in 1901, less than a decade after their marriage, Allie was left a wealthy forty-two-year-old widow with boys aged six and two. She never remarried but continued to travel, as she had for many years, between the United States and Europe, now joined by her children. Stevens Austin, then a young man of twenty, was with her when she died in July 1919, just short of her sixtieth birthday, at the magnificent villa she owned in Monte Carlo, Monaco.

A death notice in *The Baltimore Sun* reported that Allie was a daughter of the "late Peter Remsen Strong and the Countess de Limolan [*sic*], of New York." Mary's second husband, Philippe, was not a count, nor she a countess. The writer had enthusiastically if mistakenly elevated Mary, Allie's formerly disgraced mother, to the rank of a French aristocrat. Any old New Yorkers still living would not have been impressed.

Afterword

———— ❧ ————

RESEARCHING THE LIVES of the Strongs felt like a guilty pleasure, not so different from reading tabloid gossip about today's celebrity breakups. So much about the warring clans of Stevenses and Strongs captivated me. I suppose the sheer pile-up of misfortunes was compelling: two well-off families; an ill-matched couple who once seemed to be the perfect pair, betrayal, adultery, abortion, abduction, two trials, bribery, a hung jury, and, finally, divorce. I was astonished at the shenanigans that took place among these two old New York families, shielded behind the façade of genteel Victorian America, where maidenly innocence, matronly propriety, and masculine discretion were said to prevail in all matters sexual.

"Vice was not rarer in those elder years," Mrs. John King Van Rensselaer wrote in the 1920s, "but the whole social organization conspired to conceal its existence."

Although the Strongs hoped to conceal it, their marital catastrophe hadn't remained hidden for long. The publicity engendered by the suit helped explode the wall of privacy around the world of old New York, revealing that the rich and powerful were as flawed and sinful as everyone else. Already in transition and now exposed in the press, old New York as a potent force in American society was diminishing, swamped not only by scandal but by the ever-expanding size, complexity, and diversity of the nation: the rise of new money and vast wealth; prevalence of deep corruption; dismantling of Reconstruction; increase in immigration; and clamor for women's and workers' rights that characterized the postwar decade and the Gilded Age.

For all the publicity around the Strong suit, newspaper reports and trial testimony provide surprisingly few answers to specific questions about the couple's marriage. What can be garnered from the clashing versions of events, the absence of a jury verdict and the subsequent referee's decision? What motivated Mary to have an affair with Edward—if she did? Who was the seducer? Did Peter in fact force Mary to have an abortion, after receiving help from Electa Potter? Was his collaborator in crime also his lover? Were the holdout jurors bribed?

I can tell you what I believe. As I am neither a lawyer, nor juror, nor legal scholar, I will not try to argue the facts beyond a reasonable doubt. What I can do is construct likely scenarios, opinions based on the information I've gathered and shared with you.

It seems to me incontrovertible that Mary and Edward had an affair under the Strong family's very noses, driven by lust or boredom, loneliness or affection, desire or fear. Her confessions feel to me authentic, whether told to Fanny or Julia or written in notes. I can envision Edward—soldier, deacon, and widower, who had a flair for the dramatic—excitedly waving a pistol at Mary, threatening to kill her or himself if their flirtation wasn't consummated. Sexual assault can assume many different forms, manipulative threats can be frightening and misinterpreted, women's relationships with their abusers have been known to continue beyond a single event.

On the other hand, it's possible that Mary was an equal participant in committing adultery. Perhaps she was, as suggested at the trial, depressed by her purported illness or deeply disappointed by her husband's lack of attention or his flaws, his failure to provide her with a home of her own. Perhaps she felt trapped by the swarm of in-laws at Waverly, the family of strangers who, as Fanny primly protested, "never spoke unfavorably about her as a proud, overbearing woman."

Perhaps Mary simply experienced her life as limited. The Strongs' story reminds us that even the most privileged woman in the mid-nineteenth century, while protected from the hardships and suffering of working-class and enslaved women, could not attend most institutions of higher education, participate in politics, work in a chosen occupation, sit on a jury, or speak in public—her voice was literally and figuratively curbed.

Perhaps Mary longed for connection with a sympathetic soul and developed yearnings that found their outlet in a grand passion for another man. Indeed, some of the world's great fiction is about the romantic discontent of bourgeois women.

I do believe that Peter, humiliated and enraged, pressured his wife into performing an abortion on herself, after he obtained the means from Electa Potter. However, I also suspect that Mary, too, may have been ambivalent about bearing the child, unsure of its parentage and unhappy in her marriage. If so, Mary's feelings may have made her that much more susceptible to Peter's cruel pressure.

I do not believe that Peter was ever unfaithful to Mary with the enterprising Electa. The entrepreneurial "female doctor" seems to me too busy and harried to have dallied with a clubman. Moreover, in my opinion, infidelity would have taken more cunning, sexual passion, and energy on Peter's part than he possessed. I don't see Peter as—to use the conventional meaning of his favorite word—an "awful" person or an "awful" husband, although he seems to have been insensitive, at best, where his wife was concerned, too intent on satisfying his own needs to recognize or honor hers.

The Stevens men, father and son, certainly used unscrupulous means to deny Peter his divorce, including fabricating false charges and jury tampering. One can condemn them for that, as George Templeton Strong did. On the other hand, one can also weigh in the balance their audacity in defying social convention to defend a disgraced woman, when most families would have cast her out.

It's harder to defend Edward Strong, who betrayed his brother and, when the truth emerged, betrayed Mary as well.

One can admire Lucretia Stevens Heckscher, who valiantly defended her sister and clearly had a loving heart.

The referee who ultimately recommended divorce, Henry Nicoll, made a wise decision when he advised Judge Garvin to dissolve the Strongs' disastrous marriage and grant custody of each daughter to the parent who had raised her. This was a couple that needed to be divorced, whoever was found at fault. The Strong marriage had irrevocably ruptured.

In the years after *Strong v. Strong*, the reunited nation struggled to recover from the ordeals of the Civil War. Reconstruction brought with it the promise of racial equity, a hope that would blossom, wither, and bloom again in cycles over the course of the next century and a half. Woman suffragists fought on, the necessity for Black men to vote prioritized (with controversy) over women's rights. The distance between owners and laborers grew, in physical as well as metaphorical miles, as cities expanded and neighborhoods separated, segregating the wealthy from the middle class, the middle class from immigrants and the poor. The Gilded Age, the name Mark Twain and Charles Dudley Warner gave to a novel they wrote in 1873 and bestowed on their tumultuous times, began (as it would end) in rampant corruption—economic and political deals producing vast wealth for some and poverty for many, an age of railroads, marble mansions, extravagant balls, and tenement houses, all on a scale that overpowered the modest ways of old New York.

Although the world had devoured news of *Strong v. Strong*, with its glimpse into the insular, secret lives of the well-off and those who served and surrounded them, the trial was quickly forgotten except in the pages of George Templeton Strong's diary. What wasn't fully understood were the ways in which the trial was a harbinger of change. The culture of the elite was fracturing, and with it, the values and norms that, since the Revolution, had been held up as models for the nation (as if other cultures, including those of newer European and Asian immigrants; enslaved and free African Americans; other regions; and indigenous peoples never quite counted). Exploding in population, with the daily arrival of immigrants; in territory, with the settlement of the West; and in prosperity, with the industrialization of the economy, the reunited nation was a new entity. A small group of old New Yorkers (or their longtime competitors for power and influence, Bostonians and Philadelphians) could no longer serve as paragons for the diverse nation.

Within a decade of the Strong trial, society became more tolerant of divorce, a shift made possible in part by the excesses of the Gilded Age and the demands of the women's rights movement. A raft of high-profile divorce trials and adultery scandals ensued, and the divorce rate rose, according to some estimates by almost eighty percent between 1870 and 1880, at a time when the population grew by only thirty percent. Divorce laws in some states became more liberal, and some individuals sought divorces in western states where the laws were less strict. Those with the financial means to afford train transportation and months-long hotel accommodations especially availed themselves of these opportunities, establishing residence in places like Ohio, Indiana, Nevada, and the Territory of Dakota. Nevertheless, ambivalence toward divorce remained, with pushback against what were considered dangerous threats to the institution of marriage. When and if the newly divorced returned east to their home states, they sometimes found that their "foreign divorces" were not honored. Any attempt to remarry might be labeled bigamy. Along with a few other conservative states on the issue of divorce, New York failed to reliably honor out-of-state divorces until the 1940s. California became the first state to enact no-fault divorce, in 1969. New York was the last, in 2010.

The saga of the Strongs' divorce, which provides a glimpse into the vanished world of old New York, also serves as a reminder relevant to our own times. Laws and attitudes about social institutions and issues such as marriage, divorce, child custody, abortion, and adultery—much in contention today—have never been static and God-given or irrevocably embedded in the language of the Constitution. For better or worse, they have been mutable and subject to change. Adultery, once a crime, has become a matter more for therapists than the courts. Marriage, once an unequal partnership, is now more equitable, and the law currently allows mixed-race and same-sex marriages, both inconceivable in the past. Divorce, previously decided almost always in favor of men, is now generally no-fault, and custody is often joint or favors the mother, the emphasis usually on the best interests of the child. In the 1920s, the Nineteenth Amendment granted women the vote and a political role in shaping society. In the 1970s, abortion was judged a right by the United States Supreme Court guaranteed under the Constitution. In 2022, the Court decided that there is no such constitutional right, leaving the states to address the issue individually.

The Strongs' story helps provide perspective on the nation's societal and familial issues through the poignant drama of real, flawed people from our American past—a bright, bored wife; a foolish, amiable husband; a bereft but amorous widower; hapless children caught up in family conflict. The themes, complexity of relations, and tragicomedy of the Strong family saga defy myths about Victorian life and echo (or foreshadow) those of much nineteenth- and early twentieth-century fiction, including the work of novelists such as Henry James, William Dean Howells, and Edith Wharton, Mary Stevens Strong's cousin, a writer who captured with wry wit and some melancholy the transition between the worlds of *old* and *new* New York.

To my knowledge, Wharton never commented directly on the Strongs' marriage or divorce. When the trial took place in 1865, she was just a little child, a few years younger than Allie. Still, it's difficult to believe that she never heard anything about it. Wharton's mother, Lucretia Stevens Rhinelander Jones (although famously close-mouthed about family scandals, especially her own rumored affair) was Mary's first cousin, and the story surely had a whispered place in the Stevenses' family lore.

Whatever Wharton's conscious awareness of the Strongs, their saga seems to resonate through her short stories and novels like a symphony's recurrent motif. Marriage and its social meaning in an age of transition figure prominently in her work. In her short story "Autre Temps," published in 1916, the main character is ostracized by polite society for her adultery and divorce, and she flees to Europe with her little daughter. Many years later, when her onetime American friends calmly accept her adult daughter's divorce and remarriage, she believes that she, too, may finally be welcomed back. Disappointed, she discovers that she remains an outcast, the sinner of their memories.

In *The Custom of the Country*, a novel published in 1913, the same year that Wharton's own divorce took place, a social-climbing woman marries an unsuccessful lawyer and aspiring poet from an old New York family. He requires an allowance from her father to sustain their lifestyle. Eventually they separate, and the woman takes up with a distant relative by marriage, her husband's cousin-in-law. She and her husband divorce, but she finds to her surprise that her lover cools toward her. However, she also has succeeded in charming a wealthy French nobleman. When her ex-husband dies, she is free to marry her aristocratic suitor. There is much more to this story—marriages, divorces, a custody battle, and other complications abound—but elements may sound familiar to a reader who is acquainted with *Strong v. Strong*.

At one point in the novel, two old friends are chatting, and one of the men casually wonders why the "obsolete institution of marriage" survives.

"Oh, it still has its uses," comes the answer. "One couldn't be divorced without it."

Acknowledgments

⁓

MANY PEOPLE HELPED bring this book to fruition. I want to express my gratitude to those I may have neglected to mention along with those I thank below. Of course, any errors of fact or interpretation are mine alone and no one else's.

I'm grateful first of all to my lifelong comrades from graduate school days. Leo Ribuffo encouraged me to write this book and read drafts of early chapters. He passed away several years ago, and I miss him every day. Sarah Stage patiently allowed me to deluge her with questions about nineteenth-century women's lives. Elsa Dixler shared astute and creative comments and gave me the gift of the book's ending.

My editor, Amy Cherry, provided notes that not only improved my prose but provoked me to further thought and research. Her contributions enriched my work at every turn. Huneeya Siddiqui, assistant editor, answered my queries with patience, efficiency, and good humor. Many others at W. W. Norton contributed to this project, and I'm grateful to all for turning this book from wish to reality. Among them, my appreciation for their skilled work goes to copyeditor Nancy Green, project editor Rebecca Munro, and production manager Lauren Abbate.

My dear friend and spectacular agent, Mel Berger, has been my champion on *Strong Passions* from the moment I conceived the idea to publication. I am indebted to him for his encouragement and support on this and other projects through many years.

Librarians and archivists are indispensable guides to historical resources. Laura Hankin, Law Librarian of the Columbia County Supreme Court Law Library, found essential materials for me and also suggested other librarians to contact. Joseph Van Nostrand, Senior Management Analyst of the New York County Clerk's Office, unearthed original trial transcripts from his files, including some long presumed lost. John Ansley, Director, Archives and Special Collections of Marist College, helped me identify information there about relatives of the Strong and Stevens families, and Jordyn Fitzell provided research assistance when the pandemic prevented me from working in the Marist archives. Dennis Nesmith of the New York City Register's Office advised me on navigating that agency's intimidating ledgers. Allison Morey, deputy director of the Historical Society of the New York Courts, shared information that enhanced my understanding of the court system and state law.

Largely because of the pandemic, I was unable to visit the American Antiquarian Society, a remarkable research institution and one of my favorite places. Caroline Stoffel, Online Services Librarian at the AAS, stepped in to identify resources that could be useful. Marie O'Toole, an independent archivist and historical researcher, was thorough, enthusiastic, and imaginative at finding materials and using them to reconstruct Mary's life in France and many other aspects of the Strongs' story. Jack Eichenbaum, long-time Queens Borough Historian, answered many questions about nineteenth-century life in Queens County.

Friends, relatives, colleagues, and acquaintances brought the Strongs' story to life for me in more ways than I can count or categorize. Ellen Dunlap alerted me to Mary's connection with Edith Wharton. Michael Ryan stoked my enthusiasm for this project with the news that the New-York Historical Society was putting Strong's entire diary online, and he alerted me when it was finally posted, a boon that enabled my work. When I lost focus in the isolation of these strange years, Lisa Gornick helped me regain concentration. Margaret Brooks used the internet with skill, verve, and curiosity to search the corners of the Strongs' past. Veronica Herndon agreed to take my author photo, which made the process more fun than I could have hoped.

Generous readers shared their valuable time and insights, among them Kayla Bernheim, Deirdre Sinnott, Helen Breen, Tish Musso, Alyce Myatt, Ellen Lagemann, and Tobiah Black. Other friends, Jeanne Kiefer and Joan Poole, offered suggestions for characterization and narrative approach. Still others helped me navigate difficult times, and so gave me the peace of mind to write: Marie Rudden, Richard Schiro, Barry Levin, Phyllis and John Monahan, Helen Whitney, Kent Carroll, Lisa Melamed, and Alison Blank. My sister, Joan, and all the Keisers have been there for me through thick and thin.

Tools of the trade are crucial. When I stumbled with technology, Deb Ulmer rescued me, and I am grateful also to Al and Kelly Strobel of Chatham Printing for their assistance.

I am blessed to have my husband, David Black, award-winning novelist, journalist, and screenwriter, always close by for consultation, criticism, and welcome breaks from work. He is a remarkably kind and patient man. My stepchildren and their spouses, all writers and researchers, provide inspiration and ideas as easily as they take breaths. Susannah, Tobiah, Hadley, Langan, and Alastair: thank you and much love.

Oona is our newest family member, six weeks old as I write this. Dearest Oona, we welcome you into a world filled with a wondrous variety of books.

Notes

———— ⟨⟩ ————

I WANT TO HIGHLIGHT several sources that were indispensable to my research.

For insight into the Stevens and Strong families, I relied primarily on two sources: *The Letters of Lucretia Stevens Ledyard Heckscher, 1840–1907* and the *George Templeton Strong Diary, 1835–1875*. Although the online collection of Lucretia's letters omits the years of the divorce suit, it is rich in information about the personalities, habits, and pastimes of Stevens family members. I used Strong's marvelous *Diary* in both its complete form, now generously posted online by the New-York Historical Society, and in the four-volume print edition compiled and edited by Allan Nevins and Milton Halsey Thomas in 1952.

The editors' commentary in the *Diary*'s print edition was an extraordinary resource for information about New York City, as were several other works among countless books about the city. To capture a combination of Manhattan's flavor and history, as well as facts about its inhabitants' lives and lifestyles, I am indebted to Mary Knapp's richly detailed and vivid account, *An Old Merchant's House: Life at Home in New York City, 1835–65*. The *Annals of Newtown* by James Rikers, Jr., helped form my picture of nineteenth-century Queens, as did the extensive Newtown materials in the Queens Library Archives, Queens Central Library.

Other print works that formed my sense of Peter and Mary Strong's world included David Black's biography of one of New York's most powerful bankers and his era, *The King of Fifth Avenue: The Fortunes of August Belmont*; Clifton Hood's analysis of neighborhoods and class, *In Pursuit of Privilege: A History of New York's Upper Class and the Making of a Metropolis*; and the "bible" of books for anyone interested in New York City, *Gotham: A History of New York to 1898* by Edwin G. Burrows and Mike Wallace.

While many books were useful and evocative on the subject of Americans abroad, I had the benefit of another "bible" to help me reconstruct that experience, David McCullough's *The Greater Journey: Americans in Paris*.

My interest in women's history was first sparked by and continues to be reignited each time I reread Sarah Stage's pioneering and vastly entertaining study *Lydia Pinkham and the Business of Women's Medicine*.

New York City's *Archives of the New York County Clerk* turned out to be a treasure trove. The materials I found there were not online, and I was lucky enough to visit in person just weeks before the pandemic. Opening the Superior Court's volume 16 afforded me a eureka moment. In front of me, a folder of actual court documents, preserved in pages of spidery handwriting.

I, for one, have come to take Ancestry.com for granted. Of course, I could summon passport applications with the click of a key, or visit a gravesite, or peruse a census without leaving my desk. It's easy to forget what a miracle that is. Another resource that places information at one's fingertips is the extraordinary (for many reasons) New York Public Library, which provides access not only to its remarkable collections at its brick-and-mortar locations but also to an amazing range of databases on its website (www.nypl.org).

There are now a number of websites which feature full texts

of nineteenth-century books. The one I turn to most frequently is Hathitrust.org. And, of course, this project could not have been completed in the days of the pandemic without online access to nineteenth-century newspapers. I used *America's Historical Newspapers* extensively, a resource that is jointly provided by Readex and the American Antiquarian Society and that is accessible through the New York Public Library's website, other libraries, and elsewhere online. The online archives of *The New York Times* were essential.

Accounts of the *Strong v. Strong* trial throughout Parts 3 and 4 are a synthesis of the press coverage in *The New York Times*, the *Herald*, the *Tribune*, and *The World*, filtered, of course, through my sensibilities. Journalists condensed thousands of pages of trial testimony in their reporting, and I condensed five weeks of press coverage. Quoted material from the trial, such as witness testimony and lawyers' questions, is taken from an original source, generally one of the above-named newspapers, most often from the *Times*. While the reports were remarkably similar, I sometimes chose material from one paper rather than another because of more comprehensive reporting, a particularly interesting fact, or especially colorful phrasing. In addition to the newspapers already noted, sources include a variety of other newspapers, depositions, letters, and diaries.

I have included citations only for direct quotations, generally identified by their first few words. If a series of quotations across several paragraphs or pages comes from a single source, that source is identified by the first words of the initial quotation in the series. However, each time there is a change in source, a citation marks the change.

The following chapter notes and my Selected Bibliography include further information about the online and print resources on which I have relied.

Introduction

xiv **"divorce for incompatibility"**: Adam Goodheart, "Divorce, Antebellum Style," *The New York Times*, March 18, 2011. Accessed December 7, 2021, https://opinionator.blogs.nytimes.com/2011/03/18/divorce-antebellum -style.

xiv **"We are divorced"**: Mary Boykin Chesnut, *A Diary from Dixie*, ed. Ben Ames Williams (New York: Houghton Mifflin, 1949; originally published by D. Appleton, 1905), 20.

Chapter 1: A Marriageable Girl

3 **"sweet as a rose"**: Emeline (Em) Weld to Abby Stevens, July 7, 1842, in *Letters of Lucretia Ledyard Stevens Heckscher 1840–1909*, 2 vols. (transcribed and printed by Gustave A. Heckscher II, 1992), vol. 1, 12. Accessed December 7, 2021, www.scribd.com/document/74895269/ Letters-of-Lucretia-Ledyard-Stevens Heckscher.

4 **"old New York"**: Edith Wharton, *Old New York*, in Wharton: *Novellas and Other Writings*, ed. Cynthia Griffin Wolff (New York: The Library of America, 1990), 313.

4 **"The Schermerhorns"**: Edith Wharton, *A Backward Glance*, in *Novellas and Other Writings*, 784.

4 **"stern high-nosed good looks"**: Wharton, *Backward Glance*, 788.

5 **"too perfect to live"**: Lucretia Ledyard Stevens to Caroline Weld, March 6, 1842, Heckscher, *Letters*, vol.1, 8

6 **"have so much spirit"**: Em to Abby, July 7, 1842, Heckscher, *Letters*, vol.1, 12.

6 **"dear little scholar"**: Em to Lucretia, May 13, 1841, Heckscher, *Letters*, vol.1, 3.

6 **"The proprietor of almost any house"**: Nathaniel Parker Willis, 1840s, quoted in *Manhattan Moves Uptown*, Charles Lockwood, quoted in Mary L. Knapp, *An Old Merchant's House: Life at Home in New York City, 1835–1865* (New York: Girandole Books, 2012), 37.

8 **"strange and disreputable anomaly"**: *The New York Herald*, June 1, 1841, quoted in Timothy J. Gilfoyle, *City of Eros: New York City, Prostitution, and the Commercialization of Sex, 1790–1920* (New York: Norton, 1992), 34.

9 **"remain a healthful appetite"**: Lucy N. Godfrey, "Aunt Sophie's Visits," in *Godey's Lady's Book*, 1863 (repr. London: Forgotten Books, 2018), 542.

9 **"Lascivious thoughts"**: Sylvester Graham, *Lecture to Young Men on Chastity: Intended also for the Serious Consideration of Parents and Guardians*, 4th ed. (Boston: George W. Light, 1837), 36. Accessed February 25, 2023, https://archive.org/details/7704062.nlm.nih.gov/page/n7/mode/2up.

10 **"the sexual feeling is now"**: Frederick Hollick, *The Origin of Life: A Popular Treatise on the Philosophy and Physiology of Reproduction in Plants and Animals* (St. Louis: Nafis and Cornish, 1845), 231.

Accessed February 25, 2023, https://babel.hathitrust.org/cgi/pt?id=osu
.32435079833133&view=1up&seq=9.

11 **"yet the crowd is so uncomfortably"**: James Silk Buckingham, "America:
Historical, Statistic, and Descriptive" (London, 1841), in *America through
British Eyes*, ed. Allan Nevins (New York: Oxford University Press, 1948),
232.

11 **"I was in Mrs. John A. Stevens' house"**: Strong, *George Templeton
Strong Diary*, 4 vols. MS 2472, New-York Historical Society, December
25, 1857, vol. 3, 209, Digital Collections. Accessed February 25, 2023,
https://digitalcollections.nyhistory.org/islandora/search/George%20
Templeton%20Strong%20Diary%201835-1875?type=edismax&cp=island
ora%3Aroot.

12 **"young girls, especially"**: Catherine E. Beecher, *Treatise on Domestic
Economy for the Use of Young Ladies at Home, and At School*, rev. ed. (New
York: Harper and Brothers, 1848), 5. Accessed February 25, 2023, https://
babel.hathitrust.org/cgi/pt?id=wu.89042046995&view=1up&seq=9.

12 **"high toned puritanical"**: Lucretia to Gertrude Stevens Rice, January 16,
1887, in Heckscher, *Letters*, vol. 2, 91.

13 **"the pale student"**: Luther V. Bell, *An Hour's Conversation with Fathers
and Sons*, 1840, quoted in Helen Lefkowitz Horowitz, *Attitudes toward
Sex in Antebellum America: A Brief History with Documents* (Boston: Bedford, 2006), 77.

13 **"they have run wild the last three months"**: Caroline Weld to John Austin Stevens, Jr., undated, Heckscher, *Letters*, vol.1, 15.

14 **"a very businesslike air"**: Lucretia to John Austin Stevens, August 30,
1847, Heckscher, *Letters*, vol. 1, 23.

14 **"domestic fidelity, social cheerfulness"**: Buckingham, *America*, 232.

14 **"Mary is . . . so strong in habit"**: Lucretia to Em, September 17, 1850,
Heckscher, *Letters*, vol. 1, 32.

14 **"will few could withstand"**: Lucretia to Abby (mother), June 1, 1881,
Heckscher, *Letters*, vol. 2, 155. Accessed March 30, 2023, www.scribd
.com/document/74895718/Letters-of-Lucretia-Ledyard-Stevens
-Heckscher-Volume-II-1875-1907.

Chapter 2: A Good, Honest, Warm-Hearted Fellow

18 **"Artists, Literary Men"**: quoted in Edwin G. Burrows and Mike Wallace,
Gotham: A History of New York City to 1898 (New York: Oxford University
Press, 1999), 713.

18 **"mere Institutions for the Doing"**: Strong, *George Templeton Strong
Diary*, 4 vols. MS 2472, New-York Historical Society, May 11, 1845, vol.
2, 128.

18 **"Pete was indefatigable"**: Strong, *Diary*, August 18, 1846, vol. 2, 192.

18 **"High Art"**: Strong, *Diary*, December 25, 1863, vol. 4, 48.

19 **"history of mankind"**: "Declaration of Sentiments and Resolutions," in

American Women's Suffrage: Voices from the Long Struggle for the Vote 1776–1956, ed. Susan Ware (New York: The Library of America, 2020), 36–37.

22 **"Home is the empire":** J. N. Danforth, *The Token of Friendship or Home* (1844), quoted in Mary L. Knapp, *An Old Merchant's House: Life at Home in New York City, 1835–1865* (New York: Girandole Books, 2012), 2.

22 **"legally to exist":** Ernestine L. Rose, Speech to the Second National Woman's Rights Convention, 1851, in *American Women's Suffrage,* 47.

23 **"lively & cordial":** Strong, *Diary,* January 3, 1852, vol. 2, 346.

24 **"God prosper this to them both":** Strong, *Diary,* May 22, 1853, vol. 2, 386.

Chapter 3: Initiations

26 **"The sexual feeling":** Frederick Hollick, *The Origin of Life: A Popular Treatise on the Philosophy and Physiology of Reproduction in Plants and Animals* (St. Louis: Nafis and Cornish, 1845), quoted in Helen Lefkowitz Horowitz, *Attitudes toward Sex in Antebellum America: A Brief History with Documents* (New York: Bedford, 2006), 105.

27 **"First, to the reluctant wife!":** Orson S. Fowler, *Love and Parentage Applied to the Improvement of Offspring* (New York: Fowler and Wells, 1851), quoted in Horowitz, *Attitudes,* 101.

27 **"Nothing, perhaps" he wrote:** William Andrus Alcott, *The Young Wife, or Duties of Woman in the Marriage Relation,* quoted in Mimi Matthews, *"19th Century Marriage Manuals: Advice for Young Wives,"* 3. Accessed February 25, 2023, www.mimimatthews.com/2015/11/01/19th-century-marriage-manuals-advice-for-young-wives/.

29 **"Every well-regulated home":** *Report of the Select Committee, March 27, 1854,* in *History of Woman Suffrage,* vol. 1, eds. Elizabeth Cady Stanton, Susan B. Anthony, and Mathilda Joslyn Gage. 2nd ed. (1888), 617. Accessed January 31, 2022, www.gutenberg.org/files/28020/28020-h/28020-h.htm.

30 **"It is to a thousand little delicacies":** Washington Irving, "Wives," in *Irving: Bracebridge Hall, Tales of a Traveller, The Alhambra* (New York: The Library of America, 1991), 58.

Chapter 4: A Handsome Young Matron

35 **"as often as she wanted":** *The New York Times,* November 11, 1865.

35 **"the strong points of character":** Elizabeth Cady Stanton, "The Solitude of Self," quoted in Marilyn Yalom, *A History of the Wife* (New York: Harper Collins, 2001), 203.

37 **"I read of the wreck of the *Argo*":** Margaret Fuller, 1850, quoted in Joseph Jay Deiss, *The Roman Years of Margaret Fuller* (New York: Crowell, 1969), 306.

38 **"the faculty of putting thought":** Nathaniel Hawthorne, 1858, quoted in "A New Review of the Career of Paul Akers 1825–1861," by William B. Miller, *Colby Quarterly* 7, no. 5 (1966): 228. Accessed March 27, 2023, www.digitalcommons.colby.edu/cq/vol7/iss5/4.

39 **"I saw Edward":** *The New York Times,* November 11, 1865.

Chapter 5: Weddings, Baptisms, and Funerals

40 **"no rights which":** *Dred Scott v. John F.A. Sandford*, Supreme Court, December Term, 1865. Accessed March 28, 2023, www.archives.gov/milestone-documents/dred-scott-v-sandford.

43 **"I can't remember ever seeing him":** *The New York Times*, November 28, 1865.

44 **"Secession died at Newtown":** quoted in Harrison Hunt and Bill Bleyer, *Long Island and the Civil War: Queens, Nassau, and Suffolk County During the War Between the States* (Charleston: The History Press, 2015), 25.

46 **"Oh, forgive me":** *The New York Times*, November 25, 1865.

Chapter 6: Revelations

49 **"That domestic troubles should":** Mrs. John King Van Rensselaer and Frederic Van De Water, *The Social Ladder* (New York: Henry Holt, 1924), 48.

50 **"from bed and board":** Hendrik Hartog, *Man & Wife in America: A History* (Cambridge, MA: Harvard University Press, 2002), 36.

51 **"The most outrageous":** Van Rensselaer, *Social Ladder*, 48–49.

51 **"Women should be":** William Cobbett, *Advice to Young Men and (Incidentally) Young Women in the Middle and Higher Ranks of Life* (New York: John Doyle, 1831), 156–57, quoted in Deborah L. Rhode, *Adultery: Infidelity and the Law* (Cambridge, MA: Harvard University Press, 2016), 36–37.

52 **"In that day":** Van Rensselaer, *Social Ladder*, 49.

53 **"the recognized paramount right of the father":** *The People ex rel. Brooks v. Brooks*, 85 N.Y. Super. Ct. 35 Barb (1861). Accessed February 27, 2023, courtlistener.com, www.courtlistener.com/opinion/5615431/people-ex-rel-brooks-v-brooks/.

53 **"signs of the deepest humiliation":** *The New York Times*, October 10, 1865.

53 **"my husband knows all":** *The New York Times*, November 30, 1865.

53 **"residing under the same roof ":** *The New York Times*, October 10, 1865.

54 **"From the deck of our vessel":** Henry William Gangewer, "And Three Rousing Cheers for the Privates: A Diary of the 1862 Roanoke Island Expedition," ed. Mary Seaton Dix, *The North Carolina Historical Review* 71 (January 1994), 73. Accessed January 31, 2022, www.jstor.org/stable/23521323?read-now=1&refreqid=excelsior%3A1922dd3d73370a5ff1b73f241a15ca40&seq=12#page_scan_tab_contents.

54 **"We had to wade about":** George Washington Whitman to Louisa Van Velsor Whitman, February 9, 1862, Whitman Archive, Duke University. Accessed January 31, 2022, https://whitmanarchive.org/biography/correspondence/tei/duk.00314.html.

55 **"Every blow tells fearfully":** Horace Greeley, quoted in Shelby Foote,

The Civil War: A Narrative, Fort Sumter to Perryville (New York: Random House, 1958), 231.

60 **"disregarding the solemnity of her marriage vows"**: *Peter R. Strong v. Mary E. Strong*, Superior Court of the City of New York, Divorce Records, vol. 16 (1864–1868), Archives of the New York County Clerk.

61 **"There is a clique"**: Maria Lydig Daly, *Diary of a Union Lady 1861–1865*, ed. Harold Earl Hammond (Lincoln: University of Nebraska Press, 2000), 281.

61 **"each and every other allegation in the complaint"**: Superior Court, Divorce Records, vol. 16.

Chapter 7: Maneuvers

63 **"was with her full consent"**: Superior Court of the City of New York, Divorce Records, vol. 16.

64 **"reckless and desperate"**: Strong, *George Templeton Strong Diary*, 4 vols. MS 2472, New-York Historical Society, June 20, 1864, vol. 4, 76.

65 **"So that I may place them"**: John G. Foster to H. W. Halleck, June 19, 1864, in *The War of the Rebellion: A Compilation of Official Records of the Union and Confederate Armies*, prepared by Robert N. Scott (Washington: Government Printing Office, 1891),141.

65 **"That with the sole object"**: *The New York Times*, March 10, 1865.

67 **"You played a variety of parts"**: *The New York Herald*, December 9, 1865.

Chapter 8: The Tenant of Waverly Place

70 **"Marvelous are thy works"**: Strong, *George Templeton Strong Diary*, 4 vols. MS 2472, New-York Historical Society, June 20, 1864, vol. 4, 76.

73 **"artificially produced"**: *The New York Times*, March 10, 1865.

75 **"manslaughter in the second degree"**: *The People v. Peter R. Strong*, Minutes of the Court of General Sessions, October 16, 1865, October 25, 1865, Roll 29, Municipal Archives, City of New York.

Chapter 9: Criminal Charges

76 **"various hotels and"**: Superior Court of the City of New York, Divorce Records, vol. 16.

77 **"All this extravagant"**: Strong, *George Templeton Strong Diary*, 4 vols. MS 2472, New-York Historical Society, March 6, 1865, vol. 4, 111.

77 **"all means of securing the custody"**: *The New York Times*, March 10, 1865.

78 **"can fully realize"**: *The Brooklyn Eagle*, March 9, 1865.

78 **"Poor Peter Strong"**: Maria Lydig Daly, *Diary of a Union Lady 1861–1865*, ed. Harold Earl Hammond (Lincoln: University of Nebraska Press, 2000), March 12, 1865, 345.

79 **"Some of Pete Strong's injudicious"**: Strong, *Diary*, April 30, 1865, vol. 4, 120.

80 "LEE and his ARMY": Strong, *Diary*, April 10, 1865, vol. 4, 117.
80 "9 A.M.": Strong, *Diary*, April 15, 1865, vol 4, 118.
81 "It would be unsafe and dangerous": *The New York Times*, October 19, 1865.
81 "the utmost personal risk": Strong, *Diary*, October 20, 1865, vol. 4, 139.
82 "In the latter part of February": *The New York Herald*, October 26, 1865.
83 "The officer brushed past the servant": *The San Francisco Bulletin*, November 28, 1865.
83 "the case could not proceed": *The New York Times*, October 26, 1865.
85 "I look on this case with dismay": Strong, *Diary*, June 23, 1864, vol. 4, 76.

Chapter 10: A Civil Judge and Jury

89 "the social relations and the position": *The New York Times*, November 24, 1865.
89 "there were twelve": *Daily Ohio Statesman*, November 29, 1865.
89 "the Infamous Harris": *Massachusetts Spy*, December 1, 1865.
90 "Divorces—Private Consultations": *The New York Herald*, November 30, 1865.
91 "densely packed": *The New York Times*, November 24, 1865.
92 "The defense goes into the battle": Strong, *George Templeton Strong Diary*, 4 vols. MS 2472, New-York Historical Society, November 23, 1865, vol. 4, 144.
92 "unlawful carnal knowledge": Patricia Miller, *Bringing Down the Colonel: A Sex Scandal of the Gilded Age* (New York: Farrar, Straus and Giroux, 2018), 57.
94 "Strong was much excited": Superior Court of the City of New York, Divorce Records, vol. 16.
94 "ultra foppery in person and manner": Strong, *Diary*, October 2, 1840.
96 "wronged husband": *The New York Times*, April 10, 1894.
97 "a set of gigglers": *The New York Times*, November 24, 1865.

Chapter 11: Opening for the Plaintiff

100 "Gentlemen of the Jury": *The New York Times*, November 25, 1865.

Chapter 12: The Governess

109 "Singular Revelations": *The New York Times*, November 28, 1865.
109 "Painful Revelations": *New-York Daily Tribune*, November 28, 1865.
110 "Mr. Strong does *not* swear": *The New York Times*, November 28, 1865.
110 "modest, demure": "In the Witness Box," in *Harper's New Monthly Magazine*, August 1865, 284–87.
111 "At the house in Newtown": *New-York Daily Tribune*, November 28, 1865.
112 "always together . . . riding and walking": *The New York Times*, November 28, 1865.

113 **"I remember seeing her"**: *New-York Daily Tribune*, November 28, 1865.

115 **"When I left," she admitted**: *The New York Times*, November 28, 1865.

115 **"A wife can't be thrown"**: *New-York Daily Tribune*, November 28, 1865.

115 **"A Turkish carpet, a writing table"**: *The New York Times*, November 28, 1865.

117 **"Very different. He was cold"**: *The New York Times*, November 29, 1865.

Chapter 13: The Bishop's Wife

119 **"the Beata"**: Strong, *George Templeton Strong Diary*, 4 vols. MS 2472, New-York Historical Society, May 31, 1845, vol. 2, 131.

120 **"In nine cases out of ten"**: *The New York Times*, November 29, 1865.

126 **"The Court-room was not as densely"**: *New-York Daily Tribune*, November 30, 1865.

126 **"The case drags along"**: *The New York Times*, November 30, 1865.

128 **"was played by the wife"**: *Weekly Missouri Republican*, December 8, 1865.

Chapter 14: Eyes and Ears Everywhere

130 **"The Greatest Triumph"**: *The New York Times,* November 29, 1865.

131 **"He did not ask me"**: *The New York Herald*, November 30, 1865.

132 **"Then it was a regular family group?"**: *New-York Daily Tribune*, November 30, 1865.

134 **"In some families"**: Miss Leslie, *The House Book; or, A Manual of Domestic Economy* (Philadelphia: Carey and Hart, 1845), 320. Accessed December 26, 2021, https://babel.hathitrust.org/cgi/pt?id=ien.35556005384854&view=1up&seq=321&skin=2021.

134 **"every morning but one Sunday"**: *New-York Daily Tribune*, November 30, 1865.

134 **"a gentleman of color"**: *The New York Herald*, November 30, 1865.

135 **"so delicate and gentle"**: "The Coachman's Duties," All Things Victorian. Accessed December 26, 2021, www.avictorian.com/servants_coachman.html.

135 **"We are credibly informed"**: *New-York Daily Tribune*, November 30, 1865.

Chapter 15: The Judge's Daughter

138 **"I was married in October"**: *The New York Times*, November 30, 1865.

139 **"At Waverly I saw"**: *The New York Herald*, November 30, 1865.

139 **"Mrs. Strong decidedly sought"**: *New-York Daily Tribune*, November 30, 1865.

139 **"domestic habits"**: *The New York Times*, November 30, 1865.

142 **"a husband could throttle"**: *The New York Times*, December 1, 1865.

Chapter 16: A Fishing Expedition

151 **"Don Pedro is descended"**: Robert Barnwell Roosevelt, *Superior Fishing, or the Striped Bass, Trout and Black Bass of the Northern States* (New York: Carlton, 1865), 24–29.

153 **"In this way we went on"**: *The New York Times*, December 2, 1865.

153 **"said that ... it had been proposed"**: *The World*, December 2, 1865.

154 **"primarily to describe the Superior Region"**: *The New York Times*, December 2, 1865.

155 **"fishes only for quantity"**: Roosevelt, *Superior Fishing*, 194.

Chapter 17: Opening for the Defendant

159 **"There is no proof directly"**: *The New York Times*, December 5, 1865.

163 **"The real object of Mr. Strong"**: *The New York Times*, December 7, 1865.

165 **"Neither slavery nor involuntary servitude"**: Thirteenth Amendment to the U.S. Constitution. Accessed March 23, 2023, www.archives.gov/milestone-documents/13th-amendment.

Chapter 18: A Resolute Old Man

167 **"Complete unity of sentiment"**: *The New York Times*, December 8, 1865.

167 **"under her thumb"**: *The New York Herald*, December 9, 1865.

175 **"I will prove you bribed"**: *The New York Times*, December 12, 1865.

176 **"the hard, resolute, strong-willed old man"**: Strong, *George Templeton Strong Diary*, 4 vols. MS 2472, New-York Historical Society, December 11, 1865, vol. 4, 146.

Chapter 19: Delicate Health

177 **"Her health was very feeble"**: *New-York Daily Tribune*, December 12, 1865.

178 **"[Peter] told me that"**: *The New York Times*, December 12, 1865.

178 **"he was justified in considering"**: *New-York Daily Tribune*, December 12, 1865.

179 **"I saw arrows and bows"**: *The New York Times*, December 12, 1865.

181 **"don't make such a ____ fool of yourself"**: *New-York Daily Tribune*, December 12, 1865.

182 **"There was some disorder"**: *The New York Times*, December 13, 1865.

182 **"Mrs. Strong was the subject"**: *The New York Herald*, December 13, 1865.

Chapter Twenty: Sister, Nurse, Undertaker

185 **"When the honor of my family"**: *The New York Herald*, December 13, 1865.

186 **"I called on Mary"**: *The New York Times*, December 13, 1865.

186 **"'You lie!'"**: *The New York Herald*, December 13, 1865.

190 **"The deposition is considered a unit"**: *The New York Times*, December 13, 1865.

190 **"he was going to hell"**: *The New York Times*, December 14, 1865.

Chapter 21: A Mental Aberration

192 *"1861 Dec. 23"*: *The New York Times*, December 14, 1865.

193 "By obstetrics": *The World*, December 14, 1865.

Chapter 22: The Matter of Mrs. Potter

199 "There was some quarrel": *The New York Times*, December 15, 1865.

201 "... the assistance given in medical attendance": *New-York Daily Tribune*, December 15, 1865.

202 "I don't believe [Mrs. Potter]": *The New York Times*, December 15, 1865.

203 "Not always," Walsh stubbornly replied: *The New York Times*, December 16, 1865.

205 "the usual cloud of witnesses": *The New York Times*, December 20, 1865.

208 "In the confusion of yesterday": *The New York Times*, December 21, 1865.

Chapter 23: Accusations and Rebuttals

211 "procured instruments [for an abortion]": *The World*, December 21, 1865.

215 "What became of the child?": *New-York Daily Tribune*, December 22, 1865.

217 "Did you know that this evidence": *New-York Daily Tribune*, December 23, 1865.

Chapter 24: Closing Time

221 "First, that she is innocent": *New-York Daily Tribune*, December 27, 1865.

221 "In reference to confessions": *The New York Times*, December 27, 1865.

223 "I now come to a very important point": *The New York Times*, December 28, 1865.

228 "made her name a byword": *New-York Daily Tribune*, December 29, 1865.

228 "We blame John Austin Stevens, Jr.": *The New York Times*, December 29, 1865.

Chapter 25: A Long and Painful Investigation

232 "This has been a long and painful investigation": *The New York Herald*, December 30, 1865.

236 "They argued and slept, and discussed": *The New York Times*, January 1, 1866.

236 "hard & cold & spiteful & bitter": Strong, *George Templeton Strong Diary*, 4 vols. MS 2472, New-York Historical Society, December 30, 1865, vol. 4, 148.

237 "so long as any of the jury think": *The New York Times*, January 1, 1866.

Chapter 26: Post-Trial Battles

243 "as such will form an important chapter": Friends and associates of John Austin Stevens, March 26, 1866, in *John Austin Stevens Papers* (New York: New-York Historical Society).

244 **"a condition of moral flabbiness"**: Strong, *George Templeton Strong Diary*, 4 vols. MS 2472, New-York Historical Society, January 2, 1866, vol. 4, 148.

245 **"I have come to the conclusion"**: *Strong v. Strong*, N.Y. Super Ct. 1 Abb. Pr. 358 (1865). Caselaw Access Project, Harvard Law School, 366.

245 **"deprive any person of life"**: Fourteenth Amendment to the U.S. Constitution. Accessed March 28, 2023, www.archives.gov/milestone -documents/14th-amendment.

246 **"I want women to have their rights"**: Sojourner Truth, "Address to the First Annual Meeting of the American Equal Rights Association," May 9, 1867, in *American Women's Suffrage*, ed. Susan Ware (New York: The Library of America, 2020), 117.

247 **"Little Miss Mary is a sweet child"**: Strong, *Diary*, October 3, 1866, vol. 4, 168–69.

248 **"being desirous of bringing to a close"**: Superior Court of the City of New York, Divorce Records, vol.16.

Chapter 27: The Changing World

252 **"I had a few lines from Mary"**: Lucretia to Mother, August 1, 1869, *Letters of Lucretia Ledyard Stevens Heckscher 1840–1909*, 2 vols. (transcribed and printed by Gustave A. Heckscher II, 1992), vol. 1, 70. Accessed December 7, 2021, www.scribd.com/document/74895269/Letters-of-Lucretia-Ledyard-Stevens Heckscher.

253 **"Even Mary Strong seems to have deserted"**: Lucretia to Mother, March 21, 1871, Heckscher, *Letters*, vol. 1, 96.

254 **"I was dining at Delmonico's"**: Peter Remsen Strong, *Awful and Other Jingles* (New York: Putnam, 1871, repr. Forgotten Books, 2017), 9.

255 **"Poor Mary seems to have at last felt"**: Lucretia to Mother, January 25, 1874, Heckscher, *Letters*, vol. 1, 108.

256 **"so affectionate, so generous, just and true"**: Lucretia to Mother, November 8, 1874, Heckscher, *Letters*, vol. 1, 118.

256 **"I always got on with [Stevens]"**: Strong, *George Templeton Strong Diary*, 4 vols. MS 2472, New-York Historical Society, October 22, 1874, vol. 4, 422–23.

256 **"A most excellent old lady"**: Strong, *Diary*, December 2, 1874, vol. 4, 424–25.

258 **"ready pen in prose and poetry"**: *Newtown Register*, February 20, 1879.

258 **"a sweet, gentle affectionate girl"**: Lucretia to Mother, May 7, 1879, Heckscher, *Letters*, vol. 2, 148.

258 **"Mrs. Neill, Sr. told me"**: Lucretia to Mother, August, nd, 1880, Heckscher, *Letters*, vol. 2, 152.

260 **"She seems like a young girl"**: Lucretia to Mother, June 1, 1881, Heckscher, *Letters*, vol. 2, 155.

263 **"late Peter Remsen Strong and the Countess"**: *Baltimore Sun*, July 18, 1919.

Afterword

264 **"Vice was not rarer":** Mrs. John King Van Rensselaer and Frederic Van De Water, *The Social Ladder* (New York: Henry Holt, 1924), 59.

271 **"obsolete institution of marriage":** Edith Wharton, *The Custom of the Country*, in *Edith Wharton: Novels*, selected by R. W. B. Lewis (New York: The Library of America, 1985), 806.

Selected Bibliography

─────────⌐e⌐─────────

Books and Articles

Alcott, Louisa May. *The Feminist Alcott: Stories of a Woman's Power*. Edited and with an introduction by Madeleine B. Stern. Boston: Northeastern University Press, 1996.

America Through British Eyes. Compiled and edited by Allan Nevins. New York: Oxford University Press, 1948.

Apple, Rima D, ed. *Women, Health & Medicine in America: A Historical Handbook*. New Brunswick: Rutgers University Press, 1992.

Applegate, Debby. *The Most Famous Man in America: The Biography of Henry Ward Beecher*. New York: Doubleday, 2006.

Barrett, Walter. *The Old Merchants of New York City*. New York: Carleton, 1862.

Bash, Norma. *Framing American Divorce: From the Revolutionary Generation to the Victorians*. Berkeley: University of California Press, 1999.

Beckert, Sven. *The Monied Metropolis: New York City and the Consolidation of the American Bourgeoisie, 1850–1856*. Cambridge: Cambridge University Press, 2001.

Beecher, Catherine. *Treatise on Domestic Economy for the Use of Young Ladies at Home, and At School*. New York: Harper and Brothers, 1848.

Benstock, Shari. *No Gifts from Chance: A Biography of Edith Wharton.* Austin: University of Texas Press, 1994.

Black, David. *The King of Fifth Avenue: The Fortunes of August Belmont.* New York: The Dial Press, 1981.

Braddon, Mary Elizabeth. *Lady Audley's Secret.* 1862. Edited with an Introduction and Notes by Lynn Pykett. Oxford: Oxford University Press, 2012.

Bristed, Charles Astor. *The Upper Ten Thousand: Sketches of American Society.* New York: Stringer & Townsend, 1852.

Brodie, Janet Farrell. *Contraception and Abortion in 19th Century America.* Ithaca: Cornell University Press, 1994.

Buhle, Marie Jo, and Paul Buhle, eds. *The Concise History of Woman Suffrage.* Urbana: University of Illinois Press, 1978.

Burrows, Edwin G., and Mike Wallace. *Gotham: A History of New York City to 1898.* New York: Oxford University Press, 1999.

Cahn, Naomi. *Faithless Wives and Lazy Husbands: Gender Norms in Nineteenth-Century Divorce Law.* Urbana: University of Illinois Law Review, 2002.

Calhoun, Charles C. *Small College in Maine, 200 Years of Bowdoin.* Brunswick: Bowdoin College, 1993. Accessed March 30, 2023, https://archive.org/details/smallcollegeinma00calh.

Chadwick, Bruce. *Law & Disorder: The Chaotic Birth of the NYPD.* New York: Thomas Dunne Books, 2017.

Chesnut, Mary Boykin. *A Diary from Dixie,* ed. Ben Ames Williams. New York: Houghton Mifflin, 1949, originally published by Appleton, 1905.

Cohen, Patricia Cline. *The Murder of Helen Jewett: The Life and Death of a Prostitute in Nineteenth-Century New York.* New York: Vintage Books, 1998.

Coontz, Stephanie. *The Way We Never Were: American Families and the Nostalgia Trap.* New York: Basic Books, 2016.

Cooper, George. *Lost Love: A True Story of Passion, Murder and Justice in Old New York.* New York: Pantheon, 1994.

Cott, Nancy F. *Public Vows: A History of Marriage and the Nation.* Cambridge, MA: Harvard University Press, 2000.

Crain, Esther. *New York City in the Gilded Age.* New York: Black Dog & Leventhal, 2014.

Daly, Maria Lydig. *Diary of a Union Lady 1861–1865*. Edited by Harold Earl Hammond. Lincoln: University of Nebraska Press, 2000.

DeCourcy, Anne. *The Husband-Hunters: Social Climbing in London and New York*. London: Weidenfeld & Nicolson, 2017.

D'Emilio, John, and Estelle B. Freedman. *Intimate Matters: A History of Sexuality in America*. New York: Harper and Row, 1988.

DePew, Chauncey M. *Titled Americans: The Real Heiresses' Guide to Marrying an Aristocrat*. New York: The Handbook Library, 1890.

DeRose, Chris. *Star Spangled Scandal: Sex, Murder, and the Trial that Changed America*. Washington, D.C.: Regnery Publications, 2019.

Dreilinger, Danielle. *The Secret History of Home Economics: How Trailblazing Women Harnessed the Power of Home and Changed How We Live*. New York: Norton, 2021.

Dubois, Ellen Carol. *Suffrage: Women's Long Battle for the Vote*. New York: Simon & Schuster, 2010.

Dunlop, M. H. *Gilded City: Scandal and Sensation in Turn-of-the-Century New York*. New York: William Morrow, 2000.

Dwight, Benjamin W. *The History of the Descendants of Elder John Strong of Northampton, Mass.* Vol. 1. Albany, NY: Joel Munsell, 1871.

Ellington, George. *The Women of New York, or Social Life in The Great City*. New York: The New York Book Company, 1870.

Elson, Jane. *Gross Misbehavior and Wickedness: A Notorious Divorce in Early Twentieth-Century America*. Philadelphia: Temple University Press, 2017.

Erasmus Stevens and His Descendants. From Material Collected by Eugene R. Stevens, Revised by Colonel William Plumb Bacon. New York: Tobias A. Wright, 1914.

Faulkner, Carol. *Unfaithful: Love, Adultery and Marriage Reform in Nineteenth-Century America*. Philadelphia: University of Pennsylvania Press, 2019.

Faust, Drew Gilpin. *This Republic of Suffering: Death and the Civil War*. New York: Vintage Books, 2008.

Fuller, Margaret. *Woman in the Nineteenth Century*. New York: Norton, 1971, originally published by John P. Jewett, 1855.

Gay, Peter. *Education of the Senses: The Bourgeois Experience Victoria to Freud*. New York: Norton, 1984.

Gilfoyle, Timothy J. *City of Eros: New York City, Prostitution, and the Commercialization of Sex, 1790–1920*. New York: Norton, 1992.

Graham, Sylvester. *Lecture to Young Men on Chastity: Intended also for the Serious Consideration of Parents and Guardians*. Boston: George W. Light, 1837.

Greenberg, Amy S. *Lady First: The World of First Lady Sarah Polk*. New York: Knopf, 2019.

Greenidge, Kerri K. *The Grimkes: The Legacy of Slavery in an American Family*. New York: Liveright, 2023.

Gwynne, S. C. *Hymns of the Republic: The Story of the Final Year of the American Civil War*. New York: Scribner, 2019.

Halttunen, Karen. *Confidence Men and Painted Women: A Study of Middle-Class Culture in America, 1830–1870*. New Haven: Yale University Press, 1982.

Hartog, Hendrik. *Man and Wife in America: A History*. Cambridge, MA: Harvard University Press, 2000.

Havens, Catherine E. *Diary of a Little Girl in Old New York*. Bedford, MA: Applewood Books, 1919.

Heckscher, Lucretia Ledyard Stevens. *Letters of Lucretia Ledyard Stevens Heckscher 1840–1909*, 2 vols. Transcribed and printed by Gustave A. Heckscher II, 1992. Accessed December 7, 2021, Letters of Lucretia Ledyard Stevens Heckscher-Volume 1-1840-1875 | PDF (scribd.com), www.scribd.com/document/74895718/Letters-of -Lucretia-Ledyard-Stevens-Heckscher-Volume-II-1875-1907.

Heyrman, Christine Leigh. *Doomed Romance: Broken Hearts, Lost Souls, and Sexual Tumult in Nineteenth-Century America*. New York: Knopf, 2021.

History of Queens County, New York with Illustrations, Portraits, and Sketches. New York: W. W. Munsell, 1882.

Hollick, Frederick. *The Origin of Life: A Popular Treatise on the Philosophy and Physiology of Reproduction in Plants and Animals*. St. Louis: Nafis and Cornish, 1845.

Homberger, Eric. *Mrs. Astor's New York: Money and Social Power in a Gilded Age*. New Haven: Yale University Press, 2002.

Hone, Philip. *The Diary of Philip Hone 1828–1851*. Edited by Allan Nevins. New York: Dodd Mead, 1927.

Hood, Clifton. *In Pursuit of Privilege: A History of New York City's Upper Class and the Making of a Metropolis*. New York: Columbia University Press, 2017.

Hoover, Ethel D. "Retail Prices after 1850." In *Trends in the American Economy in the Nineteenth Century*, The Conference on Research on Income and Wealth. Princeton University Press, 1960. Accessed March 30, 2023, www.nber.org/chapters/c2476.

Horowitz, Helen Lefkowitz. *Attitudes Toward Sex in Antebellum America: A Brief History with Documents*. Boston: Bedford / St. Martin's, 2006.

Hunt, Harrison, and Bill Bleyer. *Long Island and the Civil War: Queens, Nassau, and Suffolk County During the War Between the States*. Charleston: The History Press, 2005.

Keller, Allan. *Scandalous Lady: The Life and Times of Madame Restell, New York's Most Notorious Abortionist*. New York: Atheneum, 1981.

Knapp, Mary L. *An Old Merchant's House: Life at Home in New York City, 1835–1865*. New York: Girandole Books, 2012.

Knox, Clement. *Seduction: A History from the Enlightenment to the Present*. New York: Pegasus Books, 2020.

Lacey, Nicola. *Women, Crime, and Character: From Moll Flanders to Tess of the D'Urbervilles*. Oxford: Oxford University Press, 2008.

Leadon, Fran. *Broadway: A History of New York City in Thirteen Miles*. New York: Norton, 2018.

Lee, Hermione. *Edith Wharton*. New York: Vintage Books, 2008.

Lewis, R. W. B. *Edith Wharton: A Biography*. New York: Fromm International, 1985.

Lockwood, Charles. *Bricks and Brownstones: The New York Row Houses 1783–1929*. New York: Rizzoli, 2003.

———. *Manhattan Moves Uptown: An Illustrated History*. Boston: Houghton Mifflin, 1976.

Long, Di. "Divorce in New York from the 1850s to the 1920s." Master's thesis. The University of Georgia, 2013.

Longstreet, Stephen. *We All Went to Paris: Americans in the City of Light 1776–1971*. New York: Macmillan, 1972; repr. Barnes & Noble, 2004. Originally published in New York by Carlton as *The Art of Conversation* in 1864 and by Dick and Fitzgerald as *Martine's Handbook of Etiquette* in 1866; repr. R L Shep, 1988.

McAllister, Ward. *Society as I Have Found It*. New York: Cassell Publishing, 1890.

McCabe, James D. Jr. *Lights and Shadows of the New York Life: Sights and Sensations of the Great City, An 1872 First Edition Facsimile*. New York: Farrar, Straus and Giroux, 1970.

———. *New York by Gaslight: Classic 1882 Edition*. New York: Arlington House, 1984.

McCullough, David. *The Greater Journey: Americans in Paris*. New York: Simon & Schuster, 2011.

Miller, Julie. *Cry of Murder on Broadway: A Woman's Ruin and Revenge in Old New York*. Ithaca: Cornell University Press, 2020.

Miller, Patricia. *Bringing Down the Colonel: A Sex Scandal of the Gilded Age*. New York: Farrar, Straus and Giroux, 2018.

Morris, Lloyd. *Incredible New York: High Life and Low Life of the Last Hundred Years*. New York: Random House, 1951.

Reynolds, David S. *Abe: Abraham Lincoln in His Times*. New York: Penguin Press, 2020.

Rhode, Deborah L. *Adultery: Infidelity and the Law*. Cambridge, MA: Harvard University Press, 2016.

Rikers, James Jr. *The Annals of Newtown in Queens County, New York*. New York: D. Fanshaw, 1852; repr. Lambertville, NJ: Hunterdon House, 1982.

Roberts, Robert. *The House Servant's Directory: An African American Butler's 1827 Guide*. Mineola, NY: Dover Publications, 2006.

Rosenblatt, Julia, and Albert Rosenblatt. *Historic Courthouses of the State of New York: A Study in Postcards*. New York: Turner Publishing, 2006.

Seyfried, Vincent F., and William Asadorian. *Old Queens, N.Y. in Early Photographs*. New York: Dover Publications, 1991.

———. *Flushing in the Civil War Era 1837 to 1865*. New York: n.p., 2001.

Seymour, Miranda. *In Byron's Wake: The Turbulent Lives of Lord Byron's Wife and Daughter*. New York: Simon & Schuster, 2018.

Showalter, Elaine. *The Civil Wars of Julia Ward Howe*. New York: Simon & Schuster, 2016.

Sinnott, Deirdre. *The Third Mrs. Galway*. New York: Kaylie Jones Books, 2021.

Smith-Rosenberg, Carroll. *Disorderly Conduct: Visions of Gender in Victorian America*. New York: Knopf, 1985.

Stage, Sarah. *Female Complaints: Lydia Pinkham and the Business of Women's Medicine*. New York: Norton, 1979.

Stansell, Christine. *City of Women: Sex and Class in New York 1789–1860*. Urbana: University of Illinois Press, 1982.

Stevens, Eugene R., ed. *Erasmus Stevens and His Descendants from Material Collected by Eugene R. Stevens, New York 1837–1905*. New York: Press of Tobias A. Wright, 1914.

Strong, George Templeton. *The Diary of George Templeton Strong, 1835–1875*, 4 vols. Edited by Allan Nevins and Milton Halsey Thomas. New York: Macmillan, 1952.

———. *George Templeton Strong Diary*, 1835–1875, 4 vols. MS 2472. Accessed December 23, 2021, https://digitalcollections.nyhistory .org/islandora/search/George%20Templeton%20Strong%20 Diary%201835-1875?type=edismax&cp=islandora%3Aroot.

Strong, Peter Remsen. *Awful and Other Jingles*. New York: Putnam, 1871; repr. Forgotten Books, 2017.

Summerscale, Kate. *Mrs. Robinson's Disgrace: The Private Diary of a Victorian Lady*. New York: Bloomsbury, 2012.

Taine, Hippolyte. *Notes on Paris*, translated with notes by J. A. Stevens. New York: Holt, 1875.

Tichi, Cecelia. *What Would Mrs. Astor Do? The Essential Guide to the Manners and Mores of the Gilded Age*. New York: Washington Mews Books, 2018.

Underwood, Richard H. *Gaslight Lawyers: Criminal Trials and Exploits in Gilded Age New York*. Lexington, KY: Shadelandhouse Modern Press, 2017.

Van Rensselaer, Mrs. John King, and Frederic Van De Water. *The Social Ladder*. New York: Henry Holt, 1924.

Van Wyck, Frederick. *Recollections of an Old New Yorker*. New York: Liveright, 1932.

Ware Susan, ed. *American Women's Suffrage: Voices from the Long Struggle for the Vote 1776–1965*. New York: The Library of America, 2020.

Wharton, Edith. *Old New York: Four Novellas*. New York: D. Appleton, 1924.

———. *The Collected Stories of Edith Wharton*. Selected and introduced by Anita Brookner. New York: Carroll & Graf, 1998.

———. *A Backward Glance: Novellas and Other Writings*. New York: The Library of America, 1990.

White, April. *The Divorce Colony*. New York: Hachette Books, 2022.

White, Richard. *Who Killed Jane Stanford? A Gilded Age Tale of Murder, Deceit, Spirits, and the Birth of a University*. New York: Norton, 2022.

Wineapple, Brenda. *The Impeachers: The Trial of Andrew Johnson and the Dream of a Just Nation*. New York: Random House, 2019.

Woo, Ilyon. *The Great Divorce: A Nineteenth-Century Mother's Extraordinary Fight Against Her Husband, The Shakers, and Her Times*. New York: Grove/Atlantic, 2010.

———. *Master Slave Husband Wife: An Epic Journey from Slavery to Freedom*. New York: Simon & Schuster, 2023.

Wright, Jennifer. *Madame Restell: The Life, Death, and Resurrection of Old New York's Most Fabulous, Fearless, and Infamous Abortionist*. New York: Hachette, 2023.

Yalom, Marylin. *A History of the Wife*. New York: HarperCollins, 2001.

Archives and Online Resources

American Antiquarian Society
America's Historical Newspapers
Ancestry.com
Archives Départementales de Seine-et-Marne
Archives of the New York County Clerk
Columbia University, Rare Book & Manuscript Library
Harper's Magazine
Indiana University, Lilly Library
Marist College, James A. Cannavino Library
Municipal Archives, City of New York
Newington-Cropsey Foundation
Newport Historical Society, Rhode Island
Newtown Historical Society, Queens, New York
New York City Register's Office

New-York Historical Society, Patricia D. Klingenstein Library
New York Public Library, Manuscripts and Archives Division, Irma and
    Paul Millstein Division
Queens Library Archives, Queens Central Library
The New York Times
Yale University, Beinecke Rare Book and Manuscript Library

Index

Cram, Henry (*continued*)
deposition of Lucretia Strong
Heckscher, 81, 187–89,
202–3
on James Strong's will, 149
during jury deliberations and
final verdict, 238–40
during jury selection, 96–97
motion to dismiss Mary's
countercharge on Peter's
adultery, 79–80
motion to dismiss Peter's manslaughter charge, 79, 80
opening arguments, 100–108,
167
post-trial attack by Austin Stevens, 243–44
presenting Lucretia's deposition, 187
reopening the divorce case, 249
on the subpoena to Madame
Barbier, 83
testimony of Benjamin Lynch,
134–37
testimony of Dr. Gunning
S. Bedford, 193–95
testimony of Ellen McArdle,
133–34
testimony of Fanny Hoff-
man Strong and her letters,
139–48
testimony of John Austin Stevens, 170–76
testimony of Madame Barbier,
187–89
testimony of Marie Tondre,
131–33
testimony of Matilda Mussehl,
110–18

testimony of Old Nurse,
120–22
testimony of Rachel Walsh,
201
testimony of Richard
Heckscher, 179
testimony of Robert Roosevelt,
150–56
on the unreliability of certain
assorted witnesses, 206, 215,
218–19
Cropsey, Jasper Francis, iv, 150
cuckolding, 51, 100
"Cup of Cold Water, A" (Wharton), xi
custody, xiv, 269
adultery and, 52
child welfare as factor in battles
over, 52–53, 269
conflict as cause of Peter and
Mary's public divorce, 61,
65–68, 76, 77, 84, 98, 147,
163, 195, 223, 227, 233–34
in Peter and Mary's final
divorce settlement, 248–51,
267
welfare of children as factor in,
52–53
Custom of the Country, The
(Wharton), 271

Daily News, 201
Daly, Joseph, 217
Daly, Maria, 61, 78–79
Danforth, J. N., 22
Darien, Connecticut, 93, 144,
247, 253
Davis, Jefferson, 80
Davis, P. J., 207

women's virginity, 26
See also divorce; Strong, Peter
and Mary
Married Women's Property Act
of 1848, 28
masculinity. *See* men and
masculinity
Massey, Horace, 218
Massey, Sarah Bixby, 77, 94, 106–
7, 110, 175, 204, 206, 218
masturbation, 13
McArdle, Ellen, 131, 133–34,
137
McKeon, John, 95, 96
during closing arguments, 220
cross-examination of Benjamin
Lynch, 135–37
cross-examination of Old
Nurse, 122
earlier prosecution of abortionist Madame Restell, 72–73,
74
on Lucretia Stevens
Heckscher's deposition,
202–3
objections during trial, 121,
141, 203–4
opening statement, 162–67
on Peter's character, 151–54
on Peter's manslaughter case,
203–4
reopening the divorce case, 249
testimony of John Austin Stevens, 168–74, 175–76
testimony of Louis Gazinsky,
198–200
testimony of Mary Smith,
204–5

testimony of Rachel Walsh,
200–4
testimony of Rev. John Cotton
Smith, 167–68
testimony of Richard
Heckscher, 178–79
men and masculinity
cuckolding, 51, 100
gentlemen's clubs, 18, 35, 41,
136, 169, 254
identity as "gentlemen," 31
male sexuality, 25–26, 29, 182
paternal privileges and rights,
65–66, 105–6, 233–34
prostitution, 8, 10, 25–26, 29, 52
"separate spheres" and gender, 29
the "sporting man," 25–26, 29
menorrhagia, 182, 183, 193–94
menstruation, 182–83
"mental aberrations" of women,
193–94
Metropolitan Police of New York
City, 206–7
Metropolitan Society for the
Relief of Widows and Families of Deceased Soldiers, 71,
200–202
Mexico, 18–19, 109
miscarriage, 36
Mary's alleged abortion or possible miscarriage, xiii, 38–39,
73–74, 181, 192, 195, 197,
225–26
Mrs. Potter's, 213–16
Monte Carlo, Monaco, 263
Moore, Clement, 11
motherhood. *See* children; pregnancy and childbirth